WE LIVE
TOO SHORT
AND DIE
TOO LONG

WE LIVE TOO SHORT AND DIE TOO LONG

WALTER M. BORTZ II, M.D.

BANTAM BOOKS
NEW YORK TORONTO LONDON SYDNEY AUCKLAND

WE LIVE TOO SHORT AND DIE TOO LONG
A Bantam Book/March 1991

"What Can You Do Today to Age Successfully?", pp. 276–277,
first appeared in *Runner's World* magazine, August, 1990, and
is reprinted with their permission.

Library of Congress Cataloging-in-Publication Data
Bortz, Walter M.
   We live too short and die too long / by Walter M.
Bortz II.
     p. cm.
   Includes bibliographical references and index.
   ISBN 0-553-07227-7
   1. Longevity.   2. Aging.   I. Title.
QP85.B66   1991
612.6'8—dc20   90-48255
                                                  CIP

Published simultaneously in the United States and Canada

PRINTED IN THE UNITED STATES OF AMERICA
RRH   0 9 8 7 6 5 4 3 2 1

ACKNOWLEDGMENTS

The sources for this book are many. Family, patients, colleagues, friends, and teachers have all provided rich background for the syntheses that I have sought. Unique assistance has been infused by Linda Perigo Moore, whose abilities gave light to my density, and by Toni Burbank, who has been a gentle shepherd throughout the whole process.

CONTENTS

PREFACE

T his is a book about aging. It will challenge everything you ever thought about the subject.

First, *We Live Too Short and Die Too Long* will challenge the boundaries you probably place on the human life span. Exactly how *long* do you expect to live? The life insurance industry bets that for most of us it will be 75 years. But you're an optimist, right? So you'll plan on beating the odds and reaching your nineties. I contend, as do other scientists who have studied the dynamics of human life, that both of those estimates are far short. Several lines of evidence clearly place the human life span at a remarkable 120 years.

I will detail my case in the chapters that follow; but for now, the most convincing facts may be those which are the most simple. Newspapers in Oakland, California, recently reported the death of local resident Arthur Reed, age 124. In Asan, Japan, Shigechiyo Isumi died on February 21, 1986, in his 121st year. Such longevity provides an inescapable inference—what is possible for one is possible for others.

That's quite a leap from the time of the first Caesar, when human life expectancy was 25 years; or from the beginning of the twentieth century, when the average American lived to the age of 49. Traditionally, this increase in life span has been explained by factors such as decreased infant mortality, eradication of communicable disease, and improvements in both nutrition and public hygiene. These most certainly are significant developments, but they only skirt the periphery of a more fundamental fact. We live longer because we are *designed* to live longer. And when we control anomalies such as disease, trauma, behavioral maladaptation, and self-destruction, the natural order of our lives prevails.

Expanding our definition of longevity means expansion of terms such as *middle age* and *old age*. For example, if you are now 40 and a member of that bold, exceptional generation known as the baby boomers, you've been

1

told by much of the media that you are reaching midlife. I challenge this contention. With prudence of prevention and health maintenance, you should think of yourself at a much younger life stage—capable of living far longer, and in a far more healthy status, than did your forebears. In essence, the opportunity to experience these additional years can be thought of as a "gift of found lifetime."

Still, some may fear this gift because of misconceptions regarding the physical nature of the aging human body. This is the second and perhaps the most important way in which my book will challenge you.

Imagine now that you have reached the magic centenarian mark. How do you envision the quality of your life? Are you climbing a tree or a mountain; or living numb in a nursing home, praying for death? I believe the fear of being old and infirm is what keeps us from being old and healthy. My hypothesis comes as a physician who for decades has watched with astonishment as his patients actively avoided all manner of preventive health care. As our knowledge of aging rapidly advances, such a tragedy is unnecessary, wrong, and inappropriate. I am not speaking now of medical technology, for I do not believe we will find miracles in youth pills or in physical gadgetry. I believe the miracle is with us today. This is because much of what passes as age change is really not due to age at all—but to disuse. Put a broken leg in a cast and in a few short weeks it will wither and appear as a leg many decades older. Similarly, all of our bodily functions— digestive, cardiovascular, respiratory, sexual, and mental—are highly keyed to use. "Use it or lose it" is far more profound than its colloquial tone suggests. Thus, the length of life is determined much by its content. Will you—will we—be a liability or a resource? The issue becomes not just how long or how well, but how long *and* how well. Quality of life and length of life cohere.

Others have described life span as a bell-shaped curve, growing to fullness and richness, only to decline into age and dependency. I deplore the decremental model, preferring instead to think of life as a "square-edged existence"—passionate and forceful to the end. We may achieve the square-edged existence only when we appreciate this remarkable final stage just as we have learned the joys of every other stage of life. A child takes his first steps, and we are exalted. The stages of later life can and must obtain this same status in the human experience.

A dominant source for my thesis on aging comes from my father, a physician before me, whose vision and wisdom perpetually reveal themselves to me—particularly as I sense that I have just derived a new and precious insight, only to discover that Father had preempted my discovery by decades. In his book, *Creative Aging,* he defined man as a Converter of Energy, an Intellectual Catalyst, an Emotional Dynamo, and a Spiritual Wanderer.

Such description, to me, was inspired and encompassing.

Aging is neither disease nor villain—that which must be cured or vanquished. Aging is a part of our natural growth process.

My father, when asked, "Dr. Bortz, how do you prevent aging?" replied, "I'm not interested in arrested development."

Such an intrinsic and *developmental* process is in communion with the anthropological history of our species and the physical laws of our universe. When we can view aging from this perspective, it is no longer something to fear or avoid. Our responsibility, upon receiving the gift of found lifetime, is then to acquire the most and the best that aging can offer.

"But what of the body?" you may persist. "Even if the spirit is bold, the body will falter."

Mark Twain, in *Letters from The Earth,* wrote, "Man seems to be a rickety poor sort of a thing. He is always undergoing repairs. A machine that was as unreliable as he would have no market."

I intend to explore these flaws in the human condition—our foreshortened life span and our protracted demise. My examination will search out evidence drawn from hosts of sources. I will present to you only the best of the research—both those discoveries which have served as historic benchmarks and those which are just now on the outer frontiers of our medical understanding.

Using anthropologic and thermophysical concepts, as well as examples from my clinical experience, I intend to trace the logic of our natural life span. For example, one perspective comes from my research in Africa into physical exercise as an evolutionary force. Over 4 million years ago the biologic transition from the shelter of the jungle canopy to the open savanna was the most important journey of our existence. I propose that the plain was a new ecologic niche for which we had much preadaptation. What set us apart from competing species and allowed us to endure with otherwise modest physical endowments was the unique ability to run long distances in the heat. "Persistence hunting," as it has come to be called, was —and is—our innate ability to run down food (in early times, the plains antelope) simply by keeping it moving in the midday sun. Such long, hard running is an activity most of civilization has forgotten. Our biologic selves have not.

As I have said, this is a book about aging. More important, it is a book about living. The story of one is the story of both. It will prove to you that you are capable of living to the ripe old age of 120. It will explain why many of us will not. And it will show the rest of us how to do it.

Others have experienced their Golden Age or their Industrial Age. We have entered the "Age Age."

We cannot paint our *Mona Lisa* and leave
the last third of the canvas blank.
We cannot build our house and leave off the roof.
We cannot run our race and stop before the final lap.
We cannot have dinner without dessert.
We cannot sing our Battle Hymn without the
"Glory, Glory, Hallelujah."
We should sing all our song.

W. M. B.

ONE

ONE MILLION HOURS

To know how to grow old is the master-work
of wisdom, and one of the most
difficult chapters in the great art of living.

Henri Amiel

O ld age is new. There has never been anything like it before—at least to any substantial degree. It is the ultimate epidemic. There have been occasional old people before, but not like this. In 1900, there were 123,000 persons in America over 85 years of age. Now there are 3 million. By 2050, some estimates predict there will be as many as 50 million. That's 16 percent of the population, compared to 1 percent now. Talk about a "megatrend"! In that same year, all of my four children will be over the age of 85. I will be 120.

How can this be? Let me begin by considering a machine—the perfect machine. Its cogs and pulleys are meshed to ultimate efficiency. Its struts and joints are sturdy. Its utility is manifest; its fuel is plentiful; its maintenance is negligible; its cost of production is minimal; its raw materials are abundant. It is friendly, versatile, and adaptable, and its operation is perpetual—or, failing that, its final disruption is abrupt.

Measured against such a design, the human body rates poorly. True, production costs are low, delightfully so; and maintenance and fuel costs are manageable. In its early years it is capable of wondrous efficiency. But a manufacturer would balk at the expense of a body's repair. It rusts out before its projected useful life is spent, and its final breakdown costs too much and takes far too long. The report of an industrial consultant would conclude that the human machine doesn't last as long as it is designed to last, and that its terminal operation is characterized by expensive decay and intolerable inefficiencies. The consultant would wonder whether these defects are secondary to blueprint errors (nature) or to environmental mishaps (nurture).

THE AGE AGE

More than one historic epoch has been labeled a "watershed moment." Each was a cohesion of population dynamics and environmental challenge which provided a change in the course of human history. Each altered the mechanisms and direction of evolution. They are the monuments of punctuated equilibrium. Historians seem to take delight in identifying certain parts of our species' calendar by "age labels." We have had the Stone Age, the Bronze Age, several Ice Ages, the Agricultural Revolution (which Dr. Richard Leakey claims represents the single most significant event in human history), and the Industrial Revolution. With some pride and justification, the historians have already labeled our current epoch the Space Age. However, with equal propriety, appropriateness, and sense of history our time can be called the Age Age. This definition of our contemporary era derives its force from two elements: first the sheer number of old people alive today, and second, and more important, the fact that we have for the first time a soundly based idea of how long we are meant to live, and the forces which disrupt this logical extent.

In the past, death appeared randomly, as an unexpected event, like a dish breaking in the dishwasher. Until now, growing old was an accident, a survival based upon chance rather than design. Everything was foreshortened. As a child I regarded my 70-year-old grandparents as extremely old—now, fifty years later, the seventies are increasingly acknowledged as part of middle age. For the aboriginal being—as well as for the animal—old age was the unlikely result of having survived myriad hostile encounters with unknown hazards and unexpected events. Daily existence was precarious. No one knew how many tomorrows there were to be or how to define a coherent life pattern. Such ignorance bred fear; and this accounts for much of what we see today as a starkly negative imagery concerning aging.

It is time for us to change. Present knowledge has expanded sufficiently for us to glimpse our entirety—to estimate the ultimate potential of the human life span.

WHAT IS THE HUMAN LIFE SPAN?

An animal may grow old in the wild, but not often. Accidents and predators keep the old members few. Evolutionary theory would predict that the onset of age and protracted weakness would not serve the survival of the species. History's great killers—famine, pestilence, lust, and war, the four horsemen of the Apocalypse—are largely controlled. New killers—arteriosclerosis, cancer, and automobile accidents—emerge. But if all external influences were eradicated, how long would it take for our machine to self-destruct? In the past, most people died young. Now most people have the chance to grow old. In 1960, there were 3,000 centenarians counted in the United States. In 1980, there were 32,194. There will be 1 million Americans over the age of 100 in the year 2050, and 1.8 million in 2080. Kenneth Manton, a scholar and demographer of aging at Duke University, calculated that 1 percent of male boys born in 1975 can expect to reach the age of 105, and 1 percent of female babies born that same year will live to 110.

My own clinical experience is reflecting the trend. Presently, I have in my practice eight centenarians, the oldest of whom is 103, spry, and coquettish. I have had the opportunity to care for one person who was 108 when he died. I have cared for thousands of persons in their nineties. Before her death at nearly 95, my mother still went to baseball games and traveled independently.

HOW OLD IS OLD?

For how long is our machine designed to run? The 1989 edition of the *Guinness Book of World Records* observes, ". . . no single subject is more obscured by vanity, deceit, falsehood, and deliberate fraud than the extremes of human longevity. Extreme claims are generally made in behalf of the very aged rather than by them."

A few years ago our attention was drawn to three population groups, one in Hunza (a region in northern Pakistan), one in southern Russia, and one in Ecuador.

An article in *National Geographic* by Dr. Alex Leaf, of the Massachusetts General Hospital, told of these peoples—many of whom were said to be living healthy, active existences until age 130 and beyond. Shirli-baba Muslimov of the Russian republic of Azerbaijan was said to have died at the age of 168. Commissar Stalin, a Georgian, supported the claims. The state bureaucracy hastened to advertise this endorsement for the virtues of communist living. The story had a lovely, bucolic Shangri-la flavor to it. Unfortunately, it wasn't true. Careful examination of these groups has revealed that the longevity of these persons was due to exaggeration rather than to some particular invulnerability or salutary lifestyle. Zhores Medvedev, an expatriate Russian gerontologist, did much to debunk the legend by revealing the inaccuracy of the records and the incompatibility of the observed events with the reported ages. It was noteworthy that all of the "old" Russians were men who had likely taken their fathers' names in order to avoid conscription.

In 1979, Richard Mazess and Sylvia Forman, of the University of Wisconsin, studied reports of extreme aging among the native population in Ecuador. The scientists worked meticulously to construct genealogical lineages and precise dates, but ultimately found no one over the age of 86. The explanation: the Ecuadorians achieved heightened status by claiming to be very old.

One of the most celebrated oldsters of all time was Old Tom Parr of Shropshire, England. His headstone in Westminster Abbey gives his dates as 1482–1635 and notes that he lived in the reigns of ten kings. However, the attribution of Parr's age actually came from a confounding with another Tom Parr, two generations younger.

Social Security records in our own country indicate that Charlie Smith was born in Africa in 1842 and was still alive in 1980. More recent documents, however, revealed that this too was an overstatement. Mr. Smith was only 101, not 138.

The mythical Shangri-la remains undiscovered. The "super-gerons" weren't.

Documentation of true age is a relatively new practice, even in civilized countries. For example, there were no written records in Russia before 1932. Most age records must be deduced from corollary events and likelihoods thereby constructed. On a recent trip to Borneo I sought out evidences of those of long life. A few centenarians were claimed, usually dating their age and activities from the time of the Japanese invasion in 1941. I was fascinated to learn, however, of a Dayak who recalls the eruption of Mt. Krakatoa, in 1883!

HOW LONG ARE WE ACTUALLY LIVING?

Today, most of us live to approximately 75 years of age—slightly longer than the biblically predicted three score and ten. Meanwhile, scholars continue to search for proof of our upper limits. My Stanford Medical School colleagues James Fries and Lawrence Crapo published a fine, thoughtful book called *Vitality and Aging,* in which they muster evidence which indicates to them that our life expectancy is 85 years. This wouldn't give us much extra time to shoot for. More recent actuarial data seem to indicate that many of us are approaching or exceeding this projected end point. Concurrently, Dr. George Sacher has observed that there is a correlation between the life span of a number of animal species and their body and brain weights. Smaller animals with smaller brains have proportionately shorter lives than do larger animals with larger brains. Using this approach, he has calculated that mankind's maximum life span is approximately 90 years. In fact, both estimates are too low.

In a 1986 article from *The Aging Society,* Paul Siegel and Cynthia Taeuber (citing data from the Census Bureau) wrote: "If the average annual rates of decrease in age specific death rates recorded in the years since 1968 continue to prevail in the coming 65 years (to 2050), the average life expectation would approximate 100 in that year."

HOW LONG ARE WE MEANT TO LIVE?

Dr. Robert Butler, first director of the National Institute on Aging and long recognized as a master in the field of gerontology, has said, "We haven't found any biologic reason not to live to 110."

I'll go a bit further. It is my best estimate that our biogenetic maximum life span is 120 years—approximately 1 million hours. This means that at birth we have the capacity to live that long—presuming that nothing happens to us in the meantime. The lines of evidence that lead to this conclusion are several, and while no single one can constitute definitive proof, taken together they achieve a high level of probability. Such reasoning is termed the Principle of Invariance. If it rains for seven days straight, it is likely that it is the rainy season. One or another rainy day doesn't imply this; but when a whole week is wet, the conclusion is inescapable.

Using this principle, I find five lines of evidence to support my thesis. These are: observational data, biostatistical maneuvers, the correlations between longevity and skeletal maturation, studies regarding the decline of vital organ function, and research into the longevity of cells in controlled environments.

Observational Data

The first reason to state that 120 years is our longest life span lies in the fact that some of us are living that long.

I spoke earlier of Arthur Reed, who died at 124 years of age. He rode his bike on his 100th birthday, and he held a job until age 116. He was born the year Lincoln was elected; his mother had worked as a cook for the Union soldiers. He was loquacious and feisty until the time he died. He was made of "good dust."

The Social Security Administration accepted Reed's age as valid, but apparently the *Guinness Book of World Records* has not. Their latest edition lists Shigechiyo Isumi of Asan, Japan, as the oldest person, having lived from June 29, 1865, until February 21, 1986 (120 years, 237 days). I have corresponded with his physician, Dr. Yoshinobu Moriya, who reported that Mr. Isumi was healthy until the end of December 1985. "He was willing to shake hands with many visitors, especially with young ladies. Many thought that this custom was a moment [sic] for his longevity," the doctor said. Mr. Isumi also moderately drank a local sugar cane wine. His death was listed as being due to pneumonia, and heart and kidney insufficiency.

After Isumi's death, various editions of *Guinness* listed Anna Williams of Swanson, Wales (age 112), Birdie May Vogt of Akron, Ohio (age 112), and Carrie C. White (age 115) of Palatka, Florida as the world's oldest people. At the same time, the United Press International was reporting the oldest known living American to be Susan Bronson of Roosevelt, New York. The daughter of a slave, Mrs. Bronson celebrated her 116th birthday in 1986. Newspaper accounts reported that she bowled until she was 105 years of age; that she had outlived all but her youngest child (age 80); and that she had seven grandchildren and more than thirty-five great-grandchildren. Mrs. Bronson told the reporters that she was born in Bamburg, South Carolina, on December 25, 1870—while Ulysses S. Grant was president.

Then, in February 1989, UPI reported that William Duberry of Summerville, South Carolina, was celebrating his 119th birthday. Duberry, who was 6 years old when General George Custer had his last stand at Little Big Horn (1876), said that he hadn't applied to *Guinness* for recognition and he "doesn't plan to."

Biostatistical Maneuvers

Thousands of people are crowding upward; and as worldwide birth records improve, others of long life will be identified. It must be emphasized that these long lives are being achieved despite the continued presence of major health hazards such as environmental pollution, an excess of fat intake, and sedentary life styles. The Japanese have the world's longest life expectancy despite a very high incidence of stroke; and this brings us to a second line of reasoning. In a statistical projection, the California State Department of Health constructed a scenario in which it was presumed that one or another of our major killers had been eliminated. The results were quite revealing. For example, when such a hypothetical prevention of arteriosclerosis is applied, the average female achieves an expected life of 100 years. The figure of 120 is consistent with this projection.

Other such projections have been constructed by Kenneth Manton, of Duke University. By analyzing extensive U.S. Census data he calculated that in 1982 the "life endurance" of American white females was 114 years and still rising.

In *The Medusa and The Snail,* Dr. Lewis Thomas wrote, "Mankind will someday be able to think his way around the finite list of major diseases that now close off life prematurely or cause prolonged incapacitation and pain. In short, we will someday be a disease free species." Having risen to such an exalted and extended state of grace, Thomas goes on to ask, "Then what? How can you finish life honorably and die honestly without a disease?"

If our research scientists can provide us with the master protocol to eliminate disease—the ultimate vaccine—it seems to me that 120 years is the logical end point. This presumes, of course, the lack of self-destruction and of accidents—but most of those are preventable as well.

Longevity and Skeletal Maturation

George Buffon, a noted French biologist who predated Charles Darwin, observed a close relationship between the time of skeletal maturity and life span across a broad range of animal species. The intense relationship between growth and life will be elaborated upon later; but in general terms, large animals live longer than small ones. Specifically, when Buffon made his study, he recognized that animals tended to live six times the period needed to complete their growth. When one notes that skeletal maturity is reached in humans at approximately 20 years, the maximum projected life span of 120 years is affirmed.

More recently, Richard Cutler, of the Gerontology Research Center of the National Institutes of Health in Baltimore, has calculated the mean lifetime potential (MLP) of a number of animal species. He finds that longevity is related to the rate of development, length of reproductive period, maximum caloric consumption, and brain size. The MLP varies 50-fold over the animal range, from 3 years in the house mouse to 20 years for the dog, 70 years for the elephant, and 100 years for the whale. Cutler calculates that with this refinement he can estimate mankind's MLP at 110 years.

Importantly, the rate of aging in different species is also found to correlate with the MLP. For example, the loss of immune competence (or reactivity) in man and the mouse is inversely proportional to the MLP. Our capacity to reject foreign skin grafts also seems related to how long we can live. The older we become, the less able are our tissues to generate antibodies to offending agents. Physical vigor, resistance to disease, and numerous other functional markers are similarly related to MLP and (also according to Cutler) can be used to estimate man's MLP as being 110 years.

How long an animal lives also correlates with the observed decline in vital organ function, which brings us to the fourth line of reasoning.

Decline of Vital Organ Function

All organs and all vital functions show a gradual reduction in capacity with the passage of time. The noted gerontologist Nathan Shock of Baltimore, Maryland, enlightened our awareness of this fact. These declines in function occur in the absence of disease and can be construed as true "age changes." However, these changes are very slow and generally are in the range of a 1 percent decline per year after the age of 30. If one presumes

100 percent function at age 30, one notes that these changes do not become functionally important until past the age of 100. We know that most individuals operate perfectly adequately at 30 percent of maximum. In fact, it is at the approximate point of 30 percent function that most individuals begin to experience symptoms (such as shortness of breath) which would lead them to seek the aid of a doctor. My point is that for most individuals, much good function still remains at 100 years. A constant reminder of this occurs when an autopsy is performed to determine the cause of death. Presently most deaths are the result of a sharply localized problem: a hemorrhage, a block in a critical artery by a clot or a chunk of cholesterol, or a strategically placed tumor. The rest of the body is still intact and has not had the opportunity to live out its allotted time. In effect, no one has been shown to have died of "old age." It is not a justifiable death-certificate diagnosis—no matter at what age the person dies. In summary, as the decline in vital body function is plotted against time, none becomes limiting to life until 110 or 120 years.

The Longevity of Cells
in Controlled Environments

Leonard Hayflick, good friend and brilliant scientist, has given students of aging the single most critical observation in gerontologic research. Until 1974 it was thought that individual cells, when grown artificially in a synthetic culture medium, were capable of indefinite life—the cells would continue dividing ad infinitum. The reference experiments were those of surgeon and Nobel laureate Alexis Carrell, who incubated chick embryo cells in tissue culture medium. He observed that these cells kept dividing interminably, leading to the suggestion that aging, at the cellular level, did not occur. If the whole is no more than the sum of its parts, the Carrell observation lent hope to the immortalists' claims. The experiment was terminated after 34 years; and unfortunately, the experiments were flawed and unreproducible. The seeming eternal life of the normal cells was due to contamination of the culture media. (Cancer cells, on the other hand, do seem to have a limitless capacity to divide and reproduce. And this paradox deepens both our awe of the mystery and our determination to find its key.)

Hayflick contributed to this disproof. He found that DNA can replace itself only a certain number of times and that this number is species specific.

ch. 2 #19

How long a species lives correlates with the number of cell doublings, reflecting again Buffon's intuition some 100 years ago.

As Hayflick took nests of human fibroblast cells (those found in connective tissue such as cartilage), clearly only a specific number of cell divisions occurred before the cells started to show signs of aging and stopped dividing. They died after about fifty divisions. If we graph the maximum life span versus the number of all cell divisions, from the mouse to the Galapagos turtle, man's MLP (maximum lifetime potential) would be 115 to 120 years. Cells taken from 90-year-old subjects still have further (ten to fifteen) doublings. Cells taken from older donors showed correspondingly fewer divisions before senescence and death set in. When one takes the number of total cell divisions and multiplies it by the cell life of each cell, one calculates roughly 120 years as the theoretical maximum cell life of cultured human cells.

Hayflick observed, as others have before, that when tissue from older animals was grafted onto younger animals, the cells from the grafts died before the younger animals did. Hayflick personally resists making this predictive calculation, reasoning that what happens in tissue culture need not apply to the whole organism. However, I must champion a different interpretation. When his evidence is placed in context with other, very different avenues of observation, and all are found to be internally consistent—then I would argue, by the Principle of Invariance, that the point is made!

These five separate lines of evidence constitute strong evidence that our endowed birthright, or maximum life potential, is 120 years.

According to Edward Devey, of Yale, the Romans preempted this estimate by 2,000 years. From their ancient writings, Devey concluded, "Ten times twelve solar years was the term fixed for the life of man beyond which the gods themselves had no power to prolong it. The Fates narrowed the span to thrice thirty years, and fortune abridged even this period by a variety of chances against which the protection of the gods was implored."

I have devoted my personal and professional energies to the study of aging. While pursuing this endeavor, the point which astonishes me most is that we—supposedly the most inquisitive and learned species on the planet—seem collectively uninterested in clearly establishing *how long* we are intended to live.

To have such a goal, to achieve some ready sight-point on our horizon, seems critical if—as the Oracle of Delphi and others before and since have beseeched us—we are to know ourselves. We vitally need to understand *every* human capacity, but most certainly how long it is that we should live. Expectation is a vital dynamic of human existence, and unless we have some blueprint to guide us, we surely will not achieve the potential with which aeons of evolutionary experiences have vested us.

WHAT IS THE NEXT STEP?

Bernard Strehler, noted gerontologist at the University of Southern California, predicted that unless the aging process differs in some mysterious and unforeseen way from the puzzles man has faced in the past, it is essentially inevitable that he will, before long, understand what causes us to age. Understanding carries with it the vital implication that we can begin to design a lifetime strategy for optimal aging. We can write a meaningful lifetime script. We will become both sculptor and marble. We will be the designer and the design. As the unknown is erased, the fears and myths of aging will fade.

In the November 1979 issue of *Age and Aging,* Mark Novak stated, "In the past religion or philosophy provided the context for discussing old age, but today these systems of explanation have lost their explanatory power. In their place we have turned to science for an understanding of aging."

Thus, our next step may be to rid ourselves of the past.

OLD IDEAS ABOUT AGING

Throughout history, interest and involvement in the phenomenon of aging has been sparse. From Greek and Roman times, philosophers, alchemists, and other stray sorts periodically sallied forth on the mission to explore the significance of aging. All retired with fatalism and ignorance. Analytic insights have been constricted, mystical, and wishful.

For example, religious dogma has dealt endlessly with the phenomenon of death, but little with age. Aging as a religious theme has been invested generally with the notion that old age is a punishment for sins, original or otherwise. We have been made to fear the unknowns of death

and disintegration. Depending upon the sin content of our earthly existence, hell, purgatory, or heaven has been offered as our ultimate path.
Given this premise, gerontophobia was logical. Catastrophes such as the
plagues which swept the world during times past were viewed as theologic
events. Although most creeds generally include belief in immortality as an
essential ingredient of faith, our yearnings for it have never seemed to carry
much conviction. Our instincts for indulgence and self-destruction seem
more deeply ingrained than are our hopes for longer lives. Alex Comfort
wrote, "Public concern for longevity does not extend to making oneself
uncomfortable."

We seem to avoid the subject as much as we can. The youth cult is not
a twentieth-century fixation. We have always exalted the young; aging has
always been a taboo. Proust wrote that we tend to deal with aging only in
abstract. Robert Butler, first director of the National Institute on Aging, says
that we deal with aging like the Victorians dealt with sex. Erica Jong calls
age an embarrassment.

Aging as a part of life has rarely attracted artistic or literary attention.
Old age is underrepresented in cultural expression. *The Picture of Dorian
Gray, On Golden Pond, Cocoon,* and *Golden Girls* are noteworthy exceptions. Shakespeare presented King Lear as that "ruin'd piece of nature."
Aging is not good box office. A recent article by Walter Goodman in *The
New York Times* suggested that characters generally treat old age in "the
comical-sentimental mode, easy to swallow, like the coated drugs that some
old people live on." Grandparents are usually presented as "doting and
somewhat disconnected"—like a different species.

THE DOCTORS WHO PEDDLE YOUTH

My profession has contributed to the malaise in that the scientific
study of aging has often been the province of charlatans and hucksters.
Every imaginable incantation, potion, and surgical maneuver has been
proposed in the name of rejuvenation. Much of this arose in the context of
perpetuating or recapturing sexual capacities—potency for the male, physical attractiveness and secondary sexual characteristics for the female. Sex
and ideas of aging are intimately mixed.

One such example concerns the legendary oldster Tom Parr. His autopsy, performed by the great anatomist and surgeon William Harvey, made particular mention of Parr's "well-developed and heavy testicles." For years this observation, along with the inaccuracy of Parr's life span, has been taken as incontestable proof that there exists a relationship between longevity and the internal secretion of endocrine glands, in particular the sex glands. Around 1400 B.C., the Indian physician Susutra recommended that his patients eat the reproductive glands of young tigers to overcome impotency.

One thing the youth doctors have never lacked is creativity. On June 1, 1889, Professor Charles Eduoard Brown-Sequard, pupil of the godfather of physiology, Claude Bernard, addressed the Société de Biologie in Paris. Brown-Sequard was then 72 years of age. He described his personal rejuvenation (i.e., regaining his potency) after having injected himself with fluid extracted from crushed dog testicles. The reaction was intense. Soon physicians worldwide were injecting patients with extracts from various animals' organs and glands. One such imitation therapy was the work of the renowned Serge Voronoff, an expatriate Siberian physician, who in 1900 felt that only monkey glands made effective stimulants. Monkeys became scarce shortly thereafter. Today the absurd notion that pulverized rhinoceros horn is an aphrodisiac has nearly doomed this noble beast.

In the United States, John Romulus Brinkley of Milford, Kansas, developed a technique for inserting whole goat testes into human scrota. It is estimated that from 1915 to 1942 he grafted 16,000 goat testicles.

The most incredible link in this chain of pseudoscience was yet to come. Back in Europe, a Swiss surgeon, Paul Niehans of Vevey, entered the field of rejuvenation. Niehans had studied with Voronoff, who had since fallen from esteem among his colleagues. Nonetheless, early in his career Niehans had grafted parathyroid gland tissue into a patient with parathyroid deficiency. The patient made an excellent recovery, thus baffling every conventional corrective remedy and prompting the amazing career which followed.

In 1948, Niehans began using cells from lamb fetuses for the purpose of rejuvenation. Before dying at the age of 86, Niehans had treated 40,000 patients, many of whom were world renowned. Winston Churchill, Gloria Swanson, and Somerset Maugham were among the most notable. Probably the most famous case was that of Pope Pius XII, who at age 78 summoned Niehans to Rome. The Pontiff was believed to be dying of gastric problems or some obscure kindred disorder, and upon two separate occasions Niehans guided him to recovery. The ranks of the faithful grew.

In April 1987 I visited the Niehans Cellular Therapy Clinic in Vevey.

It is now maintained by his daughter, having previously split from the proprietor of the original clinic several miles away. The present facility is located in an elegant hotel on the banks of Lake Geneva and provides a glorious view of the Alps. The charge for the basic package of seven days, six nights was then 6,600 Swiss francs (approximately $3,000). The cellular therapy could be supplemented with "bioenergetic treatments" such as acupuncture (of the traditional Chinese, electric, and laser varieties), shiatsu (a Japanese treatment also known as acupressure), injections of procaine (a local anesthetic), and aroma therapy (consisting of massage and compresses with vegetable and plant essences). These cost extra.

Currently most of the clinic's patients come from the Middle East and Central America.

I did not take the treatment.

The most famous of today's youth wizards is Ana Aslan of Budapest. Her potion of Gerovital, vitamin H_3, is composed nearly exclusively of novocaine (the common local anesthetic) and small amounts of benzoic acid and potassium metadisulphate. Among her patients Aslan numbered Nikita Khrushchev, Charles de Gaulle, and Ho Chi Minh. A recent full-page newspaper ad was headlined, *Doctor's Rumanian Youth Restoration Formulas Seem to Defeat Aging!* The source is the Biomedical Revitalization Center in Lawrence, New York, which, for $39 plus shipping and handling, will send a month's supply of Prozene 3, an "improvement of Gerovital." But hurry, because "supplies are limited." Unfortunately, neither Aslan's nor Niehans's patients have been shown to live to extraordinary old age—the oldest of Niehans' followers is 92.

There is a reason, however, why youth doctors should make a difference. This difference is rooted in the placebo effect. As I will explore later, aging is to a major extent a quality of the mind, and as such is susceptible to a large degree of mental imprinting.

The situation is ready-made. The eager and susceptible come humbly seeking a gift of nature, the restoration or extension of youth. They are met by a strong, promising figure who holds out the possibility of new vitalities, recapture of lost opportunities, and revisit of yesterday's horizons. The tactic is invested with sufficient hierarchical mystique to tempt and convince. Conviction is a major part of cure, and every controlled hard-science research project must factor in the reality of the placebo effect. The effect is at its most potent under just these circumstances. And as someone once wisely observed, no hometowners have ever been cured at Lourdes.

It is unfortunate that there are no sound studies of glandular therapy, Gerovital, or anything else which claims rejuvenation. One would presume that if the partisans of these immensely successful commercial enterprises were truly committed to the products and ideas they promulgate, they would seek confirmation of the effects in the scientific community by performing double-blind studies in which neither the subject nor the experimenter knows which is the *real* test compound. Sadly, the absence of such efforts implies that the youth practitioner cares more for the preservation of the mystique and its attendant rewards than for the assertion of real truth.

If the myriad anecdotes of the wonders of the youth doctors were valid, such examples would account for more than the placebo effect, which causes sugar pills to work 10 to 20 percent of the time (for whatever condition they are prescribed) merely because of the strength of positive thinking. Those who attend today's health and beauty spas do so in an effort to find a second adolescence, a second puberty. The multibillion-dollar cosmetic industry feeds on their lust for rejuvenation.

WHERE IS THE HAND OF HARD SCIENCE?

Pseudoscientific approaches are the heritage of aging research because sound science has been slow to address the issue of aging. The word *geriatrics*—the medical aspects of aging—was first coined by Dr. D. G. Nascher in 1914. The National Institute on Aging was founded as recently as 1974, the last of the National Institutes of Health. The American Geriatrics Society was founded in 1942, the Gerontologic Society of America a short time later. To put this timetable in perspective—the American Medical Association was founded in 1843.

Still, geriatrics is part of the curriculum in only a minority of our nation's medical schools. The first professorship of geriatrics was established at Cornell in 1978; the first department in a medical school, at Mt. Sinai in 1983. Geriatrics has no honored traditions. Everyone in the field is still a pioneer.

Until now, the issue of aging has not had significant impact on American social and political policy. When I recently traveled to Africa, I observed a different experience. Repeated inquiries of "How are you handling the old people?" were greeted by blank unresponsiveness. It seemed an irrelevant question. It wasn't that there weren't any old people (10 percent of the Kalahari bushmen are over 70 years of age), but they were not perceived as being a group set apart. Not a "them or us" situation—only "us."

But for the Western world the emergence of the compelling demography listed at the beginning of this chapter creates an awareness and urgency which Anne Somers of Rutgers University has appropriately termed the "Aging Imperative." We face this imperative ill armed, without a satisfactory data base or adequate social philosophy upon which we can create policy. This policy is not just for "them," the aged, but for all of us. It affects decisions at every level of involvement—personal, community, national. Arnold Toynbee remarked, "A society's quality and durability can best be measured by the respect and care given to its elder citizens." We now have the opportunity—the mandate—to discharge this responsibility intelligently and ethically. As the popular cartoon character Pogo might say, "I have met the elderly and they are us."

A MORE PRODUCTIVE OUTLOOK

The winter 1986 issue of *Daedalus*, the publication of the American Association of Arts and Sciences, was entitled "The Aging Society." It consisted of a series of excellent essays compiled by Alan Pifer and Lydia Bronte of the Carnegie Foundation. Its main message was that we are living an historic moment—a moment when a new, third age of life is appearing. Until the present there were only two ages, youth and adulthood—youth consisting of the years from birth to 20 years, adulthood lasting from the ages of 20 to 65 or so. Youth was characterized by growth, learning, and maturing. Adulthood involved productivity, reproduction, and youth care. At approximately 65 years, we died—erratically, but with high probability. Survivors past 65 were rare, but during the late nineteenth century they became common enough for Prince Otto von Bismarck, chancellor of the German Empire, to propose a social security system for that individual who unexpectedly lived beyond the second age of life. Five decades later, our nation followed suit, instituting our own social security system to help support those few who didn't die according to the predicted schedule. Medicare followed in 1965 to heal the ailing survivors.

We now identify the falseness of this model. Not only are a few of us living beyond age 65, tens of millions are. There are 53 million Chinese over 65. Also on the Asian continent, 33 million Indians and 26 million Russians live past this benchmark. Here in America, 29 million people are older than 65—that's more than the entire population of Canada. Calculate the number of those who reached age 65 during the past 100 years and you would have a sum equal to the number of people over age 65 who existed on the planet for all of previous history. By the year 2035, one in every four Americans will be over 65. The average family will have four generations.

THE THIRD AGE—
A NEW LIFE SEGMENT

We have most recently inherited a new life segment—the third age. This new phenomenon has burst upon us bringing with it new decades of opportunity, and (somewhat ominously) the potential for profligate waste. We are not prepared.

In part this is because the new third age lacks definition—biologic, psychologic, sociologic, economic, and political. We have no encyclopedias, textbooks, experiments, or models to guide us to our new age. The chances for interage conflict are real. The younger generations do not defer to the older simply because they *are* older—some equity of resource allocation is sought. We are ill armed to confront the novel challenges. We lack a conceptual framework as to what our new years can and should represent. In effect, we are in the position of defining our new, complete life. Until now everything has been an artifact. We confront the potentials of our full lives for the first time in the history of our kind. This, now, is one of the most significant epochs of the human species.

Our first challenge is to recognize our 120-year natural lifetime and redefine its subsegments. There are three segments of life: youth, middle age, and old age. Youth is 0 to 40 years, middle age is 40 to 80, and old age 80 to 120. Each major segment is then halved to produce the following segments:

1. Youth
   • young (0–20)
   • old (20–40)

2. Middle Age
   • young (40–60)
   • old (60–80)
3. Old Age
   • young (80–100)
   • old (100–120)

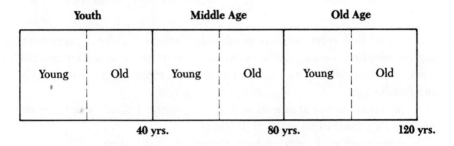

No one should die until old, old age—over 100 years. Any earlier deaths are premature. As I recently passed my 60th birthday, halfway, it is like a golfer just starting the "back nine."

If we plotted the longevity of plates in the dishwasher as an exercise in random statistics, we would see a survival slope as follows:

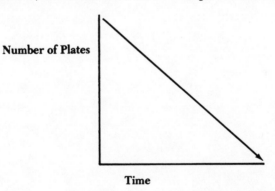

Until recently, human longevity curves have resembled this same "triangular" pattern—not much different from projections of the "life span" of a set of dinner plates.

Clearly our present goal should look very different. Ideally, each of us wants to live to our full design—the "rectangular" life span curve.

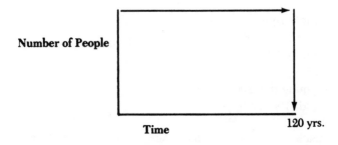

As we look at recent demographic data, we see that we are approaching the idealized rectangularized curve: more of us are living longer; but since 75 is the median year for death in America, most of us are still dying in old middle-age.

If we are dying at age 75 and have a potential of 120 years, we are faced with a current shortfall of 45 years!

Our machine is only partway through its work time.

We die too soon.

T W O

WHY THINGS
GROW OLD

Chaos is the law of nature;
order is the dream of man.

Henry Adams

W e view Ponce de León as a tragicomic figure devoting his life to finding
the fountain of youth. The story has a whimsical fairy-tale ring to it.
Nonetheless, it reminds us that in the corner of every ego is the thought
that "having to die" is a fundamental annoyance.

In Greek mythology Eos, the goddess of the dawn, loved Tithonus, a
mortal. She begged Zeus to grant her lover eternal life. Unfortunately for
all, Aphrodite also had her eye on Tithonus; and when she heard about
Zeus's concession to Eos, she jealously arranged that Tithonus's immortality
not be accompanied by eternal youth. And so he aged, and aged, and aged.
Until now he still survives, but only as the wretched chirp of the grasshop-
per.

Therefore, immortality must be qualified. We come to the recognition that length of life is not sufficient. Quality must accompany. Duration
and content cohere.

I will explore this relationship extensively in later pages; but for now,
what of Ponce de León's search? Is immortality a human possibility? Can
science discover enough and cure enough until someday age itself will be
preventable? Must we die at all? My firm guess is that death is inevitable,
and that the fountain of eternal youth is as illusory as the perpetual time
machine. Emotionally we may yearn for everlasting life, since death rarely
seems that it should apply to "us." Religions have used this longing as an

instrument of belief; but unfortunately (or fortunately), wishing does not make it so. We must look at aging and death with an unbiased eye. In chapter 1 I presented the concept that we are living in the "Age Age"; and one characteristic of this epoch is that for the first time in history, we have been provided the tools, or knowledge base, with which we may propose a workable and universal definition of aging. Such knowledge will allow us to strip away the emotional clutter of our past and to devise strategies to live our best lives.

WHAT IS AGING?

The answer to this profound question takes us close to an explanation of the very essence of life. To define aging we must probe into the heart of the question, "What is life?"

So far we haven't had much help from medical science. In fact, when we explore all the textbooks on geriatrics and gerontology, we find that very few of them even attempt to define aging. What they do is describe in elaborate detail the myriad structural and functional changes which accompany aging. But they do not provide a unified, basic causation. This is not dissimilar to the parallel failure of biologic science to provide a definition of life. Once again, the textbooks are full of the general characteristics of life, reproduction, movement, etc.; but they fail to give precious insight into the fundamental nature of life. Medicine is too close to aging, as biology is too close to life. Both are inside the topic—unable to see its whole. As with the parable of the committee of blind men trying to describe an elephant after feeling separate parts, it's hard to define an elephant from the inside. Edwin Schrodinger observed that it would be impossible to guess the purpose of an electric motor by analyzing separately its components of iron, copper, and rubber. And it has been said that a physicist is the atom's way of understanding itself.

Albert Szent-Gyorgy, a Nobel laureate, wrote prophetically in 1938, "Biologic phenomena, possibly, are to a great extent the expression of subtle changes which take place in dimension unknown which belong to the realm of quantum mechanics and can be described only in its language."

That may not be very reassuring, but let's give it a try.

AGE EQUALS THE EFFECT OF
ENERGY ON MATTER OVER TIME

At the most simple level, the components of aging are three: energy, matter, and time. Further, since everything in the universe ages, any definition must transcend biology. Stars, canyons, and Chevrolets age, as do redwoods, tadpoles, and ourselves. We search for a theorem which is therefore universal in how it relates matter, time, and energy. These terms are described in the Second Law of Thermodynamics—a sort of cosmic Murphy's Law, which states that an isolated system left to itself will, in the course of time, go toward greater disorder.

To understand how the Second Law of Thermodynamics affects your life, think of yourself as a complex set of molecules. These molecules need a certain amount of energy if they are to maintain an orderly system or pattern. (Your body is, of course, the specific pattern in question.) Too much energy (referred to as "stress"), and the system is disrupted—we commonly refer to this phenomenon as "burnout." Too little energy, and the system cannot cohere—the molecules become random and the pattern is disrupted.

To maintain ourselves—to maintain our molecular order—takes a great deal of energy. In the most simple physical terms, this is what constitutes life—literally using energy to keep ourselves together before succumbing to the natural order of decay. Time is the element of progress and aging is what we see and experience in the course of this effort.

Sir Arthur Eddington wrote, "Whenever you propound a new theory, of high attractiveness, be sure that it conforms to the Second Law, because if it doesn't it is surely wrong."

The Second Law is one of the fundamental pillars of our understanding of the universe, and therefore of ourselves. If we are to define the elements of our small machine, we need to understand how the big machine, our universe, runs.

In the last decade, the new science of nonequilibrium thermodynamics (the study of chaos) has illuminated our understanding of the Second Law. Its principal protagonists (Ilya Prigogine of Brussels, Harold Morowitz of James Madison University, Freeman Dyson of Princeton, and others) provide the rest of science with a new way of seeing. Prigogine wrote, "On the dry bones of the nature of atoms and the distribution of energy in the universe are assembled the flesh and blood of life." Biologic phenomena are ultimately the consequences of the laws of physics. Ernst Mayr of Harvard wrote, "There is general agreement that all biologic principles are basically derived from the hard sciences of physics and chemistry." What remains is to understand how these laws are inscribed onto biologic processes.

Prior to this powerful and encompassing view of the universe, physicists were concerned with equilibrium dynamics, a study field which got its start in the 1800s when there was great economic motivation for perfecting the steam engine. It was therefore involved mainly with the transfer of energy. The First Law of Thermodynamics asserts the conservation of energy. (For example, the form and distribution of energy may vary; but that the amount is constant.) But equilibrium thermodynamics is a largely theoretic construct. It does not describe adequately the workings of the real world. Specifically, the theory seemed not to involve time. Clearly time *must* be factored into our major life design—not doing so would flout common everyday events. Time, transition, and evolution are the stuff of the universe. To deny this is an incomplete theory.

Change is everywhere evident. Nothing stands still. Time marches on.

WHAT IS TIME?

Again we face a vital, simple, and yet complex question. Is time merely the flicker of a digital watch, the tolling of a church chime, or the striking of a grandfather clock? On a broader scale, is time merely an expression of the rotation of the earth on its axis or around the sun? If it is, how does one deal with the dimensions of temporal change in remote galaxies?

In 1937, Roy Helton wrote a brilliant essay for *Harpers,* the title of which I have borrowed for this chapter. In it he asserted that time is not necessarily human-related. Rather, time is a cosmic phenomenon—really an assertion of entropy, an expression of the state of change. In his bestseller *A Brief History of Time,* Stephen Hawking uses the Big Bang as the start of time (an estimated 10 to 20 billion years ago), reckoning that anything that occurred before this is simply irrelevant to current existence.

Carrying this premise of cosmic time further, we see that it is an assertion of matter and energy going from one level of organization to another—from position A to position B. Further, this transition is unidirectional. Time is irreversible. These simple observations indicate that all existence, human and otherwise, is time-driven. The Second Law encompasses this imperative when it states that an isolated system left to itself will, in the course of time, go toward greater disorder.

WHAT IS ENERGY?

Throughout the universe, heat is the form in which most energy is spent. Heat, whether generated by combustion, friction, gravity, or any other means, generally goes from a high energy source (concentration) to a low energy residue (diffuse). The burning of our sun at X-number of tons per second is the easy example. Hot things cool, cold things don't warm without the addition of energy or work—but that is a later part of the story. For now, it is enough to recognize that orderly things get disorderly.

Such universal disorder (labeled "entropy" by the physicists) is in turn temperature-dependent. Hot things tend to have higher degrees of entropy, while cold things have less. Think back to your high school science class and when the teacher drew your attention to the agitated molecules in a flask of boiling liquid. When water boils it converts to water vapor. Lowering the temperature of this vapor would produce a more orderly, crystallized, state—ice.

Yet, it was the work of the last few years which illuminated the universality of the Second Law. This was achieved primarily by the brilliant scholar Ilya Prigogine, winner of the 1977 Nobel Prize for Physics. Prigogine (and his colleague Isabelle Stengers) presented his conclusions in a book called *Order Out of Chaos.* I was introduced to this work several years ago when I gave a speech to the American Geriatrics Society in San Francisco. A fellow in the back of the room raised his hand and suggested that I get Prigogine's book, and upon taking the suggestion I experienced one of those "Eureka!" moments which can change one's life. Prigogine's insights provided incredible illumination to all sorts of partial recognitions, vague glimpses and fractions of knowledge that had been a part of my sparse understanding of aging. His applications spread out to touch on every aspect of my awareness—not just biomedical interests but activities of daily life as well. I feel privileged to live in the lifetime of this new way of knowing. The newfound interest in Chaos Theory is a derivative of Second Law analysis.

THE PHYSICS OF LIFE
ACCORDING TO PRIGOGINE

The description thus far of the implications of the nonequilibrium, thermodynamic, time-driven Second Law needs to be reconciled with the phenomenon of life. Or perhaps it would be best to say that the phenomenon of life needs to be reconciled with the Second Law. Even though the Second Law ordains that a physical system always tends toward disorder, it does allow for islands of order. Harold F. Blum, noted evolutionist and scientist, points out that whereas the entire system tends toward disorder, parts of the whole are capable of increasing order. The classic example is the formation of a crystal in a solution. A crystal represents the coalescence of a number of molecules into a tightly bound, highly ordered form. When these molecules are dispersed in solution, they have low order and no recognizable structure.

Nevertheless, such localized increases in order must inevitably be accompanied by an overall increase in entropy of the system as a whole. The food chain is the classic example of progressive ordering, but always accompanied by a net loss of energy as heat.

Professor Peter W. Atkins of Oxford, in his book *The Second Law*, notes "the underlying awesome simplicity of complexity." In his chapter "Enumeration of Chaos" he writes, "We shall see how chaos can run apparently against Nature and achieve that most unnatural of ends, life itself."

"HE BLEW THE BREATH OF LIFE"

In order for life to occur, mechanisms for ordering are necessary. The formulation of the molecule was one such ordering. Rather than atoms being content to disperse endlessly, they bred, or were bonded into molecules. The initial observation to be made, however, is that such complexing requires a package of energy which will be spent on the effort. You can't bond without fuel. This is illustrated by one of the most centrally important demonstrations of our time—an experiment performed in 1938 by Stanley Miller, a scientist in Harold Urey's Chicago laboratory. Miller took a mixture of three simple gases: ammonia, methane, and water, containing only the basic elements of oxygen, carbon, hydrogen and nitrogen. They were the major components of the atmosphere of our primordial earth shortly after its formation 5 billion years ago. Into this simple mix he introduced a shot of electricity to mimic a lightning bolt. When the contents of the flask were analyzed, Miller found amino acids—the basic building blocks of life. Subsequent experiments showed how amino acids aggregate when given an energy supply and thus yield polypeptides—closer yet to the matter of life.

Edwin Schrodinger was later to expand upon this breakthrough in his 1947 book *What is Life? The Physical Aspects of the Living Cell.* In it he ventured a physicist's view of the business of being alive. He wrote, "To reconcile the high durability of heredity substance (DNA) with its minute size, we had to evade the tendency to disorder by inventing the molecule. In fact, an unusually large molecule which was to be a masterpiece of highly differentiated order, safeguarded by the conjuring rod of quantum theory."

A molecule is a "negentropic" device. It serves to make orderly the chaotic pattern of individual atoms. For example, H_2O is a more contented state than merely two atoms of hydrogen and one of oxygen blithely buzzing around one another. They are happier as water.

METABOLISM AND THE BIG PICTURE

On a more macroscopic level, molecules are clustered within the functional units of our bodily tissues. A plant or animal is a complex, highly organized, and improbable event. Improbable because living organisms have low entropy. The composite aggregating of the trillions of individual molecules into a working whole which represents the anatomy of plants and animals seems a miraculous and epic drama. There is a local abatement of chaos, an island of order in a sea of disorder. Life in its present form has taken 4 1/2 billion years of churning and incubating. It isn't over yet.

Linus Pauling credits quantum physics for providing the intellectual base for the new revolution in biology, "molecular biology." He writes, "Schrodinger, by formulating his wave equation, is basically responsible for modern biology. Nonlinear thermodynamic principles are just starting to be applied in medicine."

Ary Goldberger, of Harvard Medical School, is advancing this idea that the intrinsic rhythmicity of the heartbeat is an assertion of the oscillatory behavior of physical systems; and Walter Freeman, of the University of California at Berkeley, is conducting experiments which show "how the brain uses chaos to make order."

The operational plan of plants and animals is called metabolism. Metabolism is in turn defined by myriad biochemical reactions which facilitate the change in form of the molecules of our foodstuffs, our hormones, our neurotransmitters, etc. All cells, even the most simple, have metabolism. It is the "gear wheel" of our engine. The ultimate aim of metabolism is to process the food and to integrate the overall operation of the body machine—to regulate heat and thus retard entropy.

The original heat (or energy) source in our neighborhood is the sun. It sends us quanta of energy with which to do our work. The primary antennae for the capture of this energy are the plants which use it to compound carbon dioxide and water, thus forming sugar. CO_2 plus H_2O yields $C_6H_{12}O_6 + O_2$. Now even children in primary school learn that this is photosynthesis or plant growth, and plant growth is in turn scavenged by animals. In terms of energy consumed, each step in the food cycle costs increasingly more. Metabolism, then, uses the sugar to do work of many kinds; and in doing so it degrades the sugar or derivative foodstuffs into carbon dioxide. Finally, the sun's energy (after numerous cyclings in metabolism) is lost to space as heat.

The biologic implications of the Second Law have been ably summarized by biophysicist Harold Morowitz:

1. The surface of the Earth is a physical system which receives energy from the sun and gives it up to space.

2. The constant energy flow acts to organize the molecules on the Earth's surface.

3. The organization leads to life, which is maintained by the energy flow.

4. The energy flow causes cycling of many types and feedback-control mechanisms in which the products of the biochemical reactions act to augment or inhibit the reactions thus leading to metabolic order.

It is a wonderful and efficient process.

But no process is static, and so intrinsic to the entire system is the creation of oscillations—rhythms or cycles. These oscillations are an inherent quality of life and are an expression of what physicists call the Cycling Theorem. As Morowitz expanded upon this concept, "In the steady-state system, the flow of energy through this system from a source (sun) to a sink (space) will lead to at least one cycle in the system." The sum total of all these rhythmic processes constitutes life.

Continuous work leads to self-organization in ordering of the biosphere. We maintain our functional and structural integrity at the expense of the energy deeded to us temporarily by the sun.

The force which comes from entropy (decay) is what gives direction to our life processes. (In fact, physicist Arthur Eddington even called entropy "time's arrow.") As heat escaping from a steam engine is not recoverable for use as work, these life processes proceed along a course dictated by the losses of heat which are inherent in biochemical reaction. Heat is the inevitable tax on usefulness.

AGE AND THE LOSS OF HEAT

Which brings us back, finally, to aging and its definition. In my view, aging is an expression of entropic decay. It is a restatement of "time's arrow." It is inexorable, inescapable, and ultimate. But, thanks to the conceptual base provided by the thermophysicists, it is no longer inscrutable. Roger Bacon correctly guessed this in the 1500s when he defined aging as "loss of innate heat."

At age 30 or thereabout, your system is at its highest level of optimal structure and function. Thereafter, it starts to decay, in various ways and at different rates. Older animals appear less energetic. And while some tissues show little if any evidence of deterioration (for example, the lining of the intestine), others like the elastic tissue evidence clear declines. The most clear examples are the unidirectional patterns of decline in skin elasticity and the graying of hair.

Viewed in this way, death becomes the final entropic event in which a rapid acceleration of decay occurs. The physicist's viewpoint was expressed by Peter Atkins, who concluded, "Coherence is intrinsically transient, and crumbles into incoherence when the structure ceases to be driven by a flow of energy."

In short, when the bodily functions governed by metabolism stop, your tissues disintegrate rapidly. Your molecules are returned to the earth system whence they arose. Your heat is lost to space and is, like Bill Bailey, "never to return again." Ashes to ashes. Dust to dust.

VARIATIONS IN TEMPERATURES
SEEM TO AFFECT AGING

We in cool environment

Several experimental maneuvers have been shown to alter the aging rate. For instance, when fruit flies are cooled, they live longer. This was first noted as long ago as 1917, at the Rockefeller Institute. The effect holds true involving either young or old fruit flies. Conversely, when flies are heated, they die sooner.

The principle has been observed in other species. Roy Wolford, eminent gerontologist at UCLA, has confirmed this life-extending effect in fish. Specifically, cold fish can live three times their normal life span. Remember, entropy is decreased by cooling.

The problem for humans is that since we are warm-blooded, our body temperatures are not easily subject to manipulation. Nonetheless, some have seized this experimental observation and have proposed that freezing be employed as an age retardant, à la Sleeping Beauty or Rip Van Winkle, until some future propitious moment (e.g., the cure for cancer) arrives. The motto of the "cryo-longevity group" is "Freeze—Wait—Reanimate." It sounds like a football cheer.

I've even seen a coffee mug which reads:

> Now I lay me down to sleep,
> I pray the Lord my soul to keep.
> If I should die before I wake,
> Freeze me.

The technique involves the rapid draining of blood after death has occurred and its replacement with a mixture of glycerine and dimethylsulfoxide (DMSO), as in a type of antifreeze. The body is then frozen for the big sleep and stored in a cryotorium until the decision to thaw is made. A whole-body preservation costs $125,000, plus a $4,100 yearly maintenance fee. In my view, the chance of success of such an effort is virtually zero.

Dr. Paul Siegel reported recently of experiments in which a beagle named Miles (Woody Allen's character in *Sleeper*) had his body temperature chilled to three degrees centigrade for twenty minutes. During this time the dog's heartbeat, respiration, circulation, and even brain waves ceased— only to regain normalcy thereafter. But acknowledging the still remote likelihood of the extension of this work to humans, the issue remains—"Is it worth it?" Ben Franklin probably would have bought into the idea. He once asserted that he would have preferred to divide up his life so that he would live only one year in every one hundred. The science fiction opportunities provided by this scenario are rich.

Short of such extremism, however, lie several sober efforts to extend some cooling efforts to man. Several studies have been performed on swamis who have developed the capacity to lower their body temperatures, like hibernating animals. Freeman Dyson, in his work at Princeton University, observed that hibernation represents a hypothetical relief from age changes. Hibernating animals die sooner when they are prevented from deep sleep. Very old people have been observed to have lower than normal body temperatures, indicating either a true age change or the fact that they lived long because they were so cold.

And yet there seem to be contradictions. For example, attempts to alter life span in rats by raising them in a cool environment serve only to shorten their lives. Similarly, while some drugs such as marijuana, Thorazine, and L-dopa have been shown to lower the body temperatures in experimental animals and in humans, the effects are usually short-lived, and influences on life span are unproven. Concurrently, Professor R. D. Myers of Purdue University reported that the body's temperature depends on the differential balance of sodium and calcium in the thermostat in the brain. He suggested that infusing calcium into the spinal fluid of a monkey could reduce body temperature and thereby offer a hypothetical approach to extending life span.

Even if you were able to lower your temperature through increasing brain calcium content, or drugs, or meditation, the net effect on your metabolic processes, your élan vitale, is unknown. Is this slowing of entropy worth it?

As we have seen, cooling slows aging; and conversely, radiation has been used widely to induce precocious age change. This too can be easily reconciled with the proposition that aging is a statement of thermophysical decay. For example, gerontologists exposed laboratory animals to ionizing radiation to investigate its effects on the lens of the eye, on skin elasticity, on the bone marrow, and on other tissues. Such a technique represents a proxy for actual age changes which take much longer and are therefore more difficult to study. Radiation is clearly a tool which increases "the noise" in the system. Even now, the survivors of Hiroshima are being closely monitored for evidence of early age changes. But the early age changes brought on by exposure to radiation are certainly not a goal. The search continues for interventions which will positively affect or retard aging.

CAN WE AFFECT AGE BY TAKING A VITAMIN PILL?

As your machine burns energy, it produces waste materials and by-products, trash and ash, toxins and refuse. Your lungs dispose of your vapors, your skin releases your heat, your gut sloughs off fibrous residue, and your kidneys excrete degradation productions. In addition, your machine is so made as to repair itself when damaged or invaded. Skin tears are mended, bleeding stops. Microbes are engulfed and foreign, unfriendly substances are rejected—and all of this is done without conscious effort on the part of the control device. (Or is there conscious control? A point we will explore later.) All of this subserves the work, wonderful and otherwise, which you direct your machine to perform.

This has generated the very important area of research into the set of adverse "age" changes commonly termed "cross-linkage superoxidation." Professor Dennis Harmon at the University of Nebraska has been the leader of a worldwide effort to elucidate the nature of the metabolic havoc which occurs when your tissues are assaulted by the toxic compounds elaborated as by-products of your metabolism. Despite your body's wonderful reparative capacity, there is evidence that this repair is imperfect and that aging is associated with a slowly increasing rate of tissue changes due to these microinjuries. These observations have logically led to counteractive efforts. Some of these efforts, notably vitamin E and kindred compounds, dietary and otherwise, have earned their undeserved reputations as antiaging agents because of their hypothetical—but as yet undocumented—successes. An interesting study of the readers of *Prevention* magazine, age 65 or older, indicated no life extension benefits in those who took vitamin E. In fact, those who took high doses lived substantially less long.

Two other "microtheories" about the nature of aging should be mentioned. Edward Schneider, of the University of Southern California, Roy

Wolford, of UCLA, and others attribute aging to a loss of immunologic competence. As we age, there are important changes in the body's reactions to foreign substances and its surveillance of damage to its own tissues.

A number of alterations in basic repair mechanisms appear. For example, wounds still heal in centenarians, infections are fought, and foreign proteins are rejected; but the clear evidence of deterioration of immune responsiveness accompanies age. Thus, aging is manifest in a slower healing process.

Similarly, DNA, your template for cell reproduction, shows signs of wear and tear over the course of time. Your machine has found out how to repair some of the damage, to scavenge some of the debris. Angelo Economos, now in Iraklion, on the island of Crete, formerly with San Jose State University, has called this capacity "counterentropic." Despite many similarities (over 99 percent concordance of protein structure), the great apes have a life span which is only half of ours. Further, it has been discovered that your DNA repair capacities are double that of your ape cousins; and the associative relationship seems obvious. Whether this observation is causative remains uncertain.

LOWERED CALORIC INTAKE
EQUALS LONGER LIFE

The most challenging and possibly most significant of the experimental work concerned with life span was performed at Cornell, fifty years ago, by my father's good friend Clive McCay. About that time I recall visiting Ithaca with Dad on a golden May weekend, and the spirited conversation between the two. McCay had found, startlingly, that by restricting the calorie intake of growing rats he could extend their life span from 250 to 400 days. Further, not only did they live longer, but their coats kept their sheen, their eyes were bright, and their vigor was intact through the major extension of life span. This breakthrough remains today one of the most important ever made in the field of aging. It is so because of all the life-related experimental observations and theories derived therefrom. It is the only factor which has repeatedly been shown to lengthen the life span of mammals.

Morris Rose, who worked at the Institute for Cancer Research in

Philadelphia, showed that he was able to double the life span of his rats from approximately 900 days for the control group to 1,800 days for the calorie-restricted animals. The observations have been confirmed over and over now and have been replicated with mice and hamsters. There is current research at the National Institutes of Health extending this effort to primates, but the time and money necessary for such studies is immense. McCay, by restricting calories, caused rats to live longer lives and retarded age changes; but he did so by also retarding and stunting growth.

If you recall from chapter 1, French biologist Charles Buffon observed that animals tend to live six times the period of their growth. It was thought likely, therefore, that the longer life was mediated somehow by growth restriction in the underfed rats. This was in accord with Buffon's observations relating length of life and the rapidity of growth. However, it has been shown more recently by other researchers that calorie deprivation will extend the life of laboratory animals even after growth is complete. It should also be noted that these restricted rats were more physically active. (This is a point we will explore with some depth in a later chapter.)

McCay's 1935 studies were extended by other researchers who showed a life-lengthening effect by protein restriction per se. The protein story has not been shown to be consistent, however, as has the calorie-restriction one.

I have noted the alterations in immunologic competency and metabolic waste accumulation with normal aging. Once again, the calorically restricted rats show: (1) better maintenance of immune responsiveness; and (2) less toxic residue levels. The occurrence of cancer seems retarded in these animals as well.

There is a large body of evidence which links obesity with premature death. It is therefore not a far leap to propose that body fat somehow correlates with aging. In the absence of regular exercise, older persons almost always have a higher percentage of body fat than do younger persons. While it is true that the food-restricted rats of McCay's experiments had less total body fat than did their ad libitum control rats, there is so much variation as to render this causal implication unlikely.

What then is the explanation for McCay's remarkable model? The most respected worker in this field today is my old Berkeley days research chum Edward Masoro, who is now at the University of Texas Health Sciences Center in San Antonio. Ed has performed dozens of studies designed to chase down the numerous leads which are provided by the basic experimental demonstration. A great proportion of the previously cited clues have been provided by his laboratory. When I see him at meetings, I try to find a chance to ask him about his latest discovery. He is forthright enough to acknowledge that the final word is yet to be uttered on how food restriction allows the machine to last longer. As I interpret his current hypothesis (published with his co-worker Byung Yu), food restriction acts to slow aging through metabolic mechanisms which decrease the deteriorative processes leading to senescence.

What is the relevance, if any, to the human situation? Some have claimed that the whole calorie-restriction story is an artifact. They affirm that the laboratory rat widely used for experimental purposes has been successively bred for rapid growth, which itself is abnormal and leads to a restricted life span. Thus, they further contend, alleviating the tendency to grow "too fast" is merely allowing the rat to live its "normal life span." I believe such criticism is offset by Masoro's experiment showing that life span is extended even when McCay's principles are applied after growth is completed.

Others state that the experiments restricting calorie intake in rats lack significance because of something as basic as the abnormal feeding patterns of the laboratory rat. Laboratory rats can eat whatever they want; while in real life, rats (like primitive man) usually live on short rations. Consequently, giving a rat all it wants to eat is an anomaly—and by replicating the usual short-ration lifestyle, one is merely asserting the normal.

In humans we know that starvation and marked weight loss result in a lowered metabolic rate—the machine runs at a lower temperature.

The epidemic of plump, rosy-cheeked Churchillian babies seems to flout the implications of the research investigating the link between calorie restriction, lowered metabolism, and longevity. Indeed, if our babies are being overfed and their growth rates accelerated, we may actually be shortening their life spans. On the other hand, it is clear that now and in the past, billions of people have existed on restricted rations. If food restriction were truly an antiaging device, it seems logical to imply that there would be examples of persons who, like McCay's rats, had lived to extraordinary long life. This has not been observed. Of course it is a complex issue—generally, "undernutrition" in the human world is rather "malnutrition" with major deficiencies or absences of vital nutrients. The restricted rats, however, were supplemented with all the necessary ingredients—i.e., they ate good diets. All that was withheld were "unnecessary" calories. Malnutrition in the human world coexists with infection and other life-threatening mischief; so once again, the history has been obscured. It is ironic that at our time in history, when we have sufficient technologic capacity to feed all of us adequately, we still have immense islands of starvation coexisting with entire nations which are overfed.

It is difficult to imagine how we could ever mount a real experiment designed to test rigorously the calorie-restriction hypothesis in man. The inherent difficulties are so obvious that the proposition cannot even be suggested. Nonetheless, the effect is sufficient for noted gerontologist Roy Walford to have placed himself on a diet of lowered calories, fasting periodically and generally maintaining a caloric input that would make most of us hungry. Some of us are going to wait around to see if Roy is still here in the year 2100.

Two hundred years ago Buffon wrote, "Length of life depends neither on habits nor customs, nor on the quality of nutriment. Nothing can alter the iron laws which determine the number of years except a superfluity of food and a too abundantly furnished table."

THE RATE OF LIVING THEORY

Thus far I have enumerated a host of separate observations which bear on the fundamental question of why things grow old. Each has its devoted band of scientists who believe that their particular experimental domain holds the key to full understanding. In my view, it is quite possible that all these factors (chemical change, radiation injury, cooling, DNA errors, and immunologic failures) are correct; but, by themselves, they are insufficient to provide an encompassing theory. To me, the McCay model and its subsequent elucidation holds the most interest, despite the reservations noted earlier in this chapter. And so, to recapitulate Ed Masoro's interpretation: restricted feeding, and in my view all of the above theories, can be reconciled through a metabolic answer. That is, they all are examples of error, or friction, or inevitable entropic decay in the operating motor of the body. As we will see, this conclusion leads us to other observations regarding *how* this motor functions, and how both factors influence aging.

In 1908, a German professor, M. Rubner, observed crudely that the length of life of a group of domestic animals was related to their rate of caloric expenditure. This early observation was codified in 1928 by Raymond Pearl of Johns Hopkins University in what he called the Rate of

Living Theory. He proposed that the longevity of animals was a direct expression of the metabolic rate, how fast the chemical reactions, the body mechanics, and the machine run. Such a proposal is necessary to reconcile the observed various lengths of lives seen in animals. Among animals, the rate varies over 50-fold—over 15-fold in mammals alone. The mouse lives 2 years, the turtle and we over 100. We all know that, of course, but we don't stop to ponder why it is so.

Pearl's Rate of Living Theory represents a basic assertion of the thermodynamic definition of aging. As such it is virtually intuitive. The faster a machine is run, the sooner it wears out. A pair of shoes worn daily wears out approximately seven times faster than a pair worn once a week. Usually, a car driven by a male teenager lasts a shorter time than one driven by his grandmother. The Rate of Living Theory is a statement, a shaping to our own design, of the Second Law of Thermodynamics. Matter, over time, goes to greater disorder. Flesh, over time, ages—and ages at a rate proportional to the flow of energy through it. Although in cold-blooded creatures aging can be slowed experimentally, by means of cooling, it is sped by the heating process. Food spoils at high temperatures. Icebergs melt at the equator. In the tropics the siesta spares work in the heat. Metabolism, then, is a good news/bad news proposition. It is what gives life "life." It also provides repair. In so doing, it creates the seeds of its own destruction. The inanimate world doesn't have to worry about this complication to existence. Dishware simply breaks.

And so by choosing a thermophysical definition in which to frame our theories, all the observations are made whole. Each separately is insufficient.

Once we invoke a new way to define aging, we also define human time in a better term—not as an arbitrary self-relevant dimension, but as a marker of universal change, of which our aging is but a partial statement. To exploit the power of a thermodynamic definition we still have much work to do. To look at aging simply as decay is to deny a fundamental property of life, namely the capacity of self-repair. As noted earlier in this chapter, Angelo Economos used the term *counterentropy* to define the body's ability to heal degenerations such as DNA defects and toxic waste accumulation. A coal furnace can't get rid of its ashes by itself; we can. An Oldsmobile can't repair its dented fender; we can. This repair and healing capacity led George Sacher, of the Argonne National Laboratory, in Argonne, Illinois, to write, "Aging is not the result of metabolic activity per se, but rather the rate of entropy concomitant with metabolic activity. Aging no longer can be considered as simply a question of how much metabolic work: it is also a function of how well the work is done in thermodynamic and informational terms."

HOW DOES AGING RELATE TO DEATH?

If the thermodynamic explanation of aging is valid, is it helpful? Does it ease any of our fears? I believe that a great proportion of our fear derives from ignorance. I am not afraid if the plane bounces as it passes a dark cloud; I don't like it at all if it starts to buck in clear air. The mythology, emotionalism, and depression presently surrounding the aging process will disperse once we have a coherent, verifiable, unitary knowledge base regarding issues such as why we age and how long we can expect to live.

Further, it will help us to define death. Clearly, aging is not always a part of dying; we see this clearly in the affront which occurs when a child or young person dies. But the reverse is true, or should be true—namely, that dying is always a part of aging. A part of the greater continuum. Woody Allen said, "Death is nature's way of telling you to slow down."

Viewed from this perspective, death should hold little emotional content. Embalming or mummifying our dead bodies has no practical value. Such a practice merely attempts to preserve the past. It attempts to recover the unrecoverable; for as Roy Helton wrote, "The past is not recoverable, for what is recoverable is not yet past." The Second Law is reaffirmed.

My best hope is that as we demystify aging by giving it a sound, comprehensible explanation, we will go a long way toward making death more approachable and appropriate. If the car stops when the gas tank is empty, that is easily grasped; but when we sputter to a halt with a full tank, that's a big problem. Aging and death are part of our design. We cannot cure them. There is no place to hide from them. Chemicals, cell suspensions, and skin peels won't do it. Freezing or underfeeding or vitamins won't do it. In a moment of romanticism I would like to put our first glorious grandchild on hold at the present 4 years of age, like a stop-action of the VCR. In my mother's memory bank I was *always* in short pants. But such reverie does not exalt; it deludes. The Sanskrit tells us, "Yesterday is but a dream. . . . Look well to this day."

Replacing futile attempts to halt aging with the conceptualization of aging as entropy has immense medical implications. Presently we can re-place diseased or decayed hearts, lungs, livers, kidneys, skin, blood, joints, teeth, and lenses. We can rebuild and reshape noses, bosoms, buttocks, sex organs, ear drums, and skin scars. We are looking at being able to transplant glands. We pause at the prospect of transplanting nerve tissue, particularly the brain; and yet, while I'm certain I won't live long enough to see such a practice, brain transplant is at least hypothetically possible.

But what have we gained by these interventions? Have we altered the aging process in any fundamental way—or have we merely aborted premature death? Further, at what energy and dollar cost? Medicine is preoccupied with these reparative efforts and has gaudy credentials of its results, worthy of high theater. Yet, the results are all foreground. They don't affect the basic problem of aging, and they need to be separated therefrom. We can replace organs, but we can't replace ourselves.

Cloning—perish the thought. I cringe at the possibility of having more than one copy of any person, no matter how noble. It is an affront to natural process. We can replace matter, we can generate energy, but we can't restore time. My personal program is to invest in grandchildren, which is the best reach toward immortality of which I personally am capa-ble. The birth of a grandchild is my Easter.

As we grasp understanding of our outer dimensions, our wisdom will encompass an enlarging view of ourselves which is consonant with the physical laws of the universe. Conversely, for us to flout the imperative of such a general principle is a consummate vanity.

My wonderful old patients are generally in communion with their own aging. They may lament physical losses, but on the whole they demon-strate a much greater sense of wholeness, of equanimity with life, than do my younger charges. Age has its many credits; and wisdom, gained from experience, is high among them. To change that which can be changed, rather than to batter at the unchangeable. The wisdom to know the differ-ence. This resolve seems particularly evident in my older patients. Sickness always hurts, but it hurts less in the older years.

When we are young, how long we have yet to live is all dominant. Any other possibility is simply unacceptable. But as the years tick by, as the million hours pass, how much longer life is yet to be becomes quantitatively less important. Quality gains preeminence, so that by the end of life, con-tent is all that matters. A minute of good becomes an acceptable trade-off for several days of poor life. (Such a bargain could not be struck at any earlier life stage.) Quantity and quality cohere. My wonderful old patients are full up with both.

WHERE DOES THIS LEAVE IMMORTALITY?

Norman Cousins in his gemlike *Celebration of Life* looks at immortality as a continuum in which a personal life is a part of the flow of time—merged with the flow of universal experience. But what of the cancer cell, which, when grown in tissue culture as were Leonard Hayflick's cells, exhibits limitless cell division? Are not cancer cells immortal? To understand this seeming paradox, we must recognize that cancer cells metabolize very rapidly and are very disorderly. Consequently, they are incompatible with extended or full life. The mystery may be further explained when we examine a theory proposed by Stephen J. Gould, one of my favorite illuminators. Gould has written extensively on the effect of "scaling" in biology, a theory regarding how and why body shapes have the form and size they do.

In the August–September 1977 issue of *Natural History*, Gould stated:

> Small and large mammals are essentially similar. Their lifetimes are scaled to their life's pace, and all endure approximately the same amount of biological time. Small mammals tick fast, burn rapidly, and live for a short time; large ones live long at a stately pace. Measured by their own internal clocks, mammals of different sizes tend to live the same amount of time. All mammals, regardless of size, tend to breathe two hundred million times during their lives—their hearts therefore beat about eight hundred million times. Measured by sensible interval clocks of their own hearts or the rhythm of their own breathing, all mammals live about the same time.

Similarly, all animals use approximately the same amount of energy in a lifetime—about 40 million calories per pound per life. A small animal, such as a tree shrew, uses the same number of calories per unit mass in its short life as does either an elephant or a whale in a very different life span.

Further, Gould points out that the different life machines of various animals run at different rates, but that over an entire life span, the total number of breaths, heartbeats, etc. may be the same. That is to say that depending upon the rate at which energy is applied to it, flesh matter, in all of its various forms, obeys the same scaling rules in us all. Such a view is in accord with the recognition that life span and rate of living are intimately related. It takes only a small extra step to state that life span, rate of aging, and rate of living are related. Even cancer cannot be inconsistent with the Second Law.

Some maintain that the Second Law is depressing, predicting as it does an eventual demise of our world in heat death. That may be, but if it is true, it is still billions of years away. Meanwhile, we have big enough problems trying to understand our present confines and opportunities to let that remote prospect preoccupy us now. In my view, a thermodynamic interpretation of living processes carries with it a message of real hope—an ordering, age-delaying effect of energy flow. We will get to this point later, but for now I offer the hope that real enlightenment about aging and life is close at hand.

WHAT OF HEREDITY?

We cannot have a definition of aging without including a word about heredity. The hackneyed advice regarding how to live longer is that you should choose long-lived grandparents. Unfortunately, that's not helpful; and I would certainly never suggest selective breeding to achieve long life in humans.

In the 1920s, Raymond Pearl of Johns Hopkins University researched the notion that people with long lives spawn people who live longer. In his population sample, Pearl found that 46 percent of those individuals living past the age of 70 had two parents who had also survived to age 70 and older. In addition, 23 percent had one parent who had survived past age 70 and a second parent who had survived past age 50. Eighteen percent had one parent over the age of 70 and one parent under age 50; while only 13 percent of those who died over the age of 70 had no parents over 70 when they died.

Common sense seems to verify the accuracy of a genetic connection, but it overlooks the interdependency of nature and nurture. Is there a longevity gene, or do people who live longer simply teach their children how to do so? At present, we have no precise answer. The Metropolitan Life Insurance Company has calculated the correlation between length of life of both parent and child to be less than the correlation of height between parent and child.

Like politics, medicine is the art of the possible. So, if a patient comes to my office and tells me that every person in his family history died at age 50, and that his 50th birthday is next month, I do not merely say, "Good luck." Rather, I begin a rapid search for those things which I can do something about.

Chapter 3 begins our exploration of what we can do about premature death.

THREE

THE FAILURE OF MEDICINE

AUNT TO NIECE, "What do you want to be when you grow up?"
NIECE, "Alive."

Adlai Stevenson

L ife is a fatal disease. Once contracted there is no hope for survival.
There is no perpetual motion. Okay, we accept this now; but does it
have to end so soon? Does your machine last its allotted program, or does it
rust out, prematurely and protractedly? Eli Metschnikoff observed, "The
reason we are all afraid to die is that we recognize that it isn't time yet."

We are designed to last 120 years; but most of us die in late middle
age, around age 75. Such a failure would be intolerable to any industrial
consultant. The blueprint looked perfect. Did the system fail because of
external factors, as when lightning strikes a space shot; or did it fail because
of intrinsic faulty workmanship, as when a bolt is not tightened? We don't
know yet. Only one thing is certain—we are *not* dying of old age. Eminent
pathologist Robert Roessle of Berlin performed 16,000 autopsies and reported that in only *one* instance did he feel that death was due to "old age."
We haven't, yet, lived long enough to die of old age.

As we look at the reasons why we die, history gives interesting perspectives. The last 75 years have witnessed an increase in our life expectancy from 45 to 75 years of age—a gain of 30 years! It appears to have come
about as a result of four features:

1. Improvement in medical care before and around the time of birth.
Infant mortality was 200 per 1,000 births in 1900 and 10.9 per 1,000 in
1983, a decrease of 2,000 percent!

47

2. The conquest of most infectious diseases. In 1860, eight of the top killers were infections, while in 1950 only five infections made the top-ten list. Deaths from infectious diseases have declined 100-fold, so that now only pneumonia remains as a major infectious killer.

3. A general improvement in nutritional adequacy.

4. Better public hygiene (with the exception of environmental pollution).

Such a dramatic lengthening of the average life span has never occurred in history before, and may not again. But we must not become complacent. We die too soon—decades too soon; the machine is defective.

A lifetime shortfall still occurs despite two major new events which, on the surface, should have increased life span. These are:

1. The incredible amount of money that we in the United States spend on health care. These totals include the high cost of death—a figure which is presently over $15 billion a year (higher than the national budget of Bangladesh)—and the cost of legal protection.

2. The dramatic increase in medical knowledge.

THE HIGH COST OF HEALTH CARE

In 1929, the first year such statistics were kept, we as a nation spent around $3 billion on health care. By 1950, that total had risen to $12 billion. In 1960, $26 billion. In 1987, we spent $542 billion on health care. That's $1.4 billion every day. And the escalation shows no sign of letting up. The projections, probably conservative, are for $660 billion in 1990 and $1.5 trillion in the year 2000. By 2080, we can expect medical costs which will equal our present federal budget; by 2370, such costs will surpass this country's gross national product for 1989.

Colorado's former governor Richard Lamm terms health care costs "an economic cancer that is threatening our prosperity." The cost of a bed in almost any intensive care unit is over $2,000 a day ($5,000 a day in some neonatal intensive care units)—and that's before the doctor walks in, before a test is ordered, before a treatment is given. Hospital bills in excess of $100,000 are now commonplace. If the increase in health care spending is extrapolated in the near future, health care expenses will consume the entirety of our gross national product. This is obviously ridiculous, but the reality is that we will soon be facing hard choices. For example, it's projected that in the year 1990, there will be 300,000 balloon angioplasties performed in the United States. Developed in 1982, this is the technique in which a tiny balloon is inflated inside the heart artery to open up a blockage. The cost will be approximately $3 billion—a sum equal to all heart-related medical expenditures of the previous 60 years. Forty percent of these arteries will close up again in a year. Until now, rationing of medical resources has not been a major topic of discussion. Now it must be. In *The Painful Prescription*, Henry Aaron and William Schwartz from the Brookings Institute describe how such rationing of medical supplies and services is already taking place in Great Britain. It is a task that I do not anticipate with relish.

Richard Lamm commented further that America's doctors now have the chance to make the individual patient well, and the nation ill. Cure the patient, kill the country.

The reasons behind the cost surge are many and occupy the work endeavors of congressional committees, academic think tanks, corporate offices, and each of us at health insurance bill time. In my view, the major force causing the increased cost of health care is what is commonly called the "technologic imperative." For example, during the past 20 years, the average number of tests ordered at the time of appendicitis has risen from five to thirty-one. These past two decades have provided powerful new tools to tend our bodies. There is no question about the increased perceptive and therapeutic advantage that those technologies provide for *individual* patients; yet their translation into gain for the population at large is far from ideal.

My old friend Dr. Leonard Sagan recently published a fine book called *The Health of Nations*. In it he cites the statistics for 1984, during which 50,000 coronary artery bypass graft (CABG) operations were performed (at about $15,000 per) and 500,000 cardiac catheterizations were performed (at approximately $3,000 each). The new Genentech product, tissue plasminogen activator (TPA), which helps to dissolve blood clots, costs $2,200 per dose.

The contribution of these high-tech maneuvers to the decline in heart-disease deaths in our country is thought to be minor, however. Most analysts attribute the worldwide decline in such deaths to better health behavior activities. Lower smoking rates, dietary prudence, and a more vigorous populace are much better candidates for credit than are the cardiologist and the heart surgeon. An ounce of prevention is worth a ton of cure.

As we scrutinize procedures, even more suspect are the operations concerning opening up the carotid arteries in the neck. Thousands of persons have had the blood vessels leading to their brains surgically explored and scraped in the name of increasing blood flow to their heads. Unfortunately, cleaning out one segment of the pipe isn't effective if there is clogging farther upstream.

Not everything done in the name of medical science is beneficial. It is a hobby of mine to survey the things I do in my daily medical practice which ten years from now will be labeled as "bad medicine." Not many years ago a patient after a heart attack was kept in bed for days or weeks (like a woman after delivering a baby). Today our heart attack victims and new mothers are out of bed the same day or the next. A few years ago the proper diet for a person with diverticulitis was one with low roughage content. Now we prescribe exactly the opposite—bran and more bran. Maybe we don't do things as egregious as the bloodletting of the royal physicians in the past, but clearly some of our present sacred cow procedures will be cast out in the years immediately ahead. It is a local piece of folk wisdom that the death rates in Los Angeles went down a few years ago when the doctors went on strike.

THE COST OF DYING

A substantial contribution to the cost of medical care is the high cost of dying. Numerous studies have indicated the very high percentage of expenditures in the last year of life. In a recent study by health economist Ann Scitovsky of the patients at my clinic who had died revealed that the average cost of the last year of life was nearly $23,000. Doctors see death as a failure.

The logical conclusion to these implications is that it would save the system a great deal if we learned how to die just before the last year of life. A quick death saves money. It has been suggested by some wags that maybe we should encourage more people to smoke because then they won't live long enough to collect their contributions to the Social Security system. This tongue-in-cheek reflection is odious. Yet, someone who dies in an auto accident doesn't generate much societal cost. Someone seriously injured in an auto accident is going to cost someone, probably all of us, a lot.

THE HIGH COST OF LEGAL INVOLVEMENT

The runaway increase in malpractice insurance—caused primarily by the excesses of the legal profession—also emerges as a substantial contributor to the erupting medical costs. Many American communities are without an obstetrician simply because malpractice claims have been outrageous. Any newborn with any birth disorder immediately triggers a lawsuit regardless of dereliction on the part of the doctor. It would be my firm bet that over 90 percent of malpractice suits which are brought to the courts are without merit—but fed by the glut of lawyers.

The sum total of these forces, fueled by the increasingly older population with their attendant higher medical bills, creates a situation in which we as a nation spend about three times as much on health care and social programs as we do on national defense. Who is to say this isn't okay; but are the dollars well spent? Certainly people in other countries seem to be living longer with a cheaper system. Individuals living in Japan, Greece, and Iceland, for example, have greater life expectancies; but their per capita health expenditures are one-fifth of our own.

THE KNOWLEDGE EXPLOSION

Having established conclusively that we are spending a vastly greater amount of money on the maintenance and repair of our collective personal machinery, it becomes important to establish how much more we know about the whole health and illness process than we did in our reference year of 1929. Knowledge is obviously a harder thing to quantify than dollars spent, but nonetheless there are several reasonable yardsticks we might use as rough approximations. For example, a paper published a few years ago in the transactions of the New York Academy of Sciences contained a section called "The Growth of Science." In his article "The Knowledge Explosion," Julius Lukagiewicz notes that since 1760, the number of scientific journals has been increasing at a constant exponential rate, doubling every 15 years (increasing 10-fold every 50 years) until the present total of approximately 200,000. There were over 1 million separate scientific articles published in 1968. Now, over 7,000 scientific articles are published throughout the world every day! This brings the yearly total to over 2.5 million! Closely paralleling the journal and separate-publication increases is the count of scientists and engineers active in the United States. Since 1930, their numbers have doubled every 12 to 14 years, indicating, not surprisingly, a direct relationship to the growth of the publication. Other growth parameters, such as the number of patent applications and the increases in medical research and development budgets show similar 10- to 15-year doublings. For example, the research budget for Massachusetts General Hospital was $50,000 in the year 1935, and $7 million in 1965. In 1990, that figure is approaching $100 million a year. The computer era has only served to accelerate these increases.

Personally, I relate to the knowledge explosion when I reflect on my accreditation process. I was graduated from medical school in 1955 and began a postgraduate training which included: internship, residency, and fellowship in biochemistry in Philadelphia, Charity Hospital in New Orleans, the University of California at San Francisco, and the Max Planck Institute in Munich. My study was interrupted for two years while I fought the battle of Schofield Barracks in Hawaii, and ended upon my seeing my first, personal patient in September 1963. (My wife and I were blessed with four great children en route.) When I decided to attempt to certify my competence in internal medicine—I felt ready. After a grueling two-part examination (consisting of both written and practical aspects), I became a "specialist in internal medicine." I had passed my Boards! This is a great moment in the life of a young doctor.

What all of this meant was that I was entitled to hang another certificate on the wall, and put the initials F.A.C.P. (Fellow of the American College of Physicians) after the M.D. on my prescription pad and letterhead.

I was hot stuff—but that was 27 years ago. What has happened to the knowledge base, the information curve, during this time? It has probably doubled two or three times! I don't think my patients would be very happy if they thought their doctor was operating on a know-how learned 27 years ago.

Recognizing this, the various medical specialty certifying organizations have created "recertifying exams"—similar to the process of renewing your driver's license. Several years ago, a number of my colleagues and I decided it was appropriate to bone up and take this re-exam. For several months, we met every Wednesday night to study the various "ologies" (cardiology, gastroenterology, nephrology, etc.) which collectively comprise internal medicine. I took and happily passed the re-exam; the point being that if I had to take the exam based on my 1963 knowledge, I not only could not have answered the questions, I would not even have recognized what they were about.

My father used to tell me the story of his first day as a student at Harvard Medical School. His dean told the collective freshmen, "Ladies and gentlemen, I welcome you to the richest intellectual experience of your lives. In the next four years you will learn the intricacies and wonders of the human body, and of the myriad of things which can go wrong with it. Unfortunately, ten years from now, half of what we have taught you will no longer be true; and furthermore, we can't tell you which half that is."

HAVE KNOWLEDGE AND EXPENSE EXTENDED LIFE?

I have established that we are spending over 100 times as much on our health as we were 60 years ago, and that we know perhaps 60 times as much about ourselves as we did then. It seems appropriate to find out what has been accomplished by this increased expenditure and knowledge base. Obviously we could hold up a number of outcome measures as a test of success for this input; but for demonstration purposes, I propose that we look at the further life expectancy of the average, white, 40-year-old American male. In 1929, such a man would have had an additional 29 years of life left to him. Said in another way, the actuary could calculate that in 1929 a white, 40-year-old male would, on average, die at age 69. Today we could predict that a white, 40-year-old male would have an additional 34 years of life left in him, or until the approximate age of 74. Thus, as illustrated by the graph below, despite immense increases in knowledge and expense, our "sample patient" can expect to live a mere 5 years longer than did his grandfather. It is true that the gain has been somewhat better for blacks and females; but the net gain for this tremendous new input has been marginal at best. It is not a very good bargain.

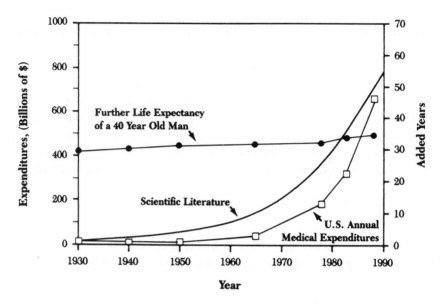

For a physician this realization is sobering. We all like to think that the fruit of our labor translates into manifest good, including, of course, longer life. The reality is that most medical care and costs address symptoms which may or may not affect the length of life. These figures should make my profession highly aware of the marginal benefits of many of the wonderful technologies which are coming off the bioengineers' drawing boards. Technology assessment is the critical new buzz term in medicine. Does the new platinum-coated Magnetic Resonance Imager (MRI) scanner save lives? At what cost? Does every diabetic "deserve" a pancreas transplant? Can we afford it? Daniel Callahan, director of the Hastings Institute, has recently published a widely cited book, *Setting Limits.* It focuses attention on this increasingly constricting area. For the first time in history large-scale rationing of medical resources is at hand. (More on this later.)

Back to our 40-year-old, average white male. We have just discovered that money and knowledge have netted him only 5 more years of life than he could have expected had he lived six decades earlier. In 1900, our 40-year-old had 27 years more left to him, so those three cheap and blissfully ignorant decades until 1930 yielded proportionately the same life expectancy gain. In other words, the gain from 1900 to 1930 was 2 additional years, and the gain from 1930 to 1990, 5 additional years. What is wrong?

We can begin to answer that question by looking at the biggest killers of middle-aged persons. I have come to call these killers the New Riders of the Apocalypse, and they are identified as the following: heart disease, cancer, stroke, and trauma.

HEART DISEASE

It is general knowledge that heart disease is our major modern demon. For the most part, heart trouble isn't basically heart trouble at all; rather, it is artery trouble (known to doctors as arteriosclerosis or atherosclerosis—hardening of the arteries). The French sage Henry Cazalis (1840–1909) rightly observed, "A man is as old as his arteries." A 40-year-old with bad pipes can be old; an 80-year-old with clear pipes can be young. It has been estimated that if arteriosclerosis were eliminated, a person 65 years of age could accrue from 10 to 16 years of additional life. I wrote my honors thesis at Williams College in 1951 on the subject of arteriosclerosis. I have done research into its basic nature with rats, rabbits, and monkeys in Hawaii, New Orleans, Munich, Philadelphia, and Palo Alto. I have written dozens of research papers in my humble effort to understand its complexities and mechanisms. We have found out a tremendous lot about it, but it is still far and away our biggest killer. Irvine Page once remarked about arteriosclerosis, "If you are not confused you are not informed." Nearly 800,000 Americans die each year in the *confusion* we call heart disease.

How do I as a practicing physician hear about it?

The phone rings. "Dr. Bortz, Harry just developed a terrific squeezing pain in his chest. He's sweating; he's short of breath."

I try to reassure. "Take it easy. Call the paramedics. Take him to the emergency room. I'll call and tell them he is coming. I will meet you there."

Once in the ER, a rapid assessment of the situation is made. We may find a critical decrease in blood pressure, rhythm abnormalities, and fluid congestion. Once stable, Harry is transferred to the coronary care unit, where the terrific nurses serve as an instant antenna to detect any adverse changes in the situation. This intensive care can cost $2,000 a day. The main responsibility of the CCU is to detect any change in how the heart is beating. This is detected by the electrocardiogram attached to Harry's chest and transmitted to the central monitor, where the monitor nurse pays constant attention. Any significant alteration can be addressed immediately. If, however, there are no arrhythmias, no blood pressure changes, and no signs of lung congestion with fluid, a British study suggests that Harry could, with equal safety and much less cost, do just as well at home. However, this decision takes a fair amount of bravado because of the afore-mentioned *technological imperative.* If I were to send Harry home and he were to get in trouble, I would feel terrible. Not to mention how Harry and his wife would feel. Therefore, if a heart attack is thought likely, Harry will go to the CCU despite the evidences that he would probably do just as well at home.

If it is found that the heartbeat is skipping erratically, medicine has developed an elaborate set of maneuvers to counteract the situation. The electrical part of heart attacks is something we can handle pretty well. But what if the heart attack has resulted in so much damage to the heart that it no longer can adequately perform its job of moving blood? Our jargon term for this is "pump failure," and it is the final arbiter in whether Harry survives. The heart, after all, is the pump of your machine, processing hundreds of gallons of blood throughout your body every day. If the pump stops pumping, the blood pressure fails. The lungs fill with fluid, death lurks.

What is a heart attack? This central bag of muscle seated so comfort-ably in the middle of your chest gets its own blood, not from the blood within its four chambers, but from the coronary arteries—three small tribu-taries of the aorta just after it leaves the heart. When one of these arteries is plugged up with a chunk of cholesterol or by a clot, the segment of the heart muscle served by that artery is robbed of oxygen. Just like tightening a tourniquet around your finger, the heart muscle swells, turns purple, and hurts. If the block is to a large portion of the heart—that's it. If it is a peripheral blockage, less damage results.

The painful fact is that half of the people who die of heart attacks do so before a doctor can be called—witness the cases of former Vice President Nelson Rockefeller and runner Jim Fixx. Having a faster ambulance, a smarter cardiologist, or a more elaborate CCU doesn't matter if you're dead before you can get into the system.

By the time a patient like Harry makes it to the system, the mischief has already been done. In fact, we have only a few minutes after the actual blockage before irreversible scarring has occurred. With hope, he will be placed in the CCU so that we may "make do" with what is left.

And "making do" can involve some rather remarkable efforts. We can measure pretty accurately the residual pumping capacity of the heart (commonly called the "ejection fraction"). In fact, we have wonderful new tools with which to address this phase of the problem. Thus we can deter-mine if a damaged heart can still squeeze and pump enough blood to serve the body's needs while shaving, or working, or making love. This is the time at which I regularly encounter my patients after they have brushed up against our number-one killer.

There is clear evidence that deaths from heart disease have decreased in our country and elsewhere in the past decade; but we must ask ourselves the reason for such improvement. Is it because of our new technical faculties or CCUs? Because we have more cardiac surgeons, or because of better in-the-field CPR? Or is the improvement the result of a general change in lifestyle which addresses a different stage of the problem?

Despite the advances, heart trouble—Harry's chest pain—is still our dominant killer. And in many ways it's no different today from what it was 60 years ago in a cheaper and less enlightened era. Despite the advances, once the artery blockage has occurred, all of medicine's horses and all of medicine's men cannot make Harry whole again.

CANCER

Our number-two killer is cancer. Two hundred thousand Americans die of it each year. Certainly we know incredibly more about cancer than we did 60 years ago, and we certainly spend a great deal more on it than we did then. As I graduated from medical school in 1955 and my wonderful mother-in-law was dying of ovarian and breast cancer at age 53, I despaired of our ever understanding the root nature of this basic evil. I felt that to understand cancer was to understand life, and I felt then that this was not ours to know. I have come to change my view totally. I now believe that because of our advances in protein chemistry, and possibly by application of the new insights provided by Prigogine, we will—within my lifetime—develop penetrating insight into the heart of the beast.

Several years ago an article published in the *New England Journal of Medicine* concluded that death rates from cancer had not fallen in the preceding 50 years. In other words, as many Americans were dying of cancer then as they were decades before. This, of course, was met by howls of protest from the *poohbahs* of the cancer camp. Even today it is uncertain whether there has been "progress" in the public-health sense of the word regarding the management of cancer; but clearly there have been notable achievements with thousands of individuals. It is still unclear whether this translates into an overall benefit.

How do I, as a practicing physician, see cancer? Several years ago, a lovely 54-year-old lady was referred to me by one of our clinic's gynecologists. On a routine visit, this doctor had discovered that the patient had high blood pressure.

"You go see Bortz," the doctor suggested. "He's a nice fellow, and he'll advise you further regarding what you should do."

The patient visited me, and we had a very cordial visit, during which I took her history, did my physical examination, confirmed that her blood pressure was up a little, sent her off to the laboratory for routine blood and urine analyses, sent her to the heart station for an electrocardiogram, and sent her to X-ray for a picture of her chest. Finally, I made a date for her to return so that we could go over her test results, take one more blood pressure measurement, and then plan her therapy. A day or so later, the tests started returning to my desk. I was jolted by the typed report on an innocent-looking X-ray slip. It read, "In the middle of the left upper lung field, there is an irregular 3 × 5 centimeter density, probably indicating malignancy." This awful information hit like a sledgehammer, because I recognized that despite all heroic efforts on the part of the medical care team, myself, the pulmonary expert, the chest surgeon, the therapeutic radiologist, the oncologist—despite everything that could be brought to bear upon her situation—the patient would undoubtedly be dead within a year.

The 5-year survival for lung cancer—our most common killing form of cancer in men and now in women—is about 5 percent. One person in 20 who is found to have lung cancer in this intelligent, expensive medical age will live 5 years. That's about the same as it was 60 years ago, when the world was much simpler.

Why is this? Why can't we do more? The answer is both simple and tragic. By the time the tumor has come to light, it has been growing silently, malevolently, in the lung tissue for months. During this time it has been shedding its daughter cells to the brain, to the liver, and to the bone marrow, so that by the time I, or my like, see the patient, the tumor has "splattered" throughout the body. Would you then have the surgeon cut it all out? He can't. Would you have the radiologist radiate it all away? He can't. Would you have the oncologist poison it all away? He can't. Lung cancer, our most common cancer killer, yields only 1 in 20 to 5 years.

This is dismal. I know this as I see my patient. Gently I involve her with the dread prospects which lie ahead. We try our damnedest—but when the dust settles, the numbers remain. We are not very good at curing our bad cancers. They spread too fast. They are too malignant.

Certainly we in medicine have done much good work in the treatment of cancer. At my parent institution, Stanford, hundreds of cases of Hodgkin's disease, once universally fatal, do, by intense therapeutic efforts, live long. They seem to be cured. I am personally skeptical, however, that the ultimate answer to cancer, as with the heart attack, will come from a curative approach. I share with the surgeon general the conviction that much if not most of cancer is behaviorally caused; and that as we increasingly heed lifestyle imperatives we will do much to make a major dent in this disease.

STROKE

Our third big killer comes in the form of a stroke. One hundred fifty thousand Americans die each year of this condition. What is a stroke? Biologically it is the cousin of a heart attack; but instead of the block being in an artery serving the heart, it is in an artery supplying the brain, or else a hemorrhage into the brain. Since our mental and physical capacities are generally controlled by specific areas of the brain, the effect of the stroke (like the heart attack) depends upon *where* the damage has occurred. If a person is right-handed and the block occurs on the dominant left side, say a block to the internal carotid artery on the left, the person develops a paralysis of the right side and cannot speak. If the blockage is on the other side, the left side of the body is paralyzed; but speech is spared.

How do I learn about a stroke? The phone rings. "Dr. Bortz, Millie can't talk. Her face is drawn to one side; she's slumped over; she can't stand up."

I then arrange for admission to the hospital. There is no call for the paramedics, the emergency room, or the intensive care unit, because we know that the brain has an even more limited time for rescue than does the heart—something in the range of 4 minutes. If a person were to have a stroke in the operating room, the spot of blockage immediately identified and the surgeon summoned, he or she would not have sufficient time to get to the block and relieve it before the damage occurred. Said in another way, by the time I first received the call, it was already too late to undo the damage. Again, the entirety of the stay in the hospital is preoccupied with efforts with the physical, occupational, and speech therapy departments to make do with what is left. To compensate for damage done. Again, Humpty Dumpty is not set right. The egg is not whole. Our approach to stroke is no better than it was in 1929—sobering, but true.

In an essay predicting that someday we will be a disease-free species, Lewis Thomas wrote, "It is the general belief that we need our diseases—they are natural parts of the human condition. It goes against nature to tamper and manipulate them out of existence, as I propose. 'Then what?' What on earth will we die of? Are we to go on forever disease-free, with nothing to occupy our minds but the passage of time? What are the biologists doing to us? How can you finish honorably, and die honestly, without disease?"

The answer is, by means of the "accident."

TRAUMA

Accidents (or traumas) are the fourth major cause of death in the United States and are seen in a wide variety of situations. In the younger age group, the automobile is the principal co-conspirator. With the older person, falls are the primary event. My regular and insistent advice to my otherwise well 90-year-old patients is, "Don't fall down." A hip fracture is not generally thought of as a lethal event, but for older people particularly, mobility and life are tightly linked—just as they were with our paleoancestors on the Serengeti. As long as we can move, vitality endures. Subtract movement from us, and survival is threatened. There were at least 247,000 cases of hip fracture in the United States in 1985, with a 15 percent direct mortality rate. One-third of old persons fall at least once each year. One-third of women over 90 will have a hip fracture. In 1983, hip fractures cost $7.3 billion.

Several months ago, my oldest patient (almost 107 years old) fell and broke her hip. I was crushed by the recognition of what threat this held out to her. After quick counsel, we elected to proceed with surgical repair of the fracture, reasoning that not to do so would commit her to weeks of bed rest and its attendant risk. She lived through the surgery fine; but in the recovery room she died in an instant without warning or fanfare. She succumbed to her fall. The death certificate reads, "Death due to cardiac arrest"—as almost all deaths are, but the real cause of her death was her fractured hip.

Perhaps this is as it should be. If we can enter the era where there is "disease no mo'," then the only causes of death will be old age and accidents. Certainly in the wild, trauma accounts for most deaths. Perhaps we will arrive at a point in time when this shall prevail again.

In the inanimate world there is no disease—disease is a property of living creatures—inanimate things either wear out or are broken. Obviously, the older a thing is the more likely it is to break—to die as a result of an accident when virtually worn out is not too bad a design; to die of an accident early in life is clearly an insult. If I fall off a mountain, or surfboard, or ladder at 120 years of age, I won't mind.

But the basic point, once again, is that once an accident has happened, the damage is already done. The job of the medical profession, the system, is to make do with what is left. For the budding medical student, intern, or resident, this is an affront to his or her sense of omnipotence. "I will make you well." It is a phrase with major limitations. The 40-year-old male fares little better today than he did 60 years ago, and these are the reasons why.

THE GOOD NEWS

All of this sounds very despairing and futile; it makes it all seem so worthless. But amid all the grim tidings is wonderful and glorious good news—which is strangely muffled (but that is part of the next chapter). The wonderful and glorious good news is polio.

When I was a little boy growing up in downtown Philadelphia, my parents used to send me to the New Jersey seaside in the summer. The reason for this was not to provide me with a summer in the sun, but because of their terror that their little boy would awaken in the morning paralyzed, unable to breathe, or dead. Polio was a scourge in the land. Thousands of kids were being ravaged by the unseen evil that would flow through the shuttered nighttime windows and wreak its devilment. I am sure that for my parents it was much like it was for the parents in medieval Europe when bubonic plague was alive in the streets. A monster was loose.

And what was the response of medicine to polio in those days? We had the iron lung, that monstrous huge cylinder which encased the body in an unwieldy effort to compensate for a paralyzed diaphragm. I recall going to movie newsreels and wondering at the heroism of those devoted to this low-benefit approach. And then there was Sister Kenney. I recall her from my youth as a loving gentle figure wrapping the limbs of the unfortunate polio victims in warm clothes, and delivering some measure of physical therapy. To what benefit?

What is polio? Polio is the destruction of the anterior portion of the spinal cord by the polio virus. If you ever have a chance to look in a microscope at a specimen of the spinal cord of a child with polio, you will see how ravaged the tissues are. The spinal cord—the body's main electrical cable—is made up of myriad minute nerve filaments, each wonderfully serving its movement and sensing functions. In polio these filaments are blasted, just as though one had stuck a hot poker into the spine and rammed it back and forth. The delicate nerve fibers are shredded, the connections shattered; chaos prevails.

What then could curative medicine hope to offer? Would we ask a surgeon to come in and put the cord in order again? Could the surgeon suture a million nerve ends to their correct other million nerve ends? Clearly the approach had no chance—in 1929, now, or in all future history.

But suddenly, wonderfully, there is virtually no more polio. My children, having children, will never have to go through the terror my parents experienced. This is a major triumph for mankind, by any standard; but there is no dancing in the streets because of it.

Perhaps there is an even greater triumph in our time: smallpox. For centuries smallpox scourged the world, claiming millions and millions of victims to torment and death. Smallpox is, or was, an infectious disease transmitted through the air by inhalations of the virus. It penetrated the body, producing fever, chills, nausea, and vomiting; after one to three weeks, a generalized pustular rash occurred which covered the body as well as the lining of the mouth and intestine. Death rates ranged up to 100 percent, and medical texts stated, "There is no treatment for smallpox." It was known as far back as 300 A.D. and swept through Europe in waves in the 1600s. The American Indian was particularly taken by smallpox, and some historians assign this condition a primary reason for the conquest by the white man. In my lifetime there have been epidemics in Bangladesh. But today, for the first time in history, there is no more smallpox. Not one case in a year. What a time for jubilation, but where are the headlines?

The point of this chapter is to illustrate that we die prematurely from causes that are sternly resistant to the prevailing approach, namely cure. Polio and smallpox document the established fact that most of the major advances in the state of our health have come about not by cures but by prevention. Massive interventional public health efforts at the local, national and international levels have combined to rid our Mother Earth from these scourges. These battles have been won by a combination of good scientific research and responsive governmental policies.

Prevention is the key word. The disease avoided spares the burden of being sick. It spares the cost too. Unfortunately, the medical enterprise has flourished in the "cure" tradition, and there are legitimate reasons why this is so.

ANESTHETICS AND ANTIBIOTICS: LEGITIMATE AGENTS OF CURE

Through the aeons of recorded history, medical treatment really had very little of legitimate benefit to offer. Leonard Sagan states that until the modern era, medical practice did as much to shorten life as to lengthen it. For example, review of the "regal" medical care offered to medieval monarchs reveals how sturdy these ancient rulers must have been to have withstood the bloodlettings and other pathetically misguided efforts to cure. The best that early medicine had to offer was comfort.

One hundred years ago anesthetics were introduced. They were probably the first legitimately effective medical agents. They salved our hurts and allowed modern surgery to evolve. I shudder to think of the fate of accident victims before anesthetics were available. The most impressive contributions which M.A.S.H. units could have brought to Caesar and Napoleon would have been anesthetics.

Fifty years later, antibiotics arrived with sulfa and then penicillin and the rest. I recall the hushed moments of Grandpa's house in 1939, when his two physician sons, my namesake uncle and my father, administered the first sulfa drug to him to treat his pneumonia. Grandpa went into kidney failure and died as a result of the well intended but primitive treatment. And this, only fifty years ago.

Nonetheless, the introduction of antibiotics gave medicine a second legitimate curing function. This was subsequently built upon by modern surgery, which had languished in the backwaters of sepsis until the antibiotics arose. The early surgeons had horrible postoperative results. Usually the tumor, or "blockage," or stone was removed only to have the patient die thereafter of fever and sepsis. Using both anesthetics and antibiotics, surgery built the image of medicine as a curing science—"fix it," "cut it out." The inherent drama of the operating theater became the glamour of medicine. The Mayos, Alton Ochsner, Frank Lahey, Eugene Halsted, and the rest of the surgeon headliners became the epitome of modern medicine.

THE SEDUCTIVE ILLUSION OF THE CURE

The attraction of cure as the appropriate end product of medical effort is evident. It is logical, simple, and final. Cure seems American. It is winning. It is the good guy in the white hat. It is technology. It is a quick fix, the easy way. "Nothing is going to stop us now." The physician as Rambo. Such an image conforms with the Christian ethic of an incarnate, external evil penetrating the essential primal good. The solution to which is the expunging of evil by the power of the priesthood. Disease and medicine. Sin and redemption. It all seems so appropriate and symmetrical.

It worked for a while. Antibiotics and surgery saved millions of lives. Much bad was killed and cut out. But today medicine has reached the virtual limits of its curative capacity. We can't cure heart attacks; we rarely cure lung cancer; we don't cure strokes; we don't cure accidents, diabetes, emphysema, or cirrhosis. After its curing era has been run, all that is left for contemporary medicine is palliative. We alleviate pain. We make do with what is left.

Victor Fuchs, brilliant medical economist and longtime friend at Stanford (and before), tells the "Tale of Two States" in his insightful book *Who Shall Live?* In the story, Fuchs contrasts Utah and Nevada. The two are geographically contiguous, have similar climates, topography and population, economies and urbanization, and numbers of doctors and hospital beds per capita. However, regarding death rates, there are huge differences between these states. General death rates in Nevada range from 10 to 69 percent higher than in Utah. Death rates from cirrhosis and lung cancer are 111 percent to 590 percent higher in Nevada than in Utah. Surely the medical system has as much curative capacity in Nevada as it does in Utah—

but even this cannot overcome the behavioral patterns that vary within the populations of the two states. Utah has a predominantly Mormon popula- tion, and the tenets of this religion prohibit drinking alcohol and smoking— the major contributory factors in cirrhosis and lung cancer. Nationally, Mormon mortality rates are 30 percent lower than those of the country as a whole. We can observe the same phenomenon within other groups whose religious principles advocate abstention from smoking and alcohol. For example, male members of the Church of the Seventh Day Adventist live an average of 6 years longer than the national norms. If you are dead before you can get into the system, or even after you are in the system, the system really doesn't make much difference.

Fuchs goes on to say, as do Sagan and others, "In developed countries, the marginal contribution of medical care to life expectancy is very small, that is, variations in mortality across and within countries do not seem to be related to differences in the availability of physicians or other medical care inputs." This is reflected by the fact that, despite their lesser commitment of financial and other resources to medical care, life expectancy in the United States ranks below that of fifteen other countries in the world.

Not only does medical care seem to be of marginal positive medical benefit, it can even represent a hazard. Thus emerges the phenomenon of iatrogenic (physician caused) illnesses. When my uncle Walter started his rural practice, maybe he didn't do much good, but he didn't do a lot of harm either. With the new technologies, our ability to poison, radiate, and desic- cate has multiplied immensely. Hospitals are dangerous places.

My father used to tell the story of the patient under his care whose illness had baffled all the well-intentioned efforts of the entire medical team taking care of him. One morning on rounds, the patient said to Dad, "Doc, I want you to know that I really appreciate all you're doing for me; but I wonder if you wouldn't let me go home for a few days to recuperate, and then I'll be glad to come back in and let you work on me some more." Sad, but true. If you are strong enough to live through a hospital experience, maybe you weren't so sick after all.

There is currently a widespread effort in the medical profession toward "technology assessment." We need urgently to know whether these wonderful and powerful new tools which we develop daily are truly valu- able. Should I order a test that costs $500 if there is only marginal benefit to be derived from the information that will be gained? Should I advise a treatment when the long-term side effects are not clear? In order to per- form organ transplants, for example, we need to suppress the immune system so that the new organ will take. Years later we recognize that such tinkering with the body's basic immunologic responsiveness leads to higher rates of cancer. The faster the tempo beats, the more urgent and threatening the consequences. Certainly we don't want to delay the use of a valuable new technology, but we need to be reasonably certain that its use will not cause more damage than it is designed to alleviate. Other countries have precipitously approved new drugs for human use before their safety was assured—with disastrous consequences. We must be very wise. Nonetheless, it is hard to be infinitely wise when so much is at stake, and when our ignorance quotient is so high. Decisions must be more tightly reasoned, analyses must be more clearly drawn.

Dr. John Knowles, the late, immensely esteemed administrator of Massachusetts General Hospital and president of the Rockefeller Foundation, lamented "the traditional acute, curative function of the teaching hospital." Modern medicine has drawn on itself the mantle of savior. It has a high ego coefficient; it feels good. But the data drawn earlier, the extraordinary increase in the expenditures on health care, and the spectacular growth of scientific insight, as contrasted with the minimal growth of life expectancy for the middle-aged person, shows that the design, for our time, is wrong. The ivory tower has stretched to an altitude where it is no longer relevant. We spend more and more, learn more and more, but do less and less. Obviously it is an inherently ill-designed system. We need a revamping, restructuring, and redirecting of the entire enterprise.

There is much ferment within American medicine. In 1987, the American Medical Association published a new health agenda for the American people, based on more than a decade of study and discussion. This advocates dozens of major reorientations and shifts in emphasis.

Leaders emerge. For example, Dr. Paul Elwood, president of Interstudy in Minneapolis, is making big waves by his insistence upon a revolution in the practice of medicine. Elwood was chosen to give the major oration of the Massachusetts Medical Society in 1988, which was published subsequently in our oracle, the *New England Journal of Medicine*. His title was "Outcomes Management—a Technology of Patient Experiences." "Outcomes measurement" was first conceived twenty years ago by John Williamson at Johns Hopkins University and provides a better way of looking at the complexities of human illness by including how a patient feels about his or her illness. This initial scheme was picked up and refined by workers at the Rand Corporation in Santa Monica. My present co-worker Dr. Anita Stewart is one of these pioneers. Elwood now champions this new approach. It differs from the current medical model in several important regards. First, it relies heavily on "quality of life" estimates; as such, it involves the patient in these measurements. Second, it invokes a multidisciplinary, multicompartmental approach. Third, it allows a more rational approach to the management of chronic illness—more and more the major medical mode. Fourth, it provides a comprehensive data system which will allow true technology assessment and other significant research endeavors. Elwood and many others characterize our present medical system as chaotic, irrational, cumbersome, and often perverse.

Any medical revolution will leave scars. Clearly, however, the way we are currently proceeding is not only "not doing" the job—it is bankrupting us in the process.

What I have discussed in this chapter is not new. There are no startling revelations contained. Those of us who daily, earnestly try to do right within the system know its faults; but blithely we continue our disease-based, cure-directed approach to medical care. We must redirect our focus from cure to prevention—and every thoughtful, deliberative person whom I know, from patient to scholar to economist to politician, *knows* this! Such a demand takes an increased urgency as we grow older. We won't cure aging, but we can prevent many of its premature debilities. This is obvious. This is clear. Well then, if it is so clear and so obvious—why don't we do it? To me, this is one of the most profound questions of our time.

FOUR

PREVENTION'S PROBLEMS

And lo! The starry fold reveal
The blazoned truth we hold so dear.
To guard is better than to heal,
The shield is nobler than the spear.

Oliver Wendell Holmes

One morning a while back, I picked up the chart of my first patient of the day. The name on the file was vaguely familiar, so I turned to the last entry. The patient was a 63-year-old box manufacturer from Red Bluff, California, and I had seen him a year earlier for a complete physical examination. My notations revealed that he had come into my office preceded considerably by his belly. He was red-faced, angry, and smoking heavily. Furthermore, he had high blood pressure and a very elevated cholesterol level. His face twitched. His chest heaved. A time bomb waiting to go off. That was all my notes told, as he had not been seen at the clinic since.

I stood idly musing about what might be bringing him back to me again, and how remarkable it was that he was *able* to come back, considering how lethal his condition had appeared on his last visit. Out of the corner of my eye, I caught a view of a fellow striding rapidly up the corridor toward me. He was slim and straight; he wore natty orange and white slacks. He stuck out his hand and reintroduced himself.

"Doc, I've been aching to see you! I haven't felt this good in 40 years."

He had lost 60 pounds and stopped smoking. He was jogging 5 miles a day. His blood pressure was normal. His cholesterol was low. He was truly reincarnated.

I had nothing to do with it. He had, in a secret, quiet moment, looked into the mirror and not liked what he saw. His transformation cost nothing, involved neither drugs, hospitals, nor technologies. He simply decided to link up with a better future. He has reidentified himself with his grandchildren—he has reestablished his heritage.

Of course, I was ecstatic. Such dramatic representations occur seldom, but often enough to sustain my conviction that prevention is where the action is—or should be. Unfortunately, prevention is also in the slow, slow lane. If we as a profession, community, or nation could somehow get our act together, and put our reason to work, we would all be tremendously better off.

John Knowles wrote in 1977, "Over 99 percent of us are born healthy and are made sick as a result of personal misbehaviors and environmental conditions."

Our failure to do what seems so absurdly obvious begs a single answer. Each of us has his own perspective of why he doesn't or can't do what he knows perfectly well he *ought* to do. Prevention has been best captured as a strategy by parents and pediatricians—kids don't know enough yet to take care of themselves. Hopefully, the parents do. As soon as health care becomes an "on board" responsibility, the system falls apart. The older we get the more fatalistic we seem to become about the need for "health hoarding." The reverse should be so. The older we get the more important it would seem to be that we marshal our constricting reserves. It seems so clear, and yet we fail.

The reasons for this failure are interwoven into our behavior as a society and as individuals, but I can identify eight separate factors which keep prevention from becoming a rallying strategy for our continuing good health.

1. Redundant Capacity
2. A Misplaced Responsibility for Health
3. The Simplicity of Health
4. Orientation Toward the Cure
5. Perverse Financial Incentives
6. Fatalism
7. The Physical-Exam Sham
8. The Fear of Aging

1. REDUNDANT CAPACITY

This is one of those good-news–bad-news stories. We have two eyes, two ears, two lungs, two kidneys, and two testes or two ovaries. In all of these situations we could get along perfectly well with only one. We can sense well with one eye or ear. We can run a marathon with one lung. We can excrete all of our waste materials with one kidney. We can overpopulate the world with one testicle or one ovary. The point is that we can start with 100 percent of full capacity and give away 50 percent willy-nilly, mindlessly, without apparent sacrifice of function. We can give away another 10 percent and still seem okay. Another 10 percent—down to 30 percent of original—and we start to notice some shortness of breath, or some other disability. Maybe at this point we'll decide to find a doctor. Another 10 percent—down to 20 percent of the original 100—and we are dead. So the standard clinical contact zone during which a patient seeks help is at 20 to 30 percent of the starting allotment. This 30 percent margin seems to apply to most vital functions—most important, to our arteries. As half of the artery is shut off like with a garden hose, the flow still seems pretty good. But when we get down to 70 to 80 percent shutdown, symptoms occur. Before the doctor is seen, 70 percent of capacity is gone, and only a few percentage points separate the individual from the undertaker. So, the doctor has only a slim margin to work with. He or she then strives to restrain further loss, and perhaps to restore a bit of the lost function. But restoration to wholeness? Impossible! "As good as new"—don't believe it! Because of the "false confidence" brought on by redundant capacity, we are often profligate with our most precious resources.

We squander health as we would never squander money. This point was never more apparent to me than it was on the day I was scheduled to speak before a preretirement seminar of the Hills Brothers coffee firm. I arrived an appropriate five minutes ahead of my scheduled time and sidled into the back of the meeting room. In full sway at the front was a hyperkinetic financial wizard madly drawing various investment schemes on the blackboard. Deferred annuities, investment trusts, Ponzi's schemes. I was underwhelmed, but the audience was in mad pursuit. Each new suggestion was met with a chorus of exclamation marks. My time on the schedule came and went. The speaker picked up fervor, better and more, more and better.

My fuse is long and slow to burn. What started as bemusement turned to irritation as this rainmaker intrigued and captured. I fidgeted as he filibustered my time away. Finally the retirement course director prevailed and shoveled this guy from the front, to great hurrahs.

My impatience bubbled over:

Dear people, may I say simply—I know intimately your fascination with finance. It preoccupies us. But as you grow older, how much money you have in the bank, how elaborately detailed is your retirement plan, how exquisite is your sense of financial security—forget it; because if you are not healthy at the end of life, all the best laid plans of all the world's greatest financial planners become irrelevant. Health trumps wealth every time. I think I remember that someone said, "You can't take it with you."

I recall that I quickly captured the audience to my health theme by my spontaneous reaction to my foreshortened time slot. It made my point better than if I had planned it.

Taking care of the here and now really doesn't require that much of an investment. Health demands neither a changing of our spots nor a renunciation of our basic soul. In fact, there is even a direct analogy to the way in which you handle your bank account. If you have $150,000 in your checking account, you can be a big time spender—yachts, limos, a high-risk lifestyle. If you have only $1.50 in the bank, you'd better watch how big a check you write. The proximate problem is, of course, that we all have a very firm fix on how much is in our bank account; but when it comes to knowing how much is in our health/wealth account—we seem to consider that someone else's responsibility.

2. A MISPLACED RESPONSIBILITY FOR HEALTH

The second barrier to implementation of an effective preventive-medicine strategy derives from the fact that patients feel that the doctor is the proper seat of responsibility for their health problems. Some of the most interesting reports in this area have come from a long-running observational study of the adult population of Alameda, California, as reported by Dr. Lester Breslow, now dean of the School of Public Health at UCLA.

Breslow and his co-workers surveyed 6,928 adults with regard to their personal health habits. Particularly noted were their sleep, physical activity, and nutritional patterns, as well as their use of tobacco and alcohol. The conclusion "demonstrates a relationship between the whole spectrum of physical health and actual day by day practices. . . . There was a consistent progression toward better health at each age as the number of good health habits increased." For the purposes of this study, "good" health habits were defined as:

1. seven to eight hours of sleep every night
2. breakfast nearly every day
3. only rare or no midmeal snacking
4. average body weight
5. often or sometime physical activity
6. no smoking
7. no more than 4 alcoholic drinks per day

Breslow and colleagues noted that the average health status of those over 75 years of age who followed all of the seven listed practices was about the same as those persons 35 to 44 years of age who followed only one or two practices. Also, the group 55 to 64 years of age practicing all good health habits had the same physical state as did the group 25 to 34 years of age with few good habits. The researchers concluded that "the physical health status of those who reported following the seven good health practices was consistently about the same as those 30 years younger who followed only a few of the good habits." The authors further stated, "The greater frequency of good habits among older patients is consistent with the view that those with bad habits have died off." These findings correspond to the recent pronouncement of the U.S. Surgeon General that two-thirds of the ailments encountered before the age of 65 are preventable. The ability to lengthen your life depends first on your capacity not to shorten it.

The absolute contempt many people show for their health continues to amaze. I recall well my second year of medical school and the 60-year-old man, virtually a live-in patient at Philadelphia General Hospital, who was brought before the class in a teaching amphitheater. He'd had all ten of his fingers amputated because of Buerger's disease, a condition characterized by severe spasm and shutdown of the little arteries in the extremities; but he was still puffing a cigarette between his first two knuckles. All internists commonly see persons with advanced emphysema, suffocating miserably, and still smoking. We all work at creating verbal imagery to describe to these tragic individuals what they are doing to themselves—driving through blinking red lights at the railroad crossing, or swimming with a golf bag on their backs. Death is at close hand.

Immunity does not apply to self-destruction. Some people seem to feel that they can walk through a hail of bullets, sail through torpedoes or mine fields, ski down the sides of tall buildings, and somehow land unhurt on their feet. If they are bruised up a bit, well, the docs will fix them up. Walking blindfolded along a high ledge may get you to the other side once or twice, but don't make a habit of it if survival is your aim. It can and does happen to *you*, as well as to the other guy. The numbers don't lie.

And still you may protest, "But what about the patient who drinks like a fish, smokes like a furnace, eats like a hog, carouses like a buck, and is nonetheless 85 years old?" By the same analogy, you may once in a while drive from San Francisco to Los Angeles at 120 miles an hour and still get there—but don't bet on it. Maybe suicide doesn't work the first time around, but try again; the odds get better.

Dr. Ben Okel, past president of the DeKalb County, Georgia, Medical Society observed, "I often feel that physicians today have little more to do with assuring health than a priest in the sixteenth century had to do with assuring his parishioners a place in heaven."

Medical science is a wonderful social tool for good, but it is ineffective when the damage has already been done. Health starts at home.

3. THE SIMPLICITY OF HEALTH

When I address a group, I say to the audience, "Health is three things." Members of the group inhale and ready their pencils. Then I announce, "Good nutrition, adequate rest, and ample exercise." The collective exhale is palpable as I imagine their thoughts. "Boring. Boring. Boring. Have I given up my day to hear this yahoo doctor tell me that health is rest, nutrition, and exercise? What a waste of time!"

Health is simple—too simple. The secrets to health won't sell magazines; they won't make the front of the *National Enquirer*. They aren't hot. They aren't sexy. In fact, these three basic ingredients are *so* basic that they are usually taken for granted. We all eat enough, sleep enough, and exercise? Right? Wrong! Even in this land of honey, most are ill fed, or ill rested, or ill exercised.

The cynic would challenge, "How can you *prove* that these three activities, in best amounts, confer a lifetime of health?"

My response is: Imagine the trained endurance athlete—someone we would all acknowledge as being in 'great shape'—the epitome of fitness, the most likely to survive. This athlete has nutrition, rest, and exercise in ideal measures. Eliminate one of the three, and see what happens. Allow him to eat and rest, but keep him inactive. See what happens. Feed him and exercise him, but don't let him sleep. See what happens. Exercise him and allow him to rest, but don't feed him. And again, observe the results.

For the endurance athlete, performance over the long pull (which is after all another definition of aging) is ultimately dependent on three basic ingredients—food, rest, and exercise. Simple, but boring.

A man staggers into my office with an arrow protruding from his chest. I don't need to take a history, perform a physical exam, or do any lab test to intuit the basic problem. I lay him down on the floor of my office, put my heel in the middle of his sternum, and, with a heave, extract the arrow.

He leaps off the floor and exclaims, "Dr. Bortz—you are the most wonderful arrow remover in the world. How can I thank you? Can I build a research institute for you? Can I endow a university professorship in your honor? How can I repay you?"

"That's very generous but not necessary," I say. "I'm glad you're feeling better; but before you leave, may I suggest that instead of walking through the jungle on the way home—you walk around it."

My patient arrives home in time for dinner despite his detour around the jungle. His wife inquires what has happened. He relates excitedly the bow and arrow adventure, but neglects the better fact that he arrived home safe and sound without another set of arrow marks on his chest. All of which brings us back to Zimmerman's Law—"Nobody notices when things go right." Prevention is low theater, low visibility, low interest, low investment, and low commitment.

Prevention is health; and health is the combination of our three basic ingredients—*plus* not doing anything to hurt yourself. Health presumes lack of self-destruction. That only makes sense. How can you expect your machine to run full bore, full term, if it mischievously destroys itself along the way? Teenage violence, suicide, accidents, drugs, alcohol, cigarettes— how many billions of lives have been snuffed prematurely because of this collection of bullets? Russian roulette belongs not only to the truly crazy among us—it seems to be a dominant genetic tendency. I, myself, recall crazy, crazy car rides as an adolescent; it is miraculous that I actually survived the careening postdate trips from Mt. Holyoke to Williamstown,

Massachusetts. I didn't think for a minute about it at the time, but then as my own kids entered their adolescence, the memory filled me with sullen foreboding. As I noted earlier, the ability to lengthen life consists first of the capacity not to shorten it.

James Mason and Dennis Tokma pose, "Imagine the public outcry if a thousand people died as the result of a natural disaster or three 747s crashing each day. Yet, one thousand people die every day from cigarette smoking."

Crazy, stupid, or both. In 1984, 8 percent of the Harvard Medical School faculty still smoked cigarettes. Unbelievable!

4. ORIENTATION TOWARD THE CURE

The fourth problem for prevention is that the best medicine available today is cure-oriented. In other words, it is preoccupied with disease rather than with health. Patients and physicians throughout the world cling to the notion that illness can be expunged with the stroke of a scalpel or a dip of medicine. Our training in medical school is pathology-based—meaning that we study what can go wrong. All of the glory, prestige, and honor within medicine go to the practitioners of the curing art. The research grants, the academic promotions, and the professional recognition go to those of us who dissect and refine cure to its highest order.

One perfect example of this phenomenon is Norman Shumway, my noted colleague at Stanford University Medical School and Hospital. It is quite possible that Dr. Shumway has transplanted more human hearts than have all other such surgeons throughout the world. This feat is immense—truly noteworthy—and deserving of all the professional respect and universal acclaim which it has drawn. Presently 60 people per year obtain a new Stanford heart. Our newspapers regularly feature stories of patients such as Joe Blow, the fireman from Worcester, Massachusetts, who came to see Dr. Shumway. Joe had a rotten heart—let's say from damage caused by years of chain smoking—and he has just been salvaged by receiving the healthy heart of a noble motorcyclist who insisted upon running his head into a telephone pole. The cost—financial, emotional, and social—of a heart transplant is huge. The time subsequent to the transplant is filled with drugs, doctor visits, and mega-anxiety. If Joe makes 5 years after his heart transplant, he is considered to have done very well, and he is called a "5-year-survivor." (There is only one "20-year-survivor" so far.) In comparison, the person who stops smoking immediately gains *8* years of life. And at no cost —financial, emotional, or social. In fact, the quality of life of the smoker who stops smoking, or the alcoholic who stops drinking, is immeasurably better than it was before. A direct contrast to the perpetual medicalized existence of the transplant patient. But where are the headlines? The glory? The recognition?

Rene Dubos, the great ecologist and microbiologist from Rockefeller University, wrote, "To ward off disease or recover health, men as a rule feel it is easier to depend on the healer than to attempt the more difficult task of living wisely." This tendency to rely upon others, coupled with the American attitude that we should have just about anything we can afford, affects the way we perceive "the cure." The common terms these days are "health care *provider*" and "health care *consumer*"—as if the patient has nothing to do but go out and buy health from the doctor. Such a proposition is patently false, because no matter how proud the medical profession is of its accomplishments, when the hay hits the fan, no payment capacity can bring back health. The cure cannot always be purchased.

The pharmaceutical industry also feeds off the passion which the provider-consumer model provides. Every year Americans spend billions of dollars on prescription medicines, billions more on over-the-counter medicines, and billions more on health additives such as vitamins, potions, and the rest. Health in a capsule. It would be bad enough if this preoccupation with external remedies were benign; but too many of these drugs have undesirable side effects. In fact, side effects are almost enough to keep the doctors busy and the hospitals full. But that is not the worst side of pills— pills represent the wrong way to approach most ailments. They should always be the method of last resort. Whenever I write a prescription (and I write lots), I consider it a failure. My patient and I have not been able to address the problem in any other way.

A patient comes to my office with a bad headache. I take the history, do a limited physical exam, and then ponder the likely diagnosis and treatment options. I might say, "Sarah, in my view your headaches come on because you are wound tighter than a spring. Your neck muscles are rigid and your pulse is too fast. You look exhausted. I honestly feel that the best advice I can give you is to take a week off, buy a warm-up suit, get a pair of jogging shoes, and work out an exercise program to get yourself in shape. That way you will have a good technique for managing your stress. You don't need a cure if you can learn to prevent."

Sarah will smile sweetly and thank me for the advice. A moment later, I'll hear her telling her friend in the waiting room, "Millie, that's a weird doctor. He told me to get a pair of running shoes and get in shape!" Furthermore, Sarah will resent receiving a bill for her visit to me. After all, I didn't prescribe a pill. The pill is the standard covenant between patient and physician. If the patient leaves the physician's office without a written prescription in hand, he feels cheated, as did Sarah. But what is the "right" answer to Sarah's headaches? In my view, her symptoms (like the great majority of complaints that come into the doctor's office) are best addressed by giving heed to what the body is saying. Redress of the symptoms comes much more often from a redirection of lifestyle and behavior patterns than it does from bizarre chemicals in pills.

But pills are American—an integral part of the cure. They are the quick fix and make for convenient shopping. Maalox is the answer to an upset stomach, right? Wrong. Valium is the answer to anxiety, right? Wrong. Advil is the answer to morning stiffness, right? Wrong. Milk of magnesia is the answer to sluggish bowels, right? Wrong again.

Pills merely plaster the crack; they don't repair it. Attention to the basic three elements of health are both the prevention and the treatment. Writing a prescription saves me a lot of time. By suggesting milk of magnesia for constipation, I don't have to take a dietary history or find out about daily activity patterns, fluid intake, and so forth. But this shortcut is wrong. If physicians would experience a little pang of regret, as do I, when writing a prescription because of their inability to approach the system in a simpler and more health-directed fashion, we would all be better off.

Obesity is a prime example of this phenomenon. Extra fat embarrasses body and soul. Most obese patients would rather they weren't. But those extra calories they laid on incrementally must come off incrementally. There is no possible way that the quick fix, easy way, instant cure promised by so many hucksters can work. Yet, obese patients continually seek the "weight-loss pill," spending billions of dollars and even more valuable life time.

Insomnia, diabetes, hypertension, arthritis, and many circulatory problems including hypertension and high cholesterol levels are also gold mine problems for the major peddlers of the cure—the drug manufacturers. A study at the famous Joslin Clinic in Boston showed that virtually all diabetic patients who presented themselves as taking very high doses of insulin (over 100 units) had as their underlying problem, not an unusually severe case of diabetes, but inappropriate diet.

Even the immensely popular book *Life Extension*, for all its numerous admirable qualities, was basically flawed by its emphasis on the drug approach to aging. To the authors, the enlightened approach to aging comes not from a reorientation of basic living habits and the recognition of the fundamental units involved in a healthy lifestyle, but from an assortment of potions and corrective age retardants. The megavitamin and orthomolecular medicine approaches share this conceptual defect. Salvation and immortality in a capsule.

My objections are not unfounded, as my medical training included a strong biochemical background. I have worked with some of the world's greatest biochemists including a Nobel laureate. I have spent years in biochemical laboratories in Berkeley, Munich, and Philadelphia, and I have published many articles in biochemical journals; but I am very resistant to the suggestion that the major health problems of our time—including aging—will yield to either a chemical or a pill. Visualize a lung wrecked by emphysema, or a brain pocked with stroke scars, or a wasted, shriveled leg; and then conjure me up a pill that I may give to my patient and thus restore him or her.

The quick-fix, cure orientation can be seen at all levels of the medical community, including professional societies, educational institutions, and research facilities. For example, the American College of Physicians is the mother church of us internists. It is the specialty society which publishes our major journal, sponsors our major meetings, and gives us distinction as we know it—the F.A.C.P. A few years ago the College surveyed members regarding preferences for postgraduate instructional courses. Preventive medicine was at the very bottom of the list.

The reference guide in any medical library is called the *Index Medicus.* In it are cataloged the tens of thousands of medical articles published each month in the world medical literature. There is a category for articles on preventive medicine, but the entries are precious few. Leafing through the *Index,* I found other topics (the meanings of which I could only vaguely guess) which were represented by columns and columns of articles written. Again, we see the preoccupation with disease and its co-riders.

We are so driven by the need for the cure that we will seek refuge in any port. I could set up a stand on the freeway with a sign which loudly proclaims that my "new product"—derived from, let's say, tomatoes—cures baldness. Many would buy my product. Some would swear by it; but the chances are great that mayonnaise, or toothpaste, or chocolate ice cream would work as well. The history of medicine is full of misadventures with inadequately tested remedies, such as thalidomide, that to me empower the restraint which our licensing agencies impose on the practice of medicine. *Primum non nocere* is the first commandment of the physician—first do no harm. Nothing is so painful to me as a dear patient who rejects the validated benefit of a recognized treatment to try a Mexican border remedy of laetrile or its ilk.

Yet, I recognize how the deficiency of medicine in identifying with, having enthusiasm for, and commitment to a preventive strategy leads to "alternative medicine." To me this is a sorrow.

Doctors are only as good as their training; and medical schools place little emphasis on nutrition and virtually none on either exercise or sleep. The gap has been filled by the shadow phalanx of the "health guides." These watchful guardians have usurped the rightful role of the medical profession because that profession has been derelict. But the medical establishment, myself included, has not welcomed this intrusion generously. This is held by the enthusiasts to represent a conspiracy on the part of "Medicine" to prevent those with a true vision and intent from rescuing us. This is pure baloney.

Medical practice is often hard. Decisions are often difficult. Choices are often painful. Outcomes are often uncertain. An honest medical practitioner appropriately displays lack of certainty on occasion. This real appraisal is too often read as incompetence and begs for another opinion, which is often found outside the mainstream of scientific thought, immune from peer scrutiny. Too often practitioners of "holism," alternative medicine, linger on the sidelines, always ready to enter. These shadow doctors fail to observe minimal standards for adequate reason and approach. Any of us would prefer a liniment to an amputation—but not at the cost of his or her life! I have cared for a very prominent woman with breast cancer who chose a Mexican potion instead of my advice for surgery. I cannot promise that what I had to offer would cure, but I would bet 1,000 to 1 that it would have a better chance than the "alternative" approach.

I have been privileged to attend some of the highest councils of American medicine. I have met personally with many of our leaders. The one binding, enduring devotion among them is to do right, without consideration of personal or professional gain, to give the best our profession has to offer to the most people possible. To do this demands that we have rigid standards. Before a treatment is given, a counsel offered, the evidence for that position must meet rigorous evaluation. And yet this very proviso slows the trajectory of prevention.

Research grants designed to demonstrate a prevention are much harder to obtain than are those designed to propose a cure. No one notices when things go right; as a result, hard, fixed facts about prevention are difficult to obtain. Cholesterol provides a good example. Just a few years ago, a serum cholesterol level of 275 was often passed as not being outside the normal limits. It has taken hundreds of studies (no one of which is finally conclusive, but most of which are internally consistent) to convince all but the most strident critics that the cholesterol story is not a fairy tale. Yet, the eggs, the bacon, and the butter taste so good—and refusal to accept a painful truth seems to be rather common among us mortals.

Alton Ochsner, Sr., the founder of the famous Ochsner Clinic in New Orleans and one of the pioneer thoracic surgeons of our era, loved telling the story of Ivan and Natasha. Natasha had come to suspect that Ivan was engaging in some extra bed time outside the marriage. One fated evening she feigned sleep only to watch Ivan steal from the dacha and mount his sleigh. Natasha followed through the snowy night in her sleigh until from her hiding place she saw Ivan dismount and approach a country cottage. The door opened and there was a gorgeous woman with long hair and a clinging negligee. They embraced, the door closed. Through the window, however, Natasha saw the couple fondle each other passionately, then disrobe, enter the adjacent bedroom, and approach the bed. The light went off. Natasha turned back to her darkness and said, "But there will always be doubt." Ochsner used this tale to berate the tobacco industry for its steadfast refusal to acknowledge the lethality of its product—innocence was ever proclaimed despite millions of persons crippled or dead as a result of smoking.

Whenever lecturing on the problems of prevention, I like to tell the story of a sleepy town in the western foothills. This town is so small that a haircut is a civic event. Everyone knows when a new ice cream flavor is at the soda fountain, and a dog could sleep the night in the middle of Main Street. The community was served by a tiny hospital, designed to accommodate the occasional farm injury or the rare birth.

Then the news hit. The feds came to town to build a new interstate highway. Engineers, surveyors, and bulldozing crews arrived; and in a few months, an eight-lane ribbon of concrete approached from the east, skirted town, and led off to the hills to the west.

A celebration, as big as the Fourth of July, heralded the opening of the highway. The mayor cut the ribbon, and the townfolk rushed to their cars to have a ride up the new road. What an accomplishment! The first night, however, a car occupied by a pair of newlyweds went off the road at a particularly sharp curve. By the time they made it to the hospital, they were nearly gone. Doctors and nurses came from the neighboring town to help out, and the next day two more cars and a trailer truck plunged over the same curve. The victims had to be accommodated in the hall outside the regular hospital rooms. The next week a bus with forty passengers crashed. The board of directors of the hospital held an emergency meeting to request authorization for an emergency bond issue to fund expansion of the hospital. None too soon, a new wing was built with an elaborate intensive care facility and new high-tech scanners. Neurosurgeons and orthopedists were brought on staff. The hospital became the growth industry of the town.

Several months after the interstate was operational, the mayor took his son out for a ride. "Isn't this wonderful, so smooth and easy. It cost $100 million, but now we can get to the state capital in forty-five minutes. The only tragedy is what happens on this sharp curve. Since the highway's been open, we've had 54 accidents with 23 deaths and 212 injuries. I don't think our hospital can take much more."

The son looked puzzled and reacted, "Why don't you just put up a guard rail?"

The obvious is so obvious when we pause long enough to see.

5. PERVERSE FINANCIAL INCENTIVES

This failure of medicine to enjoin a protective-shield stance is abetted by the fifth element of prevention's problems—the crass, but inevitable, issue of money. Preventive medicine is not esteemed by the payer. If a patient comes to my office for a physical exam just to assure him- or herself that the machine is in working order (and I enthusiastically believe this is the right thing for all of us to do), I carry out the exam, do the appropriate tests, subsequently go over the results with my patient, and then submit the bill for same. Most insurance companies, including Medicare, do not pay for a "health exam." Consequently, wise to the ways of the system, I and other physicians rarely submit a bill for a routine health exam, but instead tailor the bill to reflect some physical concern. On the other hand, the insurance companies will pay me and my colleagues thousands of dollars to take care of the patient who when first seen is almost ready to be embalmed because of rampant cancer or plugged-up pipes. As noted earlier, once the dice have been rolled, our capacities are very marginal in terms of undoing the wreckage. Still, that is what pays. Such a financial mechanism cannot help but reinforce the patient's preoccupation with disease. Disease is not only high profile, high gratification (recall the fellow with the arrow), and intellectually challenging—disease also *pays.*

Such an anomaly, paying for sickness instead of health, is like buying fire extinguishers but not smoke detectors. The way out of this "bass ackwards" dilemma would seem to be the embracing of the ancient Chinese style of payment for medical care, in which you pay the doctor only when you are well. When you get sick, that's on the doctor's tab. By such a strategy, the physician is enlisted in your effort to stay well, instead of encouraged to keep you sick. The HMO, or health maintenance organization, is our American technique of adopting the Chinese way. Our clinic in Palo Alto has several HMO plans, with about one-fourth of all of our patients operating under a prepaid system. This means that they pay annual premiums in exchange for "as needed" medical services. "Pay when well, no more when sick." I believe that in my clinic all patients are treated the same regardless of what payment mechanism is involved. All have the same diagnostic and therapeutic efforts regardless of the financial implication. But the theory behind the HMO is that physicians, while practicing preventive medicine on all patients equally, would nevertheless tend to emphasize prevention particularly to HMO patients. After all, as the theory goes, when the HMO patient gets sick, it is really money out of the physicians' own pockets. My evaluation is that we don't practice good enough preventive medicine on anyone.

Logically, those interested in HMO programs turn to the Kaiser medical system, which was the first large prepaid program. The Kaiser-Permanente Health Plan was launched originally by Henry J. Kaiser in 1942, to provide medical coverage for the workers in the Kaiser war plants on the West Coast. After the war, the plan was broadened to the public at large until the members now number in the millions. They have been at it for over forty years and are still the largest of all HMOs, with over 6 million participants nationally. The Kaiser system has been the object of many inquiries into the impact such a mode of medical practice has on health outcomes and the cost associated with these outcomes. A number of differences emerge between this type of prepaid medical care and the traditional fee-for-service model; but the one that I look for, a firm commitment to a vigorous program of preventive medicine, has not emerged—despite all the logical reasons to the contrary. This seems to be additional evidence of the resistance the medical system has to preventive care. If you pay me only when you are well, and it costs me money when you are sick—and I *still* don't tend to your health—the system is out of whack. We can only assume that the physician is so preoccupied with mopping up the water that he blindly fails to turn off the spigot.

The preoccupation of the medical profession with the curing function overemphasizes technical procedures and activities while neglecting the more basic cognitive ones including the preventive services and health promotion practices of your family physician.

This is particularly true in geriatric medicine. A few years ago my good friend Dr. Knight Steel, of the Boston University School of Medicine, wrote a wonderful paper titled "Geriatrics—the Fruition of the Clinician." In it he described how the medical care of the elderly should evoke from the practicing physician the highest ideals of medicine. It is the care of one of life's extremes in that the physician acts as a caring steward for the last days. This should be a precious task. But geriatrics, until recently, has not been an esteemed domain of medicine. Cure is seldom possible; it is time-consuming and untidy; and it involves complex interpersonal and intergenerational relationships. Finally, the end point is death. It is now a fact of record, however, that medicine is recognizing that this task is both vital and attractive. It occupies, properly, an enlarging portion of the medical agenda. In April 1988, 4,600 primary-care physicians took the first clinical examination in geriatrics in medicine to establish special competence. This is wonderful news. But the payment for primary care of older patients is at the low end of the scale. Medicare reimbursement for the care of older persons, particularly in their homes or in nursing homes, is woefully inadequate, and it snarls the caring practitioners in paperwork.

The issue of *who* pays is the final contributor to the lack of financial incentives to preventive medicine. I have come to call this the ostrich theory of self-health care. There is a pervasion of insurance coverage for most medical problems, and so when the unexpected medical crisis comes, the harm done is generally limited to the body—the checking account is not at risk. Such a safety net is surely in accord with an egalitarian, share-the-misery philosophy. But what if the damage done is clearly, inescapably secondary to the flagrant neglect of common sense? Whatever happened to the thesis that an individual should be both economically and physically responsible for his actions? Gradually, insurance companies are reinforcing this belief by encouraging good health habits and discouraging bad ones. For example, in California, rescue is considered a public service; but even rescue teams there are beginning to bill for their costs. In addition, automobile insurance rates are higher for teenage drivers. And the Supreme Court just ruled that the Veterans Administration is correct in its policy to consider alcoholism an act of personal volition rather than a disease. I believe that everyone should be encouraged to maintain his or her own health. It is, after all, life's most precious asset.

6. FATALISM

The sixth hurdle to a preventive strategy streams from the proposition that, "Hell, Doc, I've been at it for 60 years; it's too late to change now." The younger we are, the more remote seems the prospect of dying. The older we become, the less urgent seems the need to do anything about it. But this too is wrong. It is never too late to start. The renewal capacity of life is one of its wonders; each of us is improvable, redeemable, no matter what age, no matter how decrepit. Fatalism is a close kin to depression, and saying that nothing can be done is close to assuring that it will be true. Too often physicians share the "it's too late" philosophy. Numerous studies give evidence that older persons are treated differently from younger ones. To a certain extent this is appropriate and wise, but only when the facts justify a different approach. Age should not be a proxy for failure and inadequate quality of life. Rarely, rarely should age be the determining issue. The old joke makes the point.

Jake: "Say, Doc, what do you think is wrong with my right knee?"

Doc: "Well, Jake, you've got to remember that your knee is 85 years old."

Jake: "Yeah, but the other knee is just as old; and it's fine."

Age is too convenient a handle. The old dog *can* be taught new tricks. It is never too late to think and to act healthfully. The investment in caring is always worth it, since growing cynical invites despair and early decline.

Anne Somers, health economist from Rutgers, has shown how important it is that the physician become involved with the health promotion program. She and her co-workers set up a superior education program to provide the best health promotion practices. But the program failed, and Somers attributed this to a lack of the authoritative input of the primary-care physician. If the formulation of preventive medicine is farmed out to ancillary personnel and given only lip service by the physician—or worse—then the program carries little impact. For example, the physician who smokes will not do when taking care of patients with emphysema. In my view the physician, him- or herself, should be the paragon for good health practices. "Do as I say, not as I do" just won't cut it in real life.

7. THE PHYSICAL-EXAM SHAM

The seventh barrier to the implementation of preventive medicine concerns the principal tool of the primary physician, the general physical examination. There is a lot of current criticism of the "routine physical exam" because of its apparent lack of impact in finding reversible health problems. Its cost effectiveness is being questioned. I understand this reservation, but I feel that it is largely misplaced. To me, the principal value of a regular physical checkup is not the detection of some previously unknown disease lurking within, but the opportunity afforded both patient and physician to conduct a health inventory. If the exam is disease-focused, it probably cannot be justified, as is now formulated. But if the emphasis were to shift to *health*, I feel that the routine physical exam would be time and money well spent.

Specifically, what has gone wrong? The classical physical examination rates the patient on a scale of zero to minus ten. The best the patient can expect is a zero, meaning that nothing bad was found. Not that the physician really says, "You're fine." Rather, he says, "I didn't find anything wrong." You are then left to presume that you are fine. But this can be incorrect. Zero should not be our goal. What we need to establish is the other side of the scale—not zero to minus ten, but zero to *plus* ten. Not how sick you are, but how well you are. Under the present system, the doctor searches only for illness; and so you can score a zero (meaning nothing wrong found) and still be in trouble the next day. If you have 20 to 30 percent of your maximum in your physical "bank account," it takes only a minor additional deficit to "break the bank." The usual physical exam looks for disease, not at your functional reserve. Disease is where the interest lies, and that's where the money lies.

Personally, I would much rather have the opportunity of dealing with the box manufacturer cited at the beginning of the chapter (or better still, the same fellow thirty years earlier) than with someone who comes in when disease is manifest. A patient returning to me having made a health commitment as the result of a prior exam provides my highest moment of professional satisfaction. I have a standing offer of a bottle of champagne to any smoker who quits. I have given out several cases so far.

I have evoked a technique for the annual physical exam that I believe encompasses all of my philosophies regarding the search for health. The central element in the exam is the booklet "Health Risk Appraisal." This booklet, compiled from statistics accumulated by Harvey Geller, of the United States Public Health Service, and distributed by the Health Hazard Appraisal Department of the Methodist Hospital in Indianapolis, lists (by age, sex, and ethnic background) the likelihood of dying in the next ten years from the fifteen or so most common illnesses. This technique is now encouraged by the Centers for Disease Control of the Public Health Service.

I perform my history taking, physical examination, and appropriate laboratory testing. Then I invite my patient back for a review session. The patient really doesn't learn from me in that first session; I learn from him. In the second session, however, I spread out all information in front of us and, based upon what we have learned together, try to estimate his individual risks. For example, as I consider this process for myself—a 60-year-old Caucasian male—I learn that 32,000 out of 100,000 of my age and sex peers will not live ten more years. The actuaries know this. My life insurance premium is based on this number. The overall number is sobering enough, but then I try to tailor the group average to the individual. In my case, I don't smoke, and my alcohol intake is modest. I won't die of lung cancer, emphysema, or cirrhosis. Cancel out these factors and subtract 3,900—the number of people in my statistical unit who die from these diseases. My blood pressure is normal, and I am not diabetic. Cancel 3,000 more. I don't have rheumatic heart disease. Cancel 150. Now, instead of the group prediction of a 32 percent chance of dying in the next ten years, I have reduced my chances to 25 percent. The number-one killer, arteriosclerotic heart disease, remains. The overall figure for my group is 14 percent, but balancing the factors of my favorable family history, a good cholesterol value, my daily activity levels, plus the other features listed above, my risk of dying of heart disease (artery disease) is perhaps 10 percent. Note, however, that even at my reduced risk, it is still three or four times higher than the next cause of death for my peer group—stroke. Therefore, my personal preventive preoccupation is on arteriosclerosis.

In contrast, let's look back at my patient, the box manufacturer. Going through his litany of original woes—obesity, high cholesterol, high blood pressure, smoking, and anger—I would have predicted his personal ten-year risk at 60 percent! Lethal. I don't know how a person could wake up in the morning and have peace with himself when there was such a heavy sword hanging over him. But the ostrich syndrome prevails.

Fortunately, my box manufacturer decided to embrace his own health, and thus lowered his risk from the original figure to a death risk of approximately 15 to 20 percent. This certainly isn't perfect. But nothing is. You may die when driving 55 miles per hour, but driving at even that speed gives you a higher chance of survival than does driving at 120 mph.

As I evaluate and improve upon the health exam, I find that my current most valuable tool may be the exercise electrocardiogram. The test begins with the taking of what is called a resting EKG, the test most people receive in most disease-oriented physical exams. On its own, such a measurement is virtually worthless. It shows how your heart is beating and how open are your arteries, when at rest. There are volumes of case histories detailing individuals who, having just left the doctor's office with a normal EKG, succumbed to a fatal heart attack on the way home. The resting EKG gives no measure of reserve function. However, with the exercise electrocardiogram, a patient uses a stationary bicycle or treadmill to exercise gradually to higher and higher levels. During this time, function of the heart and arteries is monitored by means of the electrocardiogram. If there is any evidence of deterioration of the machine's wave pattern, the physician is alerted to an early warning sign of artery narrowing—the principal cause of death. Not conducting this test and *still* concluding that a patient is okay is nothing short of bad medical practice.

In addition to giving warning about the arteries, the exercise EKG can also be used with other measurements (such as the level of HDL cholesterol, to be discussed in later chapters, and the resting pulse) to evaluate a patient's general level of physical fitness.

In summary, when a patient leaves my office after having a health-oriented physical exam, it is my hope that he will have learned much of himself, and that he will be motivated to improve his chances for life. I believe this is the pure and simple role of the health professional—to use ultimate technology and training to provide the patient with the most accurate reflection of just who he is. In this task, we are discharging the sacred entreaty of the Oracle of Delphi, as well as others before and after— "This above all, know thyself!"

But my task is more than to act as a mirror—it is also to act as a prism, allowing the patient to see not only who he is but who he might be. When the visit to the doctor's office encompasses the action of both mirror and prism, then that visit is precious. Anything less is incomplete, and an excuse.

8. THE FEAR OF AGING

The foregoing seven personal insights into why we have failed to embrace a preventive medicine strategy for our health and for our aging are relevant and important. But all are possibly secondary to what I have come to call the Bortz hypothesis—we default on self-care as younger persons, because we fear our aging. The truth of the matter is that we don't want to get old, and we seem to do everything we can to avoid it. Too many young people look at the rigors and discipline of self-care and ask *Why?* Why should I take care of myself as a young person if the reward for such care is an extended lifetime of feebleness and futility? Such an attitude of fear becomes a self-fulfilling prophecy, and the very lack of attention which aided our avoidance hastens that which we fear the most. It is a cruel irony.

Chapter 5 will explore ways we may begin to attack both our personal and cultural myths about age.

FIVE

AGING IS A SELF-FULFILLING PROPHECY

Don't invite old age.

Mother

Old age is Indian country. Uncharted and dark.
Even when we have parents still living to
provide us with maps, show us over the rising
hill, the crest of the road, we don't want
to look. Fear, perhaps. Not of death so much as of
all the indignities lying in wait for us.

Nina Bawden in *Walking Naked*

One of the great philosophers of our age was Satchel Paige. The great Satchel asked, "How old would you be if you didn't know how old you were?" To me this is one of the most profound probes into the nature of aging. It asserts the centrality of attitude in the entire journey.

I saw vivid proof of this concept when I was a guest on *The Donahue Show.* My presence was strictly ancillary to the main business of the program, which was to highlight the lives of four centenarians, one of whom was having her 100th birthday on that day. The show was rollicking. The audience was bubbling, and Phil was in great high humor. Midway in the show, a salty old gal, 103 years young, from Rochester, New York, asked Phil if he had heard the joke about . . .

Phil said, "Uh-oh. What am I into now?"

The joke went on:

A genteel old man was sitting reading a newspaper on a very crowded bus. His eye was caught by the bright dress of the pretty girl standing in front of him.

Chivalrously he offered, 'I know I'm an old man, but I would be pleased if you would take my seat.'

She politely demurred. The bus went its awkward jerky way until it stopped abruptly, and most of the standees were hurled into a mess.

As they disentangled, the man offered again, "Well if you won't take my seat, why don't you just sit on my lap to decongest the crowding?"

She smiled and perched herself on his lap. The bus bumped its way along its route.

After a minute more or so, the man tapped the young lady on the shoulder and said, "Young lady, I think you had better stand up again because I am not as old as I thought I was."

The audience howled and Phil said, "And now it's time for a station break."

What was already a natural love-in became a boisterous celebration of aging.

WHAT ABOUT YOUR OWN AGING?

Who do you think you are going to be when you are 90? Most of you will answer, "Doc, don't hit me with that question because the odds are that I won't be here when I am 90."

In fact, Ken Dychtwald, popular San Francisco Bay Area psychologist, tells of a simple survey that he conducted with a group of young people. He asked, "To what age do you expect to live?" The overwhelming majority answered, "Around 65."

Even more grimly, some of you may respond, "Well, maybe I will still be here when I'm 90, but the chances are that I'll be in a nursing home somewhere with a feeding tube in my nose, endlessly contemplating the acoustic squares in the ceiling, incontinent, impotent, and impoverished. A disgrace to myself, my family, and my community."

My immediate reaction to these responses is: If you say you are going to be dead when you're 65, you will be. If you say you are going to be in a nursing home at age 90, you will be—because aging is a self-fulfilling prophecy. The accuracy of your prediction is guaranteed because of the attitudes, decisions, and health habits conspiring to assure their own fulfillment. The general consensus is that infant and early childhood habits are highly determinative of later life successes and failures, habits and actions. I propose that your expectation of who you are going to be at some future time of your life becomes as determinative of your life course and extent as do those benchmark events of early life. What you get is what you set. As Norman Cousins ventured in *Human Options*, "Nothing about life is more precious than that we can define our own destiny."

If I reached into my pocket, drew out a pad, and wrote a prescription which is simple, cheap, safe, effective, and easily accessible—and, most important, likely to confer 30 more years of life—would you fill it?

Some would grab the prescription from my hand and fill it immediately. Some would be circumspect. Most would refuse. For as I mentioned in concluding the preceding chapter—most of us hold a severely negative stereotype of the aging process.

WHY CAN'T WE GET
THE MESSAGE ACROSS?

In my view, the logic of preventive medicine, health promotion, and health preservation has failed to capture the public enthusiasm because most people fear the negative stereotype of aging.

For most of us, aging is a slow, downward, inward spiral wherein at any time we can look downward and inward and project where we are going to be—*if* we are going to be—until finally we slide gracelessly out of the bottom of the spiral and into oblivion. Put more precisely, every day in every way I am getting worse.

The gestalt of aging, the dissonant chords of the last part of life, seem a crude contrast to the bright energies and colors of the first. The face of

Scrooge is the standard caricature. Dr. Paul Pruyser of the Meninger Clinic published a paper entitled "Aging: Downward, Upward, or Forward?"

In this work he remarked, "Life views are dominated by an iconic illusion that forces the span of life into a low-high-low sequence of staging. Aging is seen as loss, decline, a downhill course."

Such a mental construction, termed the "ABA" model, conforms to the Gaussian curve (often called the "bell curve"), that profound mathematical theory expressed more than a century ago by Karl Gauss. The ABA model seems to verify the commonplace observation that the infirmities of aging appear to recapitulate the halting inadequacies of infancy: incontinency, poor communication, immobility, and dependency. We crawl. We run. We crawl. Is this what life is meant to be?

Pruyser continues:

> There it is: the overwhelming conviction that life has a peak, somewhere, with an upward and downward slope on each side . . . the visual imagination sees a peak, flattened by valleys, one rising, one declining, in an aesthetically gratifying symmetry. . . . So much in the world proclaims a tripartite or triphasic pattern with a dominant center that we come to think of this pattern as a cosmic, ordained reality, and as a *leitmotiv* of life. This powerful iconic illusion thwarts us from seeing, or making, alternative patterns.

ALZHEIMER'S DISEASE

Throughout history man has been mistaking disease for the hallmarks of aging. For example, as recently as 100 years ago we thought that tuberculosis was a natural consequence of aging. Later, arteriosclerosis was considered a sure benchmark. Recent studies in Baltimore have verified that reported declines in kidney function previously attributed to the "natural aging process" were actually due to pathology. And finally, we now believe that heart-stroke volume and cardiac output do not decline with age as previously assumed.

One by one these false prophets have fallen. Thought to herald age, they really herald disease and disuse.

The new and popular prophet is called Alzheimer's disease (AD). Much of our present energies in gerontology are devoted to convincing patients and public that this dreaded condition is a disease and not a natural part of the aging process.

Clearly the issue to be faced now is how much of our former negative imagery of aging—the melancholy of accelerating loss—is accurate. What does the new, third age of life look like?

Alzheimer's (so named because it was first identified in 1907, by the German physician Alois Alzheimer) is a condition which Lewis Thomas calls the "silent epidemic," "the disease of the century." And yet it goes largely unnoticed by many who purport to address the needs of our senior citizens. Presently there are several bestselling books on aging (one of more than 800 pages) which contain but a few lines about Alzheimer's disease. To pretend to represent a composite major view of aging without an in-depth accounting of Alzheimer's disease is to trivialize the entire subject. It is estimated that 2.5 million persons have AD; and this number is expected to double by the year 2000 and quintuple by the year 2040. We have estimates that of every 100 persons living past the age of 74, a statistical 2.4 will contract the disease every year. This is about the same as for heart attacks. Forty-eight percent of persons over the age of 85 show some evidence of Alzheimer's disease. It is the fourth leading cause of death for people over age 65, killing 100,000 persons per year.

Most persons in nursing homes are there because of Alzheimer's disease. The cost of this institutional care is estimated to exceed $38 billion a year. The total societal cost is estimated at $80 billion a year.

Yet the research budget for AD remains trivial: $132 million in 1990. (In the same year, the federal research budget for AIDS, which was widely criticized as inadequate, was $1.6 *billion.*

In my view there is no condition in medicine about which our ignorance is so complete. We don't even know what kind of disease Alzheimer's is, but it is *surely* a disease and not normal aging. It is not a natural condition. It is not an assertion of "God's will"—it is something for which there must be a treatment or a preventive.

A couple of years ago I had the opportunity to address the House of Representatives regarding the medical priorities for our aging nation. At that time I said, "Ladies and gentlemen, if we don't soon develop some insight into this disease, we can pretty well forget the rest of the business of this country, because we will surely be so occupied with the care of these certain to be vastly increased numbers of demented people that we won't have any time or money left to take care of the rest of the business of running America."

I feel this is even more true today. We need a Manhattan Project–level effort to root out the basis of this awful disease.

The Human Face of Alzheimer's

How do I as a practicing physician see Alzheimer's disease? Almost every day I see an unfortunate new patient, usually brought in by a distraught family member. The predominant symptom is loss of memory—generally the recent memory. Commonly the affected person is either unaware of this creeping deficit or has developed a very clever defensive strategy to hide it. Concealment is often a major issue. In these cases, the person recognizes his or her mental frailty but tries to trivialize it or otherwise shelter it from recognition. For example, I may ask, "What day is this?" and the patient will turn and instruct the accompanying family member to answer.

Another moving and typical scene is often played out in the following manner. I will ask my new patient, "Who is our president?"

He or she will try to deflect with a laugh and the response, "Everyone knows that."

There will be a pause to see if that suffices; and after an embarrassed interlude, my patient will reply, "Roosevelt."

My responsibility to this patient is to provide a diagnosis—because it is on this basis that further planning will be based. I do my history taking and include a brief inventory of intellectual capacity. Then I do a physical exam and go through a set of laboratory exams. Because of its cost (from $600 to $1,000), there is an ongoing debate as to whether a brain scan need be a part of this workup. Generally, I do order it. While the scan may not reveal any information of value, it can sometimes provide the basis for a viable plan of action. Under the circumstances, I believe this is ample justification.

A week or so later, the patient and family will return for the results. I hope the next few years will provide better diagnostic tools, but at this date we have no definitive test for Alzheimer's disease; the only secure evidence comes from a brain biopsy. Today the hope for my patient is that the tests will eliminate a diagnosis of AD by revealing some remediable condition (such as thyroid deficiency, mineral imbalance, or diabetes) which is responsible for the memory loss. Unfortunately, this is rare; and about two-thirds of the time, the exam reveals nothing. The inference then is that the memory lapses are due to Alzheimer's—a disease in which gnarls of cellular debris are laid down in areas of the brain resulting in a progressive mental decline.

I give my likely diagnosis and confess the lack of clear treatment. This is *not* to say, however, that I do nothing. Hope is never withdrawn. I emphasize that although our tools do not as yet give us any way to approach the intellectual impairment, we can certainly do a lot about the often surrounding emotional disturbances.

If a patient is hyperkinetic we can calm him or her down. For example, one recent patient, a distinguished emeritus professor at Stanford, developed AD and adopted the habit of walking naked throughout his neighborhood. This indignity to himself and his family was sad.

Conversely, if the person is too low or depressed, substantial assistance can be offered. Various stimulants from coffee, to a walking program, to a little port wine, to antidepressant medicines often help.

Treating Alzheimer's doesn't stop there. Many critical issues remain, including the need to develop a care capability which will allow the patient to remain at home. When dealing with AD, the comforts and conveniences of home life can be of great benefit to both patient and family. Some communities, such as my home city, Palo Alto, are blessed with an abundance of social support systems which can provide all varieties of home help for patient and family. This is something which must be developed throughout the country, depending upon individual needs and financial considerations.

When I see my new patient, I try hard to be upbeat and helpful; but the grim reality persists that Alzheimer's disease is a condition of unknown cause, of unknown duration, and of unknown treatment. My bet is that, like polio, there will no definitive cure or effective treatment for it once the damage is done. But also, like polio, the final answer will come through prevention. But prevention of what?

The Suspected Origins
of the Disease

There are a number of theories surrounding the fundamental cause of Alzheimer's disease, but the most common involves the brain's neurotransmitters. It has been known for some time that the brains of patients with AD have lowered amounts of the crucial brain chemical acetylcholine, as well as alterations in the enzyme machinery which are involved with this compound.

It was logical, therefore, to try to treat persons suffering from AD with related chemicals. (Lecithin, in particular, contains a certain amount of choline.) Such efforts are yet to fulfill their early promise. My intuition is that the lack of acetylcholine is the *result of* rather than the *cause of* the dementia.

There is also an observable relationship between those patients with Alzheimer's disease and greater than normal amounts of aluminum in certain crucial areas of the brain which subserve various functions including the memory. However, despite sensationalizing by the media, there is no conclusive evidence that exposure to aluminum in antiperspirants, antacids, cooking utensils, or the process of renal dialysis leads to a higher incidence of Alzheimer's. Furthermore, we can't produce AD in animals by feeding or injecting them with high amounts of aluminum.

In 1988, researchers began to close in on a genetic definition of Alzheimer's disease. It has been known for some time that individuals with the genetic problem of Down's syndrome (mongolism) have a very high incidence of AD as they age. Historically it has been felt that only a small proportion of persons with AD show any familial aggregation of their disease, and certainly a genetic origin would make prevention a very tough task indeed. However, I recently learned of a village in central Russia where the incidence of AD is extremely high; this is being investigated by researchers interested in a genetic possibility.

Another distinguished group of researchers, including Joseph Rogers in Sun City, Arizona, is working on the possibility that Alzheimer's disease, like several kindred conditions, is due to an infectious agent like a virus. My most graphic illustration of this possibility came several years ago when I had a patient, a CIA agent in the Middle East, whose performance had deteriorated so markedly over a period of eighteen months that he was brought home. Judging by the pace of his decline it was obvious that he would live only a short while longer. Such rapidity is unusual, so I made arrangements with his family that when he died we would immediately transfer his brain to the National Institutes of Health in Bethesda, so that they could inject segments of the brain into monkeys to see if there was some transferable infective agent. Unfortunately, he died a couple of weeks later on a trip to San Diego, so our plans were aborted. If our scenario had worked out and we had been able to show that AD was "catching," it would have been a very important lead.

Recently I heard Sir Harold Roth of Cambridge defend his hypothesis that Alzheimer's disease has a traumatic origin. He contends that multiple brain injuries, usually suffered in younger years, lead ultimately to the scourge of AD. His primary evidence stems from the fact that boxers precociously develop brain changes which are indistinguishable from Alzheimer's disease. Certainly the idea is intriguing, and if proven could lead to coherent preventive strategies.

Regardless of which single or multiple theories of the origin of AD is correct (genetic, toxic, traumatic, infectious, chemical, or whatever), we must soon discover its secret or it truly will overcome us. The first priority is to identify loud and clear that it is a disease, and thereby subject to prevention.

The Course of the Disease

There are three levels of pain associated with Alzheimer's disease, and the first involves the patient. Paradoxically, this is the least important in the quantitative sense. Often the patient with AD is quite unaware of what is going on and blissfully proceeds through his or her decline in seeming indifference.

I have cared for a patient I will call Anna off and on for more than ten years. She and her husband are an extremely attractive couple. Some years ago they decided to move to the Monterey peninsula, where they could indulge their passion for golf. They bought a lovely home directly on a course. Soon after, however, their daughter called to say that Anna seemed to be "losing it"—she had lost her car in a mall parking lot, she endlessly repeated certain sentiments, and she had made chaos of her checkbook. I asked to see her and soon she was in my office—bright, pretty, but totally befuddled as to why she was seeing me. A few gently probing questions revealed the subtle but real deficit in her brain function. It is the same with every visit now. She leaves as she came in—unaware, or at least "unadmitting," that there is anything whatsoever wrong with her.

The challenge is in understanding what Anna is *really* thinking. Does she know she is slipping? Or is genuine indifference keeping her from recognizing her real but faulty self in the mirror? I can't always know.

Another fine patient was a former corporate executive brought to me because of increasingly repetitive and ineffective thought processes. He spent the mornings endlessly looking over his financial records and trying to comprehend what used to be virtually automatic for him. He recognized that he wasn't as good as he used to be; but he blamed it on his inability to sleep, which was not documented by his wife, who testified that he slept like a log. Additionally, he loved playing bridge, and he had been a shark at it. But when he came under my care, he was not able to recognize the patterns or sequences and so lost the wonderful camaraderie that this had once provided him. He had no insight into what was going on, and kept repeating to me, "If only I could get some sleep."

The second level of pain affects the family of the patient with Alzheimer's disease. This is a personal tragedy of immense proportions. Father used to say that there are worse things in the world than dying, and for the family of the affected person, this is certainly true. I currently have a wonderful patient whose wife with Alzheimer's disease is fully convinced that he is her long-dead brother. Nothing can shake this delusion.

Over breakfast she addresses her husband by her brother's name and asks if they will see each other after the college semester is over. The husband doesn't know whether to play-act along—which usually seems the easiest and less painful course—or do as I advise, and bring her back to reality, reminding her over and over again that her brother died fifteen years ago. Such repetitive instruction seemingly makes no impact. When I confront her over this distortion in reality, she blandly tells me that she knows her brother is dead; but the next morning at breakfast, her husband is her brother all over again. This is a very, very tough role for her wonderful husband to play.

The excellent book *The Thirty-Six-Hour Day,* by Nancy L. Mace and Peter V. Rabins, remains an immensely helpful guide for troubled family members dealing with the effects of AD.

But the major tragedy of Alzheimer's disease, in my view, is not with those with the disease or with their grieving families, but with the rest of us who mistakenly, inadvertently, but certainly take this forlorn vision to reflect the true face of aging. As we shut our eyes and visualize someone, even ourselves, at age 90, too often our image is of someone with AD. Until we can approach this disease in a sure fashion—confident of its causes—it is my concern that the best laid preventive medicine strategies will come up short.

Alzheimer's disease stands as a grim, gray obstacle in the pathway of a lifetime of good health practices. Why should I, or you, or anyone else pass up short-term pleasures or adopt a healthy lifestyle if what we are likely to reap is a decade more of distress and shame? This is a bargain none of us would make—and it is why my simple prescription for good health doesn't have as many takers as it should.

I've said it before, but it bears re-emphasis—Alzheimer's disease is not aging. It is a disease. Most people, most old people, never get it. It is neither natural nor normal, and it certainly is not inevitable. We are due for a great societal awakening. We must no longer allow the image of a disease like AD to remain such a formidable presence as to color our senses of our own futures.

HOW FAMILIES HELP
FULFILL THE PROPHECY

Someone said, "It is not how *old* you are, it is *how* you are old." The imagery is dominant as messages from both family and government continue to confirm the down side of aging. Old people are often abandoned in our society. By everyone. And the resultant loss of vitality in the extended family eliminates much of the sense of identity and purpose which we need for successful aging. This is not always so in other cultures.

When on an extended sabbatical in Africa, in 1981, I had the opportunity to ask widely, "How do you take care of your older people?" This question was greeted generally by a sense of incomprehension. Old people weren't taken care of. They belonged. They were integral to the family life. They had roles to play. They were part of a continuity that had no margins. No retirement banquets prevailed. The social tapestry was rich and long.

I have observed all too often how differently we can treat our older citizens. When I was a resident at Charity Hospital in New Orleans, in 1959 to 1960 (one of the happiest years in my life, despite a salary of $75 a month), it was striking to note the difference in circumstances between the wings of the racially segregated hospital. When an older black person was ready to be discharged from the hospital, there was never a problem. When the older white person was ready for discharge, there was almost invariably a complication as to where the person was to live and who were to be the caregivers. The blacks generally had a family member willing and ready to come forward. The whites generally ended up in an institution.

Current census data indicate the unusual longevity of "old" black women. Fewer black women get to be 85 years of age than do white women; but when they do, they tend to live much longer. There is no medical reason that I can perceive why this should be so. I suspect it is due to the black convention of the extended family and its implicit statement of role playing and continued meaning.

HOW SOCIETY HELPS
FULFILL THE PROPHECY

Russel Lee, my former mentor at the Palo Alto Clinic and a friend of my father's, termed compulsory retirement "statutory senility." Why is it that at a turn of a single page of a calendar, a person is declared no longer capable? For most of us, work is definition: "I am a carpenter." "I am a salesman." "I am a construction foreman." "I am a doctor." It is how we identify ourselves.

Sir William Osler, revered master of American medicine, wrote, "Work is the master therapy. Changes in retirement may do more good in promoting the well-being of our older selves than corps of doctors and nurses. The Social Security system penalizes the effort. It seduces us to drop out. Early retirement entices us to step down, let the younger buck or doe take over. It is their time. Who says so? Where is it writ that our time is in decline in mid-life?"

At this historic moment we have the chance to fix the misdirections that our individual and collective initiative and inertias have created. We should not, we cannot, perpetuate policies which penalize our resourcefulness and full potentials. We must identify the fallacy and impoverishment of statutes which encourage premature withdrawal from the mainstream of life.

John William Gardner wrote in *Self-Renewal,* "We know that men need not fall into a stupor of mind and spirit by the time they are middle aged. . . . A society should create an atmosphere that encourages effort."

But what if late middle life, retirement age of 65, is met with a spirit of resignation? Such as, "Well, I guess I've about had it now." Useful roles are subtracted, individual value is diminished, wholeness dissipates. Form follows function downward.

Jake was a neighborhood druggist whose emporium was more of a social center than a pharmacy. He was gregarious, generous, and a warm charmer. The word emerged that after 38 years, at age 63, he was retiring —shutting shop and taking his wife on a cruise—a plan which he had covertly nurtured for years. The signs of discord were not evident—for while he gave every evidence of loving every moment in his shop, Jake had simply had enough. One year later, his wife came to my office and complained that Jake was now a "holy pain in the rear."

"He's always underfoot," she said. "He criticizes every move I make, while all he does is watch TV and sleep."

I also recall Mamie. For over 50 years she had been the principal of a leading girls' school in Boston—it was *her* institution. Then she retired. Sometime later, I was contacted by a niece with whom Mamie had gone to live in Pennsylvania. The niece told me that Mamie had not been out of bed for weeks, spoke only when spoken to, and ate sparsely. I made a house call and walked into the bedroom to find Mamie peering suspiciously over the bedsheets at me. I was afraid she was frankly psychotic, but I slowly teased her story from her and reckoned that she was merely acting out the details of her severe reactive depression. Mamie felt that her life had become lost to her, and this was the reason for all of this behavior. She gradually got out of bed and grew into a new life. Mamie is a superior woman who has lived through a severe late-middle-life crisis—a good old age is open to her again.

The glory of action rests in its delivery of a sense of self-control, and participation, and meaning. It is involvement. An attitude which cries out, "I matter!" This theme of participation, of being part of something akin, is integral to the theme of aging. If we lose meaning, why live? Now as we start to come down to the basic nub of life, why bother? Are we here merely to run an idle course, absorbing and emitting at about the same measure? Taking others' energies in exchange for our own? Or are we here to add to the grander concourse of nature, to enliven and enrich our own little corners of the universe? The flower-touching and star-troubling of each of us is intimate to our existence. We each search for our own meaning.

Does aging mean a loss of significance—a loss of this meaning? Do our older selves matter less than our younger selves? Much of the answer to these terribly important but rarely spoken questions lies within our attitudes. If these attitudes define aging as a time ordained by the gestalt of loss and decline, we are in for real trouble. Most of the markers for decline are wrong. There are no data for this. Norman Cousins writes that "no one knows enough to be a pessimist."

It is crucial to recognize that how we posture ourselves in relationship to our aging is deterministic. The interplay of expectation and outcome is not idle—it is intimate. *Pygmalion* was not a casual insight of George Bernard Shaw. It was an observation of everyday dynamics. Someone once observed, "Those who believe they *can't* are right; those who believe they *can* are right." Aging is a self-fulfilling prophecy. We get what we set.

MORE MIND OVER MATTER

One of the most profound and interesting instances of the effect of emotional prediction on major biologic outcome is seen in the ancient practice of voodoo. For most of us voodoo is a spooky, unreal Halloween brand of weird and surrealistic witchcraft. It doesn't relate to us, or we to it. But for great portions of our world, voodoo is not magic or late-night TV; it is the stuff of everyday life.

While there is much misconception in our culture regarding the definition of voodoo, it is generally considered a religious and cultural orientation originating on the Caribbean island of Haiti and practiced sporadically throughout the world. Voodoo has evolved into a complex set of rituals many of which have roots in both Catholicism and West African tribal religions.

I first confronted voodoo when I went to one of my patients who was dying in Charity Hospital in New Orleans. The patient's bed had been adorned with strange charms, and burning candles had been placed at both the head and foot. Instinctively I knew not to intervene—I was a witness to another realm of belief. Medical efforts had been exhausted, and I had nothing better to offer. Since this first contact, I have had the opportunity to see many instances in which belief and health are intimately related. I have seen hexed (or bewitched) persons in chains in West Africa awaiting their appointed death moment. I have seen a shaman in Ladakh sucking the evil spirits from the bellies of her faithful patients. This is all happening today in our world—not yesterday on some bizarre, foreign planet.

We in the "modern medical community" have confidence in our science and in our methods of healing, but this is not always so for individuals coming to us from other cultures. For example, at Stanford University Hospital we occasionally see a patient from Central or South America for whom a hospital is only a place to die. His or her local traditions have taught that this is so. One of our first jobs is to unprogram this belief and establish the new concept that a hospital is also a place in which to get well.

I observed the strengths of a similar belief system when caring for patients who practice the tenets of the Church of Christ, Scientist (Christian Science). In one such case, an 80-year-old woman was brought to me by her children because she was doing poorly and losing weight. She was very firm in her belief as a Christian Scientist, and so when I interviewed her, she answered negatively to each question that I put to her. During her physical examination I found a huge bleeding tumor extending out of her vagina. I had to struggle to maintain my aplomb. Eventually I confronted my patient in the presence of her children and asked how she could possibly have lived with any sense of contentment with herself while this thing was growing. She must have felt like she was straddling a softball. But she was totally indifferent to it. I pleaded that unless it was attended, it would become increasingly foul and make her life totally miserable. I had invaded her belief system; however, my best persuasive guile resulted in her family convincing her that it had to be removed surgically. She did fine through the surgery, but developed shingles and died two weeks later.

In another case, I was summoned by the adult children to the home of an older woman who was also a Christian Scientist. I made a house call and found her in the sitting room, attended by her "reader" (a religious guide). When she saw me enter, the reader left, never to return again. My new patient was in florid congestive heart failure and was dying. Congestive heart failure is one of the few dramatic circumstances in which the internist may utilize a combination of therapies and thus change the tide of ill. I initiated my therapies and called the children, who arranged for some home nursing. I saw her again at home during the next several days, and she progressively improved until I felt that she was back at her baseline state. She died unaccountably two weeks later.

The ambiguity present in these two examples is intentional. I present them in the hope that they confer a most important message—that there is a spiritual, psychologic belief-system component to all human illness. Physicians see illness as a circumscribed, technical event and forget the other. I am extremely modest about medicine's ability to cure without the patient's active participation. In both of the instances I've related here, I cured the disease but may have killed the patient by usurping from her a belief system which is the fundamental wellspring of life.

The medical establishment has not been generous in its according of prominence to psychologic factors in disease situations, even though the effects of a patient's mental attitude over his or her physical condition have long fascinated scientists. One such pioneer in this field was Dr. Walter Cannon, a great man of American medicine, and a professor of physiology at Harvard Medical School in my father's era. Dr. Cannon's credentials in the medical world were impeccable. In 1929, for example, he was the first to characterize the behavior pattern of the emergency situation termed "fight or flight."

The most dramatic illustration of mind over matter concerns the ability of some practitioners of voodoo to cause others to "die by suggestion." Equally phenomenal is the reputed ability of some voodoo priests themselves to enter a state resembling clinical death—and perhaps more important, to recover from such a state.

In a 1942 paper entitled "Voodoo Death," published in the *American Anthropologist*, Dr. Cannon wrote, "The phenomenon is so extraordinary and so foreign to the experience of civilized people that it seems incredible; certainly if it is authentic it deserves careful consideration. I proposed to recite instances of this mode of death, to inquire whether reports of the phenomenon are trustworthy, and to examine a possible explanation of it if it should prove to be real."

Cannon made a thorough search of the evidence concerning the practice of voodoo, extending his studies to voodoo and voodoolike cults in West Africa, Brazil, Haiti, Australia, Hawaii, and elsewhere. In one account he reported, "In Australia, a witch doctor points a bone at a man. Believing that nothing can save him, the man rapidly sinks in spirits and prepares to die. He is saved only at the last minute when the witch doctor is forced to remove the charm."

In a concurring report, Herbert Basedow wrote in *The Australian Aboriginal*, "The man who discovered that he is being boned by an enemy is indeed, a pitiable sight. He stands aghast with his eyes staring at the treacherous pointer, and with his hands lifted to ward off the lethal medium, which he imagines is pouring into his body. His cheeks blanch, and his eyes become glassed, and the expression of his face becomes horribly distorted. He attempts to shriek, but usually the sound chokes in his throat, and all that one might see is froth at his mouth. His body begins to tremble, and his muscles twitch involuntarily. He sways backward and falls to the ground, and after a time appears to be in a swoon. He finally composes himself, goes to his hut and there frets to death."

Convinced of the reality of this phenomenon, Cannon turned to the scientific question of how these terror states manifested themselves—what was the mechanism of death? His earlier experimental work had involved cats and the way in which rage (associated with the instinct to attack) and fear are associated with flight. Both were shown to be related to an extreme arousal of the autonomic or automatic nervous system. During such agitated states, adrenaline is poured out into the system; and it was this compound which Cannon felt was responsible for the agonal results of hexing, bone pointing, and voodoo seen in man.

Cannon's pioneering work was picked up by another noted physiologist, Dr. Curt Richter of Johns Hopkins Medical School. Serendipitously Richter had found that after clipping the snout whiskers of rats, they behaved very peculiarly and died a short while later. In other experiments he compared the swimming endurance of wild and domesticated Norway rats. Without clear explanation, some rats died shortly after having been placed in a swimming chamber, while others swam for as long as 81 hours. Richter then clipped the rats' whiskers. While a few of the tame rats died when put into the water, every one of the 34 wild rats immediately sank to the bottom of the tank and died. Later experiments revealed that merely holding the wild rats also resulted in their failure to swim. He became intrigued with the mystery. Had the wild rats failed to swim because they had been held, or because they had had their whiskers clipped? He reasoned that the situation was not so much one of "fight or flight," but rather one he termed "hopelessness." The wild rats seemed to give up. Richter's next step was to see if such hopelessness could be overcome. In subsequent experiments the rats first were held and then released; next they were immersed in water for only a few seconds, and then rescued. The result was that the rats *learned* not to give up. These rats swam as long as had their domesticated cousins.

There are a number of observations made by veterinarians and zookeepers of the sudden deaths of wild and domesticated animals. There is even a newly described condition in animals known as "capture myopathy," in which, after a brief chase, a pursued animal topples over and dies with no apparent injury. Lewis Thomas has written much about how the mouse when caught by the cat seems to die without a struggle or pain. It seems to die on cue.

IMPLICATIONS FOR AGING HUMANS

What are the implications of these animal experiments and the many observations of voodoo deaths in aboriginal people to our contemporary modern world? Are there lessons to be learned, and messages to be delivered to us? There have been so many demonstrations of the morbid effects of helplessness/hopelessness that the behavior has been termed a syndrome. Dr. George Engle, of the Department of Psychiatry at the University of Rochester, reviewed 160 cases of unexplained or unexpected sudden death in adults. He found that 58 percent occurred at a time of loss, 35 percent at a time of threat, and only 6 percent at a time of pleasure. Twenty percent occurred at around the time of death of a loved one. A similar British study of 4,500 widows showed a 40 percent higher death rate in the first six months after a husband's death. Robert Butler estimates that bereavement causes 25,000 deaths per year in America.

In addition, Richter cited evidence in which persons intending suicide often die despite consuming sublethal doses of poison, or despite having inflicted relatively trivial wounds. There are other examples. A 1946 report in the *Archives of Pathology* discusses the deaths of soldiers in combat who died without wounds; and many surgeons are reluctant to operate on patients who exhibit preoperative terror or a sense of doom.

Dr. Stewart Wolf said, "Death is the solution to an insoluble problem."

I think he was correct. If we look carefully we can find many examples of seemingly inexplicable death. In Japan, for instance, there have been numerous reports of nocturnal deaths in otherwise healthy young men who appear to have suffered terrifying dreams. This ancient phenomenon has even been labeled, Pokkui disease. In the Philippines this same disorder is known as Bangangut. The anecdotal evidence coupled with observations that stress will precipitate abnormalities in the electrocardiogram lead to the conclusion that these individuals were most probably "shocked to death."

A doctor friend of mine, Paul O'Rourke, told of a similar observation he made during his internship at Sacramento City Hospital, forty years ago. There was at that time a serious epidemic of meningitis, and when doctors studied effects of the disease, they learned that most of the fatalities occurred among Catholics who had received the last rites. O'Rourke pondered whether having last rites was, in effect, a "pointing of the bone"—a granting of permission to die.

Other Factors Leading to
Death by Suggestion

Social observations reveal that poverty, overcrowding, and ignorance conspire to produce high death rates. The helpless/hopeless syndrome would find its best opportunity in just this situation. It has been
suggested too that community and family attitudes toward someone with a
terminal illness, such as advanced cancer, may be very similar to that of a
community in which a hexed person lives. For example, entry into a nursing
home can be fraught with disenfranchisement, abandonment, and a helplessness message. Loss of control. Dependency. The message contains all
sorts of hidden implications—but the power of the forces at play is without
doubt.

A kindred observation was made during the First World War. At that
time the Germans noted that after one of their ships was sunk and the
survivors confined to a lifeboat, death seemed to occur first in the younger
members of the crew while the veterans lived on. The interpretation of
this, of course, was that experience can offset the sense of the inevitable
which often preoccupies one who is uninitiated. Decades later, recognition
of this factor lead to formation of structured trainings such as the Outward
Bound program in which participants are taught self-reliance, insulation
against helplessness, and inoculation against hopelessness.

In an attempt to relate these principles to humans, Stewart Wolf,
M.D., studied the residents of Roseto, Pennsylvania. He chose this particular community because despite other health habits such as obesity and lack
of exercise (conventional threats to longevity), the 1,700 townspeople exhibited very high levels of health. After much analysis, Wolf proposed that
the unique characteristics of this community were a strong social fabric and
respect for and involvement of the older generation.

I believe that such observations were most clearly articulated in the
wonderful book *Persuasion and Healing,* by Jeremy Frank, eminent psychiatrist from Johns Hopkins University. For me, Frank's residual message was
that the effects of "caring" far outweigh any detail of what was done, or by
whom. This is similar to the Hawthorne effect so well known to industrial
psychologists studying human behavior in the workplace: what you do isn't
so important as "doing something"—caring. Many studies of normal child
development indicate that caring—from simple attentive responses to
physical touching—is essential to well-being. This is a message for all interpersonal relationships—including those with the aging adult.

In medicine we call it the placebo effect. The sugar pill has at its roots the fact that a person expects the remedy to work. Suggestibility can be negative, as in witchcraft, or positive, as in the placebo. Norman Cousins wrote, "The physician's job is to program patients to live."

A number of major national studies have come apart because of the Hawthorne and placebo effects. We at the Palo Alto Clinic were chosen to be one of the centers involved in the aspirin myocardial infarction study (AMIS) sponsored by the National Institutes of Health. Upon entering the study we selected 200 of our male patients who were survivors of earlier heart attacks and gave half of them aspirin and half a placebo in a double-blind fashion (neither the patient nor the doctors knew who was getting what). At the conclusion of the study, data analysis revealed that *all* of the subjects had done so much better than the projections of the study designers that conclusive evidence of the benefit or lack of benefit of aspirin was impossible. Merely being part of the program had become a significant factor.

What does the discussion of voodoo and helplessness have to do with aging? A lot. We fashion our lives like a carpenter builds a closet. Our totality is under our conscious steering and predicting. The compass points which we set are highly predictive.

HOW OLD WOULD YOU BE IF YOU DIDN'T KNOW HOW OLD YOU WERE?

A favorite game is to play reincarnation—who would you like to be should you return to Earth in another life? When asked this question Winston Churchill replied, "Clementine's second husband." My grace is not so easy. If I had the opportunity, I would choose to return as a symphony conductor. They have been my heroes since my boyhood days attending Philadelphia Orchestra concerts nearly every Saturday night. I have always been jealous of what appears to me the awesome opportunities for repetitive creativity and self-indulgence which accompany my Walter Mitty image of an orchestra conductor. Danny Kaye once said as he finished conducting the Boston Symphony Orchestra, "If I were any happier they would throw me into an institution."

It was therefore with this sense of wonder that I became the physician of William Steinberg. He had earlier been a conductor in Boston, New York, and Pittsburgh. He had been a protégé of Toscanini. His failing health had brought him to the good climate of Palo Alto; and although he had no close family there, he did have a number of good friends, one of whom was a close colleague of mine. Through this contact I became Steinberg's physician. I was ecstatic—to have a chance to give back a little to one of the demigods.

My initial contact with Steinberg revealed enough medical problems to fill a museum. He was sometimes taking ten medicines a day. His laboratory tests were awful. I could scarcely tell which was the top and which was the bottom of his electrocardiogram because it was so disordered. I explored each of his problems diligently; I consulted my skilled colleagues for advice. I did the best technical job that I could.

But more important, I invaded his confidence enough to dare a reassessment of his life goals. He had come to Palo Alto to die; he was helpless, hopeless. A wreck of a body, depressed, and often in pain. But despite these major infirmities, he still had a zest for life. Gradually I reintroduced him to a future. I proposed that we bind him up with the best bailing wire we could find, patch up his leaks, and soothe his discomforts. I suggested that he might consider some of the guest-conductor invitations that were in his daily mail. Early on these had been dismissed summarily, but gradually he came to the conclusion (like another patient, the box manufacturer) that life still had meaning and challenges for him.

In the two years of my care he conducted over a dozen concerts in the United States, Europe, and Israel, interspersed with trips into Stanford and other hospitals. There was one occasion when he virtually arose from his sickbed to conduct. I was in the wings as he stiffly approached the podium, shuffling uncertainly. He picked up the baton, and he became the Maestro. He commanded the orchestra with a might that would have made George Patton envious. He was sustained by the purpose of his existence.

Steinberg died on May 17, 1978, at the age of 78. He had gone to New York and suffered heart failure shortly after conducting the New York Philharmonic and Isaac Stern. Way to go, Steinberg!

Who do you think you are going to be when you are 90? *Do* you think you're going to be at 90? Animals and primitive people—ourselves until the present age—lacked the perception and the conceptual framework to address these questions. The answers were strictly left to Fate, an uncertain and nonbenevolent agency. Who we were to be—"if" we were to be—was not evidently of our choosing. It depended upon someone—something else.

Until I became president of the American Geriatrics Society, I had always naïvely presumed that this "something" was a benign, all-knowing guidance system directing my and my contacts' destinies in accord with a rational program. I didn't know where the system rested—in the Oval Office, or with my parents, or at Harvard, or Stanford, or where—but I was comfortable with the assurance that someone wise was taking care of me. My year of responsibility changed that because I had the opportunity to meet many of our nation's leaders and dialogue with them about the major problems that concerned me. I recognized that we are all in this together. Solutions stream from within, not without. The familiar quote, "If you are not part of the solution, you are part of the problem," assumed a new meaning for me.

This is my constant observation in the practice of medicine. For example, several years ago on a New Year's Day I was called to the hospital emergency room twice within a few hours to admit two patients who had had strokes. One was a fat druggist; one was a wizened, feisty lady with a French accent. They were about the same age; and as the result of artery blockage at the same brain site, both had virtually the same amount of damage.

I examined them and admitted them to their rooms, where a program of rehabilitation was begun. During this program, the druggist was always apathetic, rarely helping in his own care, demanding that everything be done for him—even the washing of his own face. The little lady, on the other hand, was full of pep and scarcely able to be contained from rushing to her next exercise session.

She walked out of the hospital under her own steam, albeit with a cane and a limp, but nonetheless erect. The druggist, conversely, was rolled out of the hospital in a wheelchair, where he spent the entirety of his next several years, to recover no further.

What made the difference? Not I, nor the nurses, nor the therapist, nor medicine. It was an assertion of will—an exclamation point of effort on the woman's part; a sorry abdication of effort on the man's.

I thought of these patients and others like them while attending a sampling of Werner Erhard's pop self-confidence-building course, EST. After days of intimidating introspection in this program it is revealed that there is no secret. *We* are the secret. *You* are the secret.

You, for the first time in history, have the opportunity to design your own future. You are not an impassive, nonparticipating witness in your own life story. You are the author and the players. You are the sculptor and the marble. If your future beckons with opportunity, creative pursuit, worthiness, and meaning, then you can live your *entire* life span. But if you abandon your later years to images of despondency and dependency, then the devil takes the hindmost—which he currently seems very adept at doing. You live too short.

SIX

USE IT OR LOSE IT

No man doth exalt Nature to the
height it would beare.

John Donne

What is a man,
If his chief good and market of his time
Be but to sleep and feed? A beast, no more.
Sure he that made us with such large discourse
Looking before and after, gave us not
That capability and God-like reason
To fust in us unused.

Hamlet, act IV, scene IV

U se it or lose it. These five little words, thirteen letters, are so small that they seem insignificant. They appear to be a whimsical, trite, and trivial aphorism of minor import. Yet, contained in this sparse statement is immense and pervasive wisdom. It applies forcibly to each part and corner of our being. It applies to every bit of the earth. An unused engine rusts. A still stream stagnates. An untended garden tangles. It is a powerful and universal truth.

In fact, "use it or lose it" is a restatement of the Second Law of Thermodynamics, in that the Second Law emphasizes the tendency of matter to go toward greater disorder—entropy. But an equally important physical corollary is the ordering effect that an energy flow provides. So that we find ourselves in a world which is tending toward disorder; while in contrast, continuous work leads to self-organization and ordering. It is this ordering phenomenon which was described by Prigogine and Stengers in their central book, *Order Out of Chaos.*

ENERGY FLOW IS AN ORDERING INFLUENCE

Life is the bundling and ordering of our substance by an energy stream. Prigogine wrote, "Life is a supreme expression of self-organization processes."

This vital ordering effect of energy has been called the Fourth Law of Thermodynamics by Harold Morowitz to indicate the tremendous importance of this life-developing process. It underlies evolution, and it underlies each dynamic of our bodies and of our function. The relationship holds from the most minute portion of ourselves (from the enzyme protein level) to the whole organism, where the principle of "practice makes perfect" is another way of saying the same thing. For the cook, the athlete, the surgeon, or the piano student, the more directed energy that is conveyed toward a task, the more effectively that task will be performed. Much of the work of your body is devoted to maintaining what is called homeostasis—the maintaining of the order, the evenness of function, and your ability to adapt and adjust.

In chapter 2 I discussed the experimental creation of amino acids by a lightning bolt. The underlying factor in that experiment was this organizing effect of an energy flow. Closer yet to the essence of life are the experiments in which an energy source can cause the complexing of amino acids and thus the formation of polypeptides. Such "ordering" seems, in a way, to be flouting the Second Law—but it isn't. It merely addresses the inevitable interactive relationship between energy and matter. It is therefore clear that "losing it" at the molecular level merely represents the entropically driven inviolable dispersion ultimately due to heat loss which cannot be recaptured for use for ordering purposes.

Perhaps a brief review is in order here. The Second Law states that all matter is moving toward disorder—entropy. This process is essentially one of heat loss. Some of that heat loss is retarded when we use energy in an ordering process (work), thus we are able, for a time, to "stave off" the total disorder.

But without the energy flow, the form of matter—the order of life (homeostasis)—deteriorates. Faster and inevitably. May the force be with you—because if it isn't you will lose it, and lose it quicker than you had to. We are all destined to lose it eventually, but what is the sense of throwing away the magic gift such a thermophysical process has given to us?

DISUSE—THE DESTRUCTIVE FORCE

For centuries scientists have been intrigued by the decremental effects which the lack of use (or disuse) has on natural processes. In 1835, Edward Blythe wrote in the *Magazine of Natural History,* "An animal supplied regularly with abundance of food, without the trouble and exertion of having to seek for it becomes in consequence, bulky and lazy, while the muscles of locomotion become rigid and comparatively powerless, or are not developed to their full size."

Charles Darwin dealt extensively with the effect of disuse on animal parts in *On the Origin of Species.* He noted particularly the loss of effective function in both the ostrich's wings and the mole's eyes; and he presumed this was because of underuse. "With animals the increased use or disuse of parts has had a marked influence; thus I find in the domestic duck the bones of the wing weigh less and the bones of the leg more, in proportion to the whole skeleton, than do the same bones in the wild duck; and this change may be safely attributed to the domestic duck flying much less, and walking more, than its wild parents. The great and inherited development of the udders in cows and goats when they are habitually milked, in comparison with these organs in other countries, is probably another instance of the effects of use. Not one of our domestic animals can be named which has not in some country drooping ears. And the view has been suggested that the drooping is due to disuse of the muscles of the ear, from the animals being seldom much alarmed, seems probable. . . . Many animals possess structures which can be best explained by the effects of disuse." Finally, Darwin concluded, "Natural selection would aid in the effects of disuse."

STRESS IS THE RESULT
OF TOO MUCH ENERGY

It is my personal conviction that this series of observations from Darwin to Prigogine has given us a powerful new tool to look at the human condition.

A similar breakthrough insight was provided the scientific world in 1936 by Hans Selye, research physiologist in Montreal. Selye popularized the term *stress*, identifying this syndrome as being any change in the natural order of a system. Through his hundreds of experiments, Selye demonstrated the multiple detrimental effects that stress has on the human body. For example, when he subjected his experimental laboratory rats to a variety of repetitious noxious situations, he noted a characteristic set of reactions, and he termed these reactions the General Adaptation Syndrome. The features that he found most commonly were ulcers, high blood pressure, diabetes, kidney changes, thin bones, and premature aging. I have heard him talk several times and have read many of his books and scientific papers—as have most physicians. The results are very impressive, and to me represent clearly what happens to a living creature when too much energy is applied to it.

The mechanism that Selye proposed for this syndrome is dependent upon an excessive stimulation of the adrenal glands—to be precise, the adrenal cortex. This is the part of the adrenal that makes cortisone, so that stress in effect is manifested by an excessive outpouring of cortisone, and the resultant set of adverse changes noted above.

Selye's popularization of stress was so successful that we now all generally identify with the very real physical burdens which excessive anxiety, tension, and labor can provoke. We all can diagnose the evidences of wear and tear.

But Selye went a step further by clearly differentiating this threat to well-being from the classical medical model of disease. The disease model presumes an extrinsic force or agent entering the body and provoking its mischief by way of its own mechanism. Infection, allergy, and injury are examples of the typical disease situation in which the body (the patient) is predominantly the passive host of the real cause of the trouble. Stress changes, on the other hand, result from a maladjustment, a breakdown of homeostasis of the basic body mechanism. Like an engine failure due to overheating, stress results from too much energy throughout. The body is designed to operate with a certain load applied to it; but when an excess burden is placed, it decompensates. It burns out.

TOO LITTLE ENERGY
IS JUST AS DESTRUCTIVE

Just as there is a situation in which excessive energy load is applied to the body, and experimentally documented adverse changes result, there is a comparable circumstance in which the body, built by and for work forces, receives too little energetic input and a set of operational and structural failures ensue. Such a suggestion conforms to intuition but has not been formally proven. For example, Dr. Calvin Hirsch recently performed an interesting study at Stanford University Hospital regarding the functional state of patients at the time of admission—their ability to walk, dress, and generally care for themselves. At the time of discharge, Hirsch resurveyed the patients and found that their levels of functioning within these basic tasks had declined. This is scarcely what one would hope for as the result of an expensive, intensive hospital experience.

It is my further sense, particularly as we age, that the sum total of adverse outcomes which can be attributed to understimulation (disuse) of the body is quantitatively more significant to our overall well-being—or lack of it—than are stress outcomes. In my view, disuse needs an expanded general consciousness so that we can plan effective counteractive maintenance strategies that will conform our biomachine to its idealized operation.

My interest in disuse has been fueled by two significant events in my life, one intellectual and the other recreational. The intellectual event was a six-month sabbatical to Africa in 1981 and 1982. My wife and I strapped on our back packs and flew initially to West Africa to pursue a quest with three goals. First was to see what aging meant to populations in Africa; second was to observe as much as we could about faith healing; and third was to search out evidences relating to the physical exercise pattern of primitive man (and woman).

By any measure the six months were among the most wonderful of our lives in that we had the opportunity to probe our primal origins, to see the great beasts close at hand, and to learn the passions of different peoples and lands. I have long been an amateur anthropologist and feel that both anthropology and astronomy should be required courses in school, since they teach us where we belong in the universe and of our relationship to the other travelers on our journey.

The bulk of our Africa time was spent in Nairobi, where I worked at the Louis Leakey Institute for the Study of African Prehistory. During my time there, I had the rich opportunity to meet some of the world's great anthropologists who had come to Nairobi and its neighboring renowned digs like golfers flock to Pebble Beach. I approached them with my largely undeveloped ideas concerning the pattern of physical activity demanded of our ancient ancestors. Most of my queries were met with genuine expressions of interest. Anthropologists have variously advanced theories of our evolutionary pattern. Tool use, feeding patterns, aggression, territoriality, bipedalism, reproductive strategies, and others have been proposed as forces which shaped human development. I was eager to inquire whether physical exertion, too, should be considered an element of selection for our survival as a species. The history lesson of this experience provided a major insight into the effects of disuse in our contemporary world.

The story goes back a long way. It starts with a geologic event—the upheaval of a crust of the earth all along the eastern edge of the African continent. This is known as the Great Rift. As a result of this great shift of the surface of the earth, the nature of the earth changed—jungle changed to plains, and new environments emerged. Many of the great archaeological finds of early man in South Africa, Tanzania, Kenya, and Ethiopia are along the great continental shift line. At the time of the Great Rift, 15 million years ago, our ancestors were jungle creatures, some of whom made the most important journey in the long history of mankind—they left the jungle and went out onto the plain. Zoologist Loren Eiseley wrote, "Man bears in his body clear signs of an early apprenticeship in the trees. Man has served his arboreal apprenticeship." Our close current cousins, the great apes, are still in the jungle, while present-day man has undergone immense evolutionary change—and all due to the exodus from jungle to plain.

The most important footsteps ever left by a humanoid (Neil Armstrong's lunar variety notwithstanding) are those found in the molten ash of Laetoli, a few miles from the Olduvai Gorge in Tanzania. These footprints, found by Mary Leakey, are dated at 3.76 million years ago—the approximate same age as the collection of bones known as Lucy, found by Don Johanssen, a few hundred miles to the north. Study of the footprints and of the structure of Lucy's skeleton shows that by this date and in accord with the descent from the trees and out onto the savanna, our antecedents were fully upright on two legs and walked with a striding gait. This major adaptive step surely served an evolutionary end, and that end was involved with the feeding strategy. In the trees we were vegetarians—but the plains provided different food options and demands. In a not uncommon parched year in East Africa, other animals were at the top of the food chain and were therefore a likely major food source for us. Bone remnants, tool evidences, and the fact that we, unlike the apes, have an obligate need for eight essential amino acids in our diet indicate the certainty that our forebears had meat as a major foodstuff for millions of years of our development. Professor Richard Lee wrote, "Bushmen eat as much vegetable food as they need, and as much meat as they can get."

I have had the opportunity to study the mountain gorillas in Rwanda and the orangutan in Borneo, and I learned that these great creatures are very territorial, moving less than a half a mile a day. The Kalahari bushmen, by contrast, move ten to thirty miles a day, in accord with the likely daily habit of our plains ancestors. But what does all this have to do with disuse and aging?

Primitive humans were small, slow, and unarmed with any lethal anatomic weapons (such as claws, venom, fangs or stingers). When contrasted with the other major predators, large differences appear. For example, the large cats have great speed, strength, and killing jaws and teeth. Early man, however, had one crucial functional advantage and that was his ability to run—long. The human endurance capacity is virtually unique. Even today the great cats chase for only a quarter-mile or so, and if unsuccessful they then give up. In addition, the biologic need to cool the body during running led to a decrease in the body hair of early man—a distinct advantage. We also developed the ability to sweat. (Specifically, we have the capacity to sweat 4.2 quarts an hour.) Endurance and this ability to sweat are evolutionary factors which have come to serve us well. As a result of my African sojourn, I published a paper in the *Journal of Human Evolution*. In it I suggested that our selective survival advantage as a species was the strategy of "persistence hunting." This means the running down of the plains animals (mostly antelope) simply by the strategy of keeping them moving—in the midday sun.

This ability has been coupled with another phenomenon veterinarians have described as "capture myopathy," in which a prey animal, when chased by a helicopter or jeep, will run full out for some distance, perhaps a mile, and then keel over in a swoon. This capture myopathy is secondary to hyperthermia (overheating) and, I propose, was exploited for day-to-day existence by our primitive ancestors.

In a 1925 book, *Pygmies and Bushmen of the Kalahari*, Samuel Shaw Dorman wrote, "A bushman will run an unwounded springbok to a standstill in the hottest part of the day, keeping the animal constantly on the run, preventing it from lying down until it is quite exhausted. It is then easily killed."

Many more-recent reports recount this relentless chase of prey and the stamina exhibited by aboriginal people. I saw it myself during a recent trip to Borneo. The journey took my wife and me upriver for four days in a dugout canoe. As the river petered out, we arrived at a longhouse occupied by Dayaks who are members of the Salap tribe. We were eager, though, to go deeper into the rain forest; so we arranged for three hunters to lead us farther. The first of our guides was the 58-year-old chief of the longhouse; the second was another Salap, age 68; and the third guide was a younger man from a neighboring tribe. They slung their baskets on their backs and their old rifles over their shoulders. The first night out, after a very rigorous and gorgeous seven-mile hike, the hunters shot two wild boar and butchered them on the spot. We had the ultimate barbecue. We ate only a fraction of the meat, however, so the remainder was packed into the baskets for the trip back. The point is that, as marathoners, my wife and I consider ourselves to be in better than average condition. But despite their tremendous burden, these primitive, wonderful people had to wait up for us repeatedly on the way home. They were in incredible shape! We have seen this same characteristic in sherpas in Nepal, who also made us feel like pantywaists.

People such as these make no particular effort to be in shape; as an integral part of daily life, they just *are*. In another example, the exercise pattern of the American Indian is the stuff of legends. The Tarahumara Indians of northern Mexico are renowned for their kickball races of a hundred miles or so. These races, and those of their cousins to the north in New Mexico and Arizona, are ritualistic reenactments of epochs of their history in which long-distance running was a part of the regular routine. In a similar way, thousands today run marathons, 26 miles 385 yards, which commemorate directly the defeat of Sparta's army. The fact that we can run this distance, and farther, is no newfound genetic freak, but rather a statement of our age-old endowment of endurance capacity.

Another remnant evidence we have of our progenitor's vigorous lifestyle is the cache of bones of these early man types. Neanderthal bones, 60,000 years old, and others are tremendously massive, virtually as iron ingots compared to our own fragile relics. There is a basic law of bone formation called Wolff's Law, which asserts that the robustness of any bone is in direct proportion to the physical stresses applied to that bone. Use it or lose it. Analyses of the bones of present aboriginal people show that they are similarly much more rugged than are our own.

We can also trace the evolution of physical activity upon other parts of our bodies. Not long ago the hearts of athletes were thought to be abnormally large—in fact, diseased. But when we calculate our heart weight compared to our body weight, we find it to be lower than that of wild animals. This indicates that our "nonused" hearts are really the abnormal ones by being too small. The imperative message derives therefore that throughout the long sweep of our evolutionary development, when our present structure and function were being formed, we lived as very active creatures. It is appropriate to ask how many of us today would last a month when confronted with the challenges of this era of our prehistory.

These aeons are known popularly as our hunter-gatherer era. Only the fittest of us survived. Darwin taught us that who lived and who died depended upon both accommodation and durability. Each day was one of physical threat and challenge. The pursuit of food, and being pursued as food, dominated our ancestors' thoughts and lifestyle.

I was again reminded of this fact when I celebrated my 51st birthday in the middle of the Kalahari desert. We threw a party and invited our host bushmen to be our guests. They were enthusiastically festive, and I concluded that it takes little there to conjure up a celebration. As they presented their good-night farewells they said, "Happy, happy long life, and may all your children be fat." (Or clicks to that effect.) This message symbolized the centrality of food in their total organizational framework.

The physically demanding, threatened, uncertain lifestyle which characterized the daily life of millennia of our predecessors lasted until the event which Richard Leakey calls the most significant moment in the history of our species—the Agricultural Revolution. This occurred 10,000 years ago. The significance of the historical time cannot be overstated. Until this calendar date we lived our lives in an extraordinarily active mode—we chased our food, which chased the rain. The food moved and we moved. However, the Agricultural Revolution changed all that. We no longer chased our food; we grew it. Hunting and gathering gave way to the pastoral life complete with its restricted physical demands and challenges. Energetic needs and stimulations slackened.

The Agricultural Revolution spawned an agronomous culture; the dramatic result of which was the explosion of population. Specifically, the provision of adequate food supply has increased world population from perhaps 1 million persons 10,000 years ago to 5.5 billion today—a 5,000-fold increase that is the present major threat to our civilized existence. For as observed by the eighteenth-century writer Thomas Malthus, when otherwise unrestricted (by war, poverty, or natural disaster), a population will always reproduce faster than its food supply.

The redirection of our hard won physical vigor took on additional restriction with the arrival of the Industrial Revolution just 200 years ago. Not only did we no longer chase our food or cultivate it, we bought it at the store. Food procurement became mechanized. We became zoo animals.

Using Carl Sagan's convention of conforming a given time span to a calendar year, we set the morning of January 1 as 3.76 million years ago, the time when we know that we were upright. Our great- . . . great grandparents, 200,000 generations of them, lived the vigorous life of the hunter-gatherer until the Agricultural Revolution of early in the morning of December 31. The Industrial Revolution arrived only at 11:59:59 P.M. on our time scale. The conclusion is that throughout the long span of our prehistory, our evolutionary development, we lived as physically active, vigorous creatures of robust vitality.

Yet, what is the standard by which we measure our normalcy today? What is the normal serum cholesterol—250 mg percent or 200 mg percent? The serum cholesterol of the Kalahari bushmen is 77 mg percent. What is a normal blood pressure, anyway? The 140/90 that life insurance allows us, or the 120/80 seen in medical textbooks, or the 105/70 of aboriginal people? Our present sense of normalcy is in fact derived from the means of the last millisecond of our biologic history. Our archive stretches far beyond.

Many of our biologic standards are simply wrong. Restating intuitive remarks made over a century ago by both Darwin and Blythe, Loren Eiseley wrote:

> The most remarkable of acquired variations are those brought about in animals in a state of confinement or domestication in which case an animal is supplied regularly with abundance of every nutritious, though often unnatural food, without the trouble and exertion of having to seek for it, and it becomes, in consequence, bulky and lazy, and in a few generations often very large: while the muscles of the organs of locomotion, from being little called into action, become rigid and comparatively powerless, or not developed to their full size.

Eiseley's remarks are punctuated by a basic anthropologic law called the Principle of Least Effort. Simply stated, it asserts that any organism when confronted with a task will seek out that method of performance of

the task that demands the least effort. The economy implicit in this principle is apparent. A hummingbird that will fly from Florida to Honduras will
take the direct route and not detour along the way. A beaver will select
local material for its dam, not those of the next valley.

Contemporary man has embraced the Principle of Least Effort for
his very own. The wheel, the steam engine, push-button tuning, and the
true embodiment of least effort—the motorized golf cart. It is my feeling
that if we were asked to embalm one item in a time capsule which would
serve to tell generations 10,000 years from now who we, as a culture, were,
the best choice would be the golf cart. It tells our story eloquently. Sports
are automatic, electronic, spectator, and vicarious. Participation in all fields
is devalued. Several years ago my children gave me an electric carving
knife for a Christmas present. I no longer need even to move my arm to
carve the roast. And then there is the electric toothbrush. Great economic
gains seem to accrue to anyone who can conceive of a technique that will
allow us to work less hard and sweat less. A month or so ago I was in the
Dallas airport with some time to spare between flights, and I decided to
conduct a controlled experiment. I watched people approach the horizon-
tal escalator. At that moment they had a simple choice, ride or walk. Everyone rode. People at Stanford Hospital cluster around the elevator to go up
one floor. A sight which would have been physically as well as intellectually
incomprehensible to our ancestors of the savanna.

In summary, our sabbatical experience in Africa provided a framework for viewing the current energy demands on our species, and the likely
immense debt we owe to our physically active heritage. It was a *Roots* kind
of experience. Descartes said, *Cogito ergo sum,* "I think, therefore I am." I
say, *Curso ergo sum,* "I run, therefore I am." There is a long and vital
message contained in our anthropologic journals.

The other major contribution to my interest in the participation of
disuse phenomena in the human condition occurred twenty-some years ago
at the bottom of the steep part of the Nose Dive ski run at Stowe, Vermont.
Absentmindedly I had dug my ski tips into a snow drift at the side of the
trail, and so when my binding did not release, I fell forward over my skis. I
tried to rise, but soon recognized the embarrassing results of my clumsiness.
Thus, I was carted down the mountainside to the derisive teasing of my
children.

When my right leg emerged from its cast after having been encased
for six weeks following the suturing of my torn Achilles tendon, I looked
down at my leg and exclaimed in alarm, "Whose leg is that?" It was shriveled, purple, weak, and painful. It couldn't have been my leg. "Why, that's

an old leg!" I cried. But it wasn't old. The other leg was just the same age, and it was fine. Neither was it the result of the fact that the tendon had been repaired, because the orthopedist could have put the cast on my good leg and the same thing would have happened. The answer therefore lay in the fact that my leg had been immobilized for six weeks and had grown precociously old as a result.

This observation intrigued me and set in motion what was to be first a major hobby—collecting evidences hither and yon of the relationships between disuse and aging. I kept notes of all sorts bearing on this simple but strange coincidence. For example, did you know that professional perfume sniffers reportedly lose their olfactory sense slower than the rest of us? Now that is an oddment—but I saved it for future use.

DISUSE AND THE FRONTIERS OF SPACE

My search into the association between disuse and the physical condition took on much momentum when my family and I moved to Palo Alto sixteen years ago. Shortly thereafter I met up again with several research chums with whom I had worked during my biochemistry fellowship days at Berkeley. At that time they were working for NASA at the Ames Research Lab at Moffett Field; and this unexpected, serendipitous reunion gave great impetus to my search. As noted above, recognition of disuse as a contribution to our health status has had a brief history. Systematic inquiry into the individual or cumulative adverse effects which physical inactivity might have upon our bodies was simply not a scientific question which could elicit interest, curiosity, or research support. If a researcher wished to study the effects of bed rest, or being in a body cast on any physical outcome, such research would not have been rated very highly by any review council. Inactivity, or laziness, or disuse was simply not a major research priority. It wasn't "sexy."

But the space program changed all of that. We all recall watching John Glenn and his astronaut colleagues stand and walk uncertainly upon their return to Earth after only a short time in space. Their systems were badly miscued, as a number of unexpected adverse conditions had been encountered. This occurred because space travel represents accelerated disuse. As we stand or sit in our daily routines, we may not identify that we are doing work—but merely the act of holding our heads or torsos erect requires work—to offset gravity. If we didn't do this, our heads would fall onto our chests or we would tumble to the floor. In space this is not the case. If we raise an arm or a leg, it simply stays where we set it—it conforms to the movement, as gravitational effects are zero. As a result, work demands are markedly diminished.

The scientists at NASA recognized immediately the health problems confronting them, so they (as well as their Russian counterparts) embarked on a crash research program to detail the multitude of deleterious effects which space travel seemed to provoke. The sum total of this new insight has been the curriculum for the newest of sciences—space medicine. This new discipline has greatly expanded our understanding of the morbid effects of the enforced rest and weightlessness which accompany us into space. By looking beyond ourselves, we started to understand more effectively what we are within.

I was excited to be put in close touch with the dozens of crucial experiments which the NASA scientists and their Russian co-workers were conducting. I found myself reading all sorts of technical bulletins of obscure nature that I would not usually have the opportunity to know about.

Consequently, my search for correlations between disuse and aging picked up speed. The end product of this effort was a paper I published in the *Journal of the American Medical Association* (JAMA) in 1982, entitled "Disuse and Aging." The conclusion reads, "A review of biologic changes commonly attributed to the process of aging demonstrates the close similarity of most of the changes subsequent to a period of enforced physical inactivity. The coincidence of these changes from the subcellular to the whole body level of organization, and across a wide range of body systems, prompts the suggestion that at least a portion of the changes commonly attributed to aging is in reality caused by disuse and, as such, is subject to correction. There is no drug in current or prospective use that holds as much promise for sustained health as a lifetime program of physical exercise." This conclusion stands unmodified in my thinking today.

The article cited 111 references, many from the space medicine literature. In effect it represented an effort which took me to the medical libraries where I first dug out all the textbooks of geriatrics, then listed all of the adverse effects of age on blood pressure, cholesterol levels, sleep, bone density, muscle strength, body function, psychological profiles, temperature control, drug reactivity, and so on. Next I turned to the books and articles on exercise physiology and on space medicine and prepared a similar list of the adverse effects on the body during a period of physical inactivity. Again I charted these factors as they related to blood pressure, cholesterol levels, et al. I held the two lists side by side and recognized that the effects were virtually the same—whether secondary to aging or to disuse.

OXYGEN TRANSFER—
WHAT YOU DO WHEN YOU "USE IT"

Of all the varied fundamental physical functions which your body is charged with carrying out regularly, its requirement to transport oxygen is by far the most centrally critical one. So, when I say that you must "use it," I define the word *use* as improving your ability to move oxygen throughout your body.

We can live years without sex (if we have to); in addition, it seems we can live a long time without thinking. We can live weeks without food and days without water, but we can live only a few fragile minutes without oxygen. How long does a candle burn when its oxygen supply is used up? Our oxygen delivery apparatus involves the nasal passages, the trachea, and the bronchial tubes—all of which serve as rather passive corridors for the oxygen from our atmosphere to reach our lungs, where the oxygen is then coupled with the hemoglobin of our blood cells. From the lungs the hemoglobin-borne oxygen goes first to the heart, then it is pumped out by the heart through the arbor of the arteries. Finally the oxygen goes to the smallest arteries and capillaries, where it is released from the hemoglobin. It is then transferred to the inside of every cell of the body, where it is used to spark the chemical reactions which make our metabolism and thus allow us to conduct the business of being alive. $C_6H_{12}O_6$ (sugar) plus 6 molecules of O_2 (oxygen) yields energy plus 6 CO_2 (carbon dioxide) and 6 H_2O (water). This basic chemical reaction learned by schoolchildren is the root reaction that virtually drives our machine. It represents how our machine takes in fuel and, in the presence of oxygen, uses it to drive our engines.

How this is accomplished involves VO_2 max, a term which sounds unduly complex but which really isn't. VO_2 max means the amount of oxygen which your body can use under maximum workload. Each of us has maxima for everything—your heart can beat only so fast, your reflexes can react only so fast, and your body can use only so much oxygen. This is the

VO$_2$ max, and to measure it means hooking up to an oxygen-measuring device while doing some kind of work, usually walking on a treadmill or riding a stationary bicycle.

When VO$_2$ max is measured over the lifetime, it is seen to decrease at about 1 percent per year. This is a true age change and represents what I would view ultimately as the sum total of entropically driven heart-lung muscle decay in structure and function. Another way to look at such a performance term is to look at the world age records for running marathon races. The absolute record in 1990 was held by Belayneh Dyusamo, from Ethiopia—2 hours, 6 minutes and 50 seconds—set when he was 30 years of age. The age-group records decline slowly over several decades. A 69-year-old has run the distance in under 3 hours, faster than the winning time in the 1908 Olympics. Amazing! Thereafter, records tend to fall off significantly; but this is probably due to the fact that until now very few people over age 70 chose to run marathons. It is fully expected that these older-age performances will improve dramatically as more participate.

Notable too is the actual decline in performance. But this is not the main story. Looking at the decline slope in a group of fit individuals (as contrasted with the slope of the conventional couch potato American), we can see that the declines are similar in slope but at very different levels.

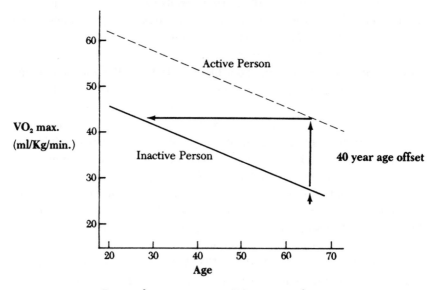

Potential improvement in VO$_2$ max age changes.

Herbert DeVries, research scientist at the University of Southern California, measured VO_2 max in a group of unfit older persons. He then started them on an active conditioning program for six weeks. He discovered that the VO_2 max increased greatly to a level equal to that of an unfit person 40 years younger. Said in another way, a fit person of 70 has the same oxygen carrying capacity as an unfit person of 30. Fitness is a 40 year age offset. More concretely, at age 78, marathon runner Mavis Lindgren had a VO_2 max measurement equivalent to that of untrained college women.

The point bears repeating—the everyday business of most doctors (not just heart and lung experts), is to improve our patients' abilities to move oxygen in their bodies. I have dozens of drugs in my practice bag which are directly or indirectly consecrated to this effort. However, if I or my colleagues can derive 5 or 10 percent of the benefit shown to be accorded by an exercise program, we think we have done a noble day's work.

Let us apply the same protocol to the television character Archie Bunker. Somehow Archie, like my 63-year-old box manufacturer of chapter 4, is at age 70 exhorted to get his rump out of the armchair, surrender his vicarious lifestyle, and begin exercising more than his jaws. Archie gets a pair of running shoes, running shorts, and starts chugging around the block. (I like the imagery.) If Archie can do it, we all can. We all can do it, so Archie can. Within a week or so the effort becomes easier—becomes the natural act that it is. Archie starts to look forward to it with pleasant anticipation. It makes him feel better. He regains his self-pride and recognizes that he is his whole self. He stops apologizing and making excuses; the transformation is complete. Edith stops worrying whether or not Archie will be breathing when she wakes up each morning.

Archie has regained his heritage, hard won by vigorous struggles on the Serengeti. His machine is tuned, he purrs. He snarls less. And this profound change in operational efficiency hasn't cost anything. Archie will appreciate this. The tune-up has provided a better oxygen supply to every body part, every niche of the engine. Moreover, it has provided a host of beneficial changes in the functioning of the heart, the lungs, the arteries, and the tissues.

THE FALSE PROPHETS OF AGING

It used to be thought that aging provoked a host of deteriorations in circulatory function. "A man is as old as his arteries." A person of 40 with "bad pipes" is functionally old. A person of 80 with "good pipes" appears young. Now we know that age is not all there is to it. Dr. Frank Williams, director of the National Institute on Aging, states, "There is no current evidence which confirms that aging *per se* is the cause of any deterioration of the blood vessel system." This means that the dogma concerning an inevitable decline in heart and lung performance needs to be reexamined in the light of the major salutary effect of exercise on oxygen delivery.

Thirty years ago Dr. James Currens and Dr. Paul Dudley White of Harvard Medical School reported in the *New England Journal of Medicine* the autopsy findings in Clarence Demar, "Mr. Boston Marathon" who over a 50 year span had run in a thousand long distance races including 100 marathons (34 in Boston, of which he won 7). He died of cancer at age 70. His autopsy revealed that his coronary arteries were "2 to 3 times the normal diameter." The effect of exercise on the size of the heart arteries has been evaluated in laboratory animals and the same relationship found.

These observations have been slow to be confirmed in humans because of lack of adequate technology. However, Dr. Edwin Alderman at Stanford has provided a new measurement technique with which we have studied 12 long distance runners. This study has confirmed what Drs. Currens and White found in Clarence Demar—exercise expands the coronary arteries.

What is the normal size for coronary arteries—those tubes which clog so frequently and thereby employ our nation's cardiologists and cardiac surgeons? Should the artery be constricted like the arteries of my cast-enclosed leg, or widely open like those of a long distance runner or Bushman? Heart disease, artery plugging, is a condition of domestication. A large artery likely offsets high cholesterol values in the blood.

It had been thought that the strength of the heart's contractions went down with aging. It had been thought that the amount of blood the heart pumps went down with age. It had been thought that blood pressure went up with age. However, in fit older persons these changes do not occur. Are they then due to aging or to disuse? All the experimental studies in which the reported changes were found were done on unfit older persons. To understand this you must only look to the logistics of research. Where can a researcher easily find vast numbers of willing subjects? Not jogging along the beaches or running paths, but clustered together in nursing homes and hospitals.

Also in the domain of circulatory changes commonly attributed to aging are increases in the amount of the blood fats, cholesterol, and triglycerides. Scientific efforts to understand the mechanisms involved with these important compounds have preoccupied the research community. Tens of thousands of research papers have been written in pursuit of their basic nature. I have contributed my share. It has been generally held that aging results in higher levels of blood fats. However, it has also been shown that physical inactivity, by itself, also leads to higher levels. Therefore, again the question arises—is it age or inactivity which provokes the association?

Older people have more blood clots; their blood shows an increased tendency to clog up the vessels. This is due in part to changes in the blood itself—namely, it coagulates too easily. In my JAMA paper, "Disuse and Aging," I cited several articles from Russian space scientists which recorded the increased "clotability" which accompanies bed rest. Surgeons have long recognized this in the postoperative period. And particularly if prolonged, it is very dangerous for the patient to be kept immobile in bed. Richard Asher, of the Central Middlesex Hospital in London, expressed it well in a 1947 piece in the *British Medical Journal* entitled "The Dangers of Going to Bed":

> Teach us to live that we may dread
> Unnecessary time in bed.
> Get people up, and we may save
> Our patients from an early grave.

THIN BONES—WEAK MUSCLES

Prominent in any description of age changes is the mention of alterations in the musculoskeletal system of bones, muscles, tendons, and cartilage. It has long been held that one of the hallmark changes of the aging body is a decrease in lean body mass—muscle tissue. I recall well a geriatrics meeting I attended several years ago in Denver in which a researcher had just delivered a paper on the beneficial effects of Transcendental Meditation (TM) on aging. The audience had listened with moderate interest. Upon the speaker's conclusion, Dr. Isadore Rossman, friend, distinguished geriatrician from New York, and past president of the American Geriatrics Society, rose and asked, "What is the effect of TM on lean body mass?" The paper presenter had no answer. The point being that Izzy had presumed that this aspect was a true marker of aging, and that unless TM could have been shown to affect it, then TM really wasn't affecting the aging process itself—whatever good it might have been doing. But what of my leg in a cast? That is the prototype of loss of muscle tissue—due not to aging, but to disuse. I am sure that if we were to measure the muscle mass in 70-plus-year-old Jack LaLanne, we would not find this "age" change. His muscle systems would do credit to any 30-year-old.

Each morning my day starts on the orthopedic floors of Stanford University Hospital, where I visit my one or two women patients who are lying there with fractured hips. These fractures have not occurred as the result of any major mechanical insult, but have usually occurred due to a rather trivial tumble. Osteoporosis is the villain (*osteo* meaning bone, *porosis* meaning porous). The women's magazines are generally full of protective remedies of estrogens and calcium. This is big business. But look at Neanderthal's bones—they are like iron ingots. A sledgehammer could do them no harm. Wolff's Law is affirmed. This precept states, "The robusticity of any bone is in direct proportion to the physical stresses applied to it."

Osteoporosis is less of an issue for men, but it still occurs. Men seem to have better calcium intakes over the life span, and generally do more skeletal work—besides, there are a lot more old women than old men.

Our contemporary zoolike existence has deeded us a life result which finds too many of us languishing on the orthopedic floors of our hospitals with fractured hips, spines, and pelvises; neither as a result of age nor of calcium or estrogen lack, but because of our cultural disuse. There are no broken hips in the jungles of Borneo.

French researchers have shown that 36 weeks in bed provoke the same amount of calcium loss from the bones as seen in 10 years of aging. It is also of interest to note that if the spinal cord is severed, the bone in the portion of the body which is paralyzed becomes disproportionately demineralized. Space travel too has its risks from calcium wastage. The *Skylab* astronauts lost 4 grams of calcium from their skeletons for each month in space. This observation prompted Dr. Don Whedon to suggest that unless corrective strategies were developed (they are now under way), space voyages of over 9 months may be precluded.

Related to the bone and muscle changes that have traditionally been assigned to the aging process is an increase in total body fat. Older animals and people have increased amounts of body fat. Master-class athletes have 10 percent of their body weight as fat, in contrast to the 30 percent or so of the average older person.

OBESITY AND INACTIVITY

To me the most critical experiment dealing with the basic mechanisms of obesity was done by Dr. Jean Mayer (now President of Tufts University) when he was in the School of Public Health at Harvard. Mayer *et al* measured the food intake of mice as they were exercised. A certain work load was met by an exactly appropriate increase in calories ingested, so that over a wide range of increased need the mice maintained their normal weight. The critical part of the experiment, however, came when the mice were restrained from their usual cage activity. With this they continued to eat as though they were still active, and thereby grew fat.

The extension of this work to the human experience is obvious. Our eating centers, planted in the hypothalamus of our brains, were programmed millions of years ago when we were hunter-gatherers. There are and were no fat Bushmen. Now our physical exercise has slackened, but our eating centers don't know that. We have two choices: either exercise up to the level of our ancestral heritage, and then there is no problem with calories, or spend most of our lives dieting as a penalty for our collective inactivity.

FUEL SUPPLY AND DISUSE

As a medical student I learned that aging was accompanied by a decreased ability to metabolize glucose—sugar. "Old-age diabetes" was a frequently used term. We used to utilize the glucose tolerance test, in which the subject drank a glass of sugar water, and then at hourly intervals thereafter the clinician drew blood samples and analyzed the level of sugar in the blood. As subjects aged, the test results deteriorated. This was taken as a true evidence of aging. But again, bed rest or any other immobilization has been shown recently to result in a similar deterioration. It takes two weeks for a normal metabolic pattern to return after confinement.

A HIGH-TECH SOLUTION?

In July 1990, a research report appeared in the *New England Journal of Medicine* that immediately made front-page news across the nation. The research, conducted by Dr. Daniel Rudman and his associates at the Medical College of Wisconsin, concluded that injections of genetically engineered human growth hormone, given three times a week for six months, could significantly offset the effects of aging. The older men who participated in the experiment gained nearly 9 percent in lean body mass, dropped nearly 15 percent in fat, and had thicker, more youthful skin. They also reported they had more energy for their daily activities.

Despite the cautions of the researchers themselves, the public responded as if the fountain of youth had opened for business. The next day, I had nearly 20 phone calls from patients requesting the experimental drug, which currently costs about $14,000 a year. My colleagues and I joked that ground for growth hormone clinics was already being broken in Tijuana.

What did I tell my patients? Apart from the expense, an excess of growth hormone has been shown to have many significant side effects—including diabetes, high blood pressure, heart problems, and even cancer. Furthermore, some older people produce as much growth hormone as younger people; the men who took part in the experiment were clearly deficient in the hormone. But, most important, the entire proposition is flawed. The loss of lean muscle tissue in old age is not due to age; it is due to disuse! (The researchers even said the men looked "more fit and in better condition.")

Physical exercise itself increases growth hormone levels, and similarly dramatic results have been achieved through exercise programs—without the potential of harmful side effects. For example, Dr. Maria Fiatarone in Professor William Evans' laboratory at Tufts University reported in the *Journal of the American Medical Association* that 90-year-old nursing home residents had increased their muscle strength by as much as 180 percent in an 8-week exercise program. When the weight lifting was discontinued, the muscle weakness returned.

So the story is a recurrent one. We search for pharmaceutical solutions to lifestyle problems. We try to find a medical "cure" for aging, as if aging were a disease.

Human growth hormone has clear value in medicine and may be appropriate in some situations—for example, to aid recovery from a stroke or other debilitating illness. But I will continue to reject the seduction of the quick fix.

DISUSE AND THE BRAIN

A host of other organ system changes, like the EEG (brain waves), have similarly been shown to exhibit a pattern in aging. This prompts the obvious repeated inquiry into how much is age and how much is disuse. But of all the areas to be addressed, probably the most significant in terms of our credential of being sapient is the effect of age on our brains. This will be dealt with extensively in chapter 8.

DISUSE AND DEPRESSION

Depression is integral to our stereotype of what aging is all about. Psychologic inventories of older persons invariably reveal that test scores relating to depression indices are much higher in older than in younger persons. Antidepressants are one of the few batches of prescriptions which I write that I really feel comfortable about because of the manifest good they provide to my older patients. It is wonderfully gratifying to see a person recapture his interest in being alive after he had previously lost the zest for life and found all the world's glories shrouded in gray. Such an individual will then reinvolve himself in making his own destiny. Neuroscientists have shown that depression is characterized by a decreased level of certain brain chemicals called catecholamines (adrenaline and noradrenaline) in specific parts of the brain. This is very similar to the discovery that Parkinsonism is due to a decreased amount of another brain chemical, dopamine, in a neighboring part of the brain, prompting our present treatment of Parkinson's disease with L-dopa.

What I hope to do when I write a prescription for an antidepressant is to restore the brain catecholamines to their proper level and thus relieve the depression. This is akin to my giving insulin to a diabetic. However, psychiatrists have found that an exercise program is also a very effective treatment for depression.

Further studies into these observations are being conducted throughout the world. For example, Russian space scientists have shown how enforced inactivity leads to depression in healthy young cosmonauts. Exercise places increased work demands on the human machine, and these increases cause a variety of body responses. Your heart beats faster, your lungs stretch, you sweat, your blood vessels dilate, energy fuels mobilize, and blood shunts from inactive areas to active ones. The modulators of all these effects are the catecholamines. They organize your response to work.

It is interesting to conjecture regarding the societal effects of this process. If we accept the proposition that our species was physically very active over the long sweep of prehistory; that this activity generated high levels of catecholamines; that these catecholamines are the counteractants to depression; and that our present society is inactive—then it follows that maybe our whole society is depressed. It follows particularly that we should insist that our world leaders go out for a long run, or swim, or brisk walk before sitting down to decide our collective fates in the confrontational mode.

Therefore, as I write my prescription for the antidepressant, it is in effect a proxy for doing it the right way—reasserting our primitive exercise pattern. Clearly the two are not mutually incompatible, so as I write the prescription I also exhort my patient to find an appropriate activity program.

The cataloging of age changes and inactivity changes reveals such a correspondence and similarity that it is always appropriate to question whether any change is actually age-related. A short while ago I wrote a paper called "Redefining Human Aging." The first sentences were, "A grandfather's clock stops running. The possible diagnoses are: it is broken; it is worn out; or it needs to be wound up. The same diagnosis applies to the human situation." When we break down we are either broken (diseased), worn out (age), or we need to be wound up (disuse). As I mentioned previously, medicine has been totally preoccupied with the broken (disease) model. It has given passive awareness to age changes, but it has neglected the most obvious issue—that in terms of physical activity, many of us need to be "wound up."

THE DISUSE SYNDROME

Disuse and aging are closely linked. In fact, it was the correspondence of a number of changes due to inactivity which prompted me to suggest that the major ones:

1. cardiovascular vulnerability
2. musculoskeletal fragility
3. obesity
4. depression
5. precocious aging

occur collectively so frequently and invariably as to merit their inclusion as a single definition, the rubric for which is the "Disuse Syndrome." The Disuse Syndrome is for inactivity what Selye's General Adaption Syndrome is for stress. Too little energy throughput versus too much.

A syndrome is a collection of features which are often found in connection with one another and as a consequence are grouped together to facilitate understanding and to provide a unitary causative mechanism. It is predictably producible in the research laboratory, and it's reversible by an appropriate counteractive strategy. My formulation of the Disuse Syndrome was similar to one proposed earlier by Professors Wilhelm Raab and Hans Kraus in a 1961 book *Hypokinetic Disease*. The common features of their grouping were cardiovascular deterioration, musculoskeletal problems, obesity, and mental alteration. I was unaware of their publication as I was doing my own study, but the coincidence of these two proposals is striking. I am sure it was their hope (as it is mine) that by providing this conceptual framework we will provoke our colleagues into rethinking some of their disease-model conceptions. By refocusing our efforts on changes that are not fundamentally due to extrinsic cause, we can prepare preventive steps that are at the root level of origin. We should identify basic issues and not preoccupy ourselves with derivative issues. We should turn off the spigot instead of mopping up the water.

My Stanford colleague James Fries has published extensively on a

very thoughtful hypothesis which he calls "the compression of morbidity."
Jim suggests that as we progressively approach our life terminus we can
diminish our time for illness by sustaining ourselves in the healthy mode. If
sustained, such a proposal has major implications for health-policy planning. We clearly wish that the end of our life trajectory will be well spent.
Sidney Katz of Brown University called this the "active life expectancy."
And of course, inactive life expectancy (disuse) is what we all hope to avoid.

I was asked to write a commentary on Jim's proposal and billed my
response, "Disuse and Extended Morbidity." I thoroughly agree with Jim's
formulation, eventually; but it is my view that we are not there yet. I think
that we are all still dying prematurely, and how we live the years leading up
to our demise is highly keyed to our disuse quotient. If we live our lives
actively until the end, the morbidity can be compressed. We die quickly,
some would even say mercifully. If, however, we allow our last decades to
be disused, then we live too short and die too long.

USE IT OR LOSE IT

The foregoing categorizing of the involutionary results of not using
our capacities falls under the simple headline "Use It or Lose It." This
principle applies to our smallest compartments, and it applies to us all. The
Second Law of Thermodynamics commands that we age, and die at the
end. We cannot avoid this. At the beginning of this chapter I introduced the
corollary of the Second Law—the ordering of random matter by flow of
energy. This is our target. It seems inescapably obvious that by searching
out the many varied strategies available to us for keeping our functions
maximal, we may reach toward our full lives.

In "Disuse and Aging" I wrote, "It is wrong to suggest that exercise
might halt the fall of the grains of sand in the hourglass. It is proposed,
however, that the dimensions of the aperture may be responsive to the
toning of physical activity, and consequently the sands may drain more
slowly."

Although the main discussion of this chapter has been directed to the
restorative effects of physical exercise on body function, it is not to be
presumed that the effect is restricted to this "use." There is a substantial
effort to encourage athletes to exercise their eye muscles in "visual train-

ing" so that higher perception skills may be achieved. When any part of the body is removed from its usual intended role, it deteriorates. When a lung collapses or a segment of intestine is bypassed, or a kidney clamped off, or the endocrine gland not stimulated quickly enough, structural deteriorations are evident. Form truly follows function. Darwin taught us that, and it is evident intuitively; but we seem to pay scant attention to the power of this truism. Goethe observed, "To be is to do." Life is not a spectator sport. Stagnation is not conducive to good function anywhere in the universe.

In the book *Entropy, A New World View,* Jeremy Rifkin extrapolated the basic physical implications of the Second Law of Thermodynamics into societal terms. Social units ranging in size from the family to the nation were evaluated in terms of the increasing tendency toward disorder. For example, he discussed the decay of several notable civilizations with the annotation that there was seeming value in an occasional revolt or revolution. In this way, Rifkin stated, people were able to interject a new social energy and order.

Basic physical scientists—accustomed to measuring energy quotients and degrees of entropy, as well as simple chemical systems—disparage Rifkin's extension of the principles of the Second Law to a complex *social* network. They resist his efforts as oversimplification of archival events.

In response, Rifkin cites the work of Nobel chemist Frederich Soddy: "The laws of thermodynamics control, in the last resort, the size and fates of political systems, the freedoms or bondage of nations, the movements of commerce and industry, the origins of wealth and poverty, and the general physical welfare of the race." Rifkin continues, "Every single physical activity that humankind engages in is totally subject to the ironclad imperative expressed in the First and Second Law of Thermodynamics."

We have no absolute proof that the Second Law is truly confined to simple systems—nor can we confirm that it can, as Rifkin believed, be applied to everything in our universe. Nevertheless, the repeated observations of the ordering effect of energy flow are generally observable. For example, a number of researchers have used the model provided by the thermophysicists to interpret the relationships between predators and prey, such as wolves and deer. As the numbers of one group increase, disorder ensues and the numbers of the other decrease until the balance shifts, and the reverse disorder occurs. This oscillatory behavior in prey/predator relationships is another characterizing aspect of the natural order.

Whether the social order of an individual (or groups of people) represents a real example of thermophysical principles at work is uncertain; but it is most clear that the thermophysicists have given us a powerful paradigm to understand our biology. All we need provide is the wisdom to utilize it.

The first justification of the claim that we live in the Age Age derives simply from the number of our older selves. We really can't boast of a place in history because of this, but we can rightfully claim an historic moment of enlightenment if we can mobilize our new insights and sustain, channel, and organize our energy.

We need to keep our clocks wound.

SEVEN

SNOW ON THE ROOF, FIRE IN THE FURNACE

> Can that one facet of our lives,
> affecting more people in more ways than any
> other physiologic response other than
> those necessary to our very existence, be
> allowed to continue without benefit of
> objective scientific analysis?
>
> **William Masters and Virginia Johnson**

Aging and sexuality are intimately linked. The pursuit of youth implies the search for renewed potency or physical attractiveness, and the mythology of aging is permeated with misconceptions and prejudices regarding sexual activity. Fortunately for us all, scientific examination of the myth brings much enlightenment.

All major human-sex researchers conclude that regular sex performance over the life span is likely to confirm an active sexual pattern into old age. In glorious other words, if you were sexy when you were 20 and 30, it is most likely that you will be sexy at 70 and 80. Masters and Johnson, the leaders in the field of sexual research, stress the "consistency of lifestyle" as being highly determinative of late-life sexual capacity. The familiar refrain "use it or lose it" is heard once again. As a male this makes a lot of simple sense to me. Sex is one form of exercise that no one should fault because of tedium. Research involving the testosterone levels in males has repeatedly shown that hormonal levels remain unchanged as long as the individual maintains general good health. For the female, Winnifred Cutler, from the Department of Biology at the University of Pennsylvania, reports that frequent sex tends to regularize the menstrual periods; and Julian Davidson of the Physiology Department at Stanford reports that frequent sex cuts down on hot flashes in menopause. These findings reflect the fact that behavioral practices have feedback effects on basic body mechanics which only serve further to support the system.

Even research with laboratory animals has interesting implications for our attitudes on aging and sex in humans. We know, for example, that female rats which have frequent coitus alter their hormonal patterns. In addition, when different hormones are administered to rats, marked effects on mating behavior result. This is not surprising and maybe even predictable. However, it has further been noted that when rats engage in frequent intercourse their hormone levels change. Therefore, the issue arises, which is cause and which is effect? Do hormones alter sexual behavior, or does sexual behavior alter hormone pattern? There is probably a circular effect.

What is the relevance for humans? David Adams and co-workers from Wesleyan found that female-initiated sexual activity in humans rises around the time of ovulation, like a female animal in heat. However, this effect is nullified in those individuals using birth control pills, as they distort a woman's hormonal patterns.

In other observations scientists have learned that when male rats are provided regular opportunity for mating, they show a lessened decline in sexual capacity; and when old male rats have younger female rats made available to them, they show a marked tendency to "spruce themselves up."

This last bit of laboratory insight made me query my friend Davidson as to any parallel research for the ladies. "What happens," I asked, "if female rats are given the same opportunities with younger males?"

He replied that the experiment probably was not "do-able." Driven by biology (definitely not by passion), female rats would accept coitus until the point of physical intolerance.

The important point for humans is that sexual activity need not diminish with aging. Moreover, the noted psychiatrist Eric Pfeiffer has reported that 15 to 20 percent of older men actually report that their sex lives improved later in life. The vernacular expression might be, "A dud at 50, a stud at 70." Pfeiffer has conjectured that this observation is due to the fact that healthy sex is a survival issue. Maybe sexy people are healthier, as well as the fact that healthy people are sexier.

For the male, there are logical reasons why sex can improve with age. There is less "ejaculatory demand"—meaning less urgency, more time, better opportunity, or less performance pressure. Conversely, women often find that sex improves with age because of emotional factors such as greater self-assurance, confidence regarding the need and/or use of contraceptives, and freedom from the fatigue of child rearing.

Additionally, sustained sexuality has been shown to correlate with educational status—the smarter we get, the sexier we remain. Knowledge frees us from taboos and prejudices; so as we grow in wisdom, we allow our sex lives to mature and ripen to their full extents. This certainly has not always been the case.

GUILT AND SEXUAL EXPRESSION

Probably no aspect of our beings is the source of so much guilt as is our sexuality. Freud made a career out of it. If we have guilt and shame and embarrassment about our sexuality as young persons, what are we supposed to do with our sexual feelings as we grow older?

Clearly, we are in a major transitional epoch with regard to sexuality. I have seen the cloistered chastity of yesterday (my childhood), the libertine "anything goes" era of my children's teen years, and now the sobering fallout from AIDS and its cousins. Generalizing from any of these three age cohorts is clearly dangerous; but at the least, sexual discourse is now an open topic. The freedom gained from this societal attitude has been one of the great gifts of our age. The opening of the closet doors has allowed better communication and self-expression, but most of all it has allowed new scientific inquiry. A sex researcher of 100 years or even 50 years ago would have had a very hard time of it. Sex was not something to be talked about openly, much less studied analytically. But the "enlightenment" is upon us. Sex is okay. It is part of us; it makes us. How we reckon with it individually and collectively goes a long way to assuring the competency of our entire lives.

SEX IS MORE THAN MERE REPRODUCTION

Most important, our new awareness of sex has taught that reproduction is but one of its dimensions. The physical act itself is only a point on the arc of adventure which sex avails to us. A far more dominant element is the bonding afforded by sexual attachment. Now more than ever we recognize that we are defined, in a very full measure, by our sexual selves.

The old mythologies of aging and sexuality ordained that sex after 40 was an unnatural act. The phrase "dirty old man" flowed too easily from the tongue. The caricatures of old, new parents were displayed to us as rank curiosities more worthy of a sneer than of happiness. I have in my files a news document from the *Weekly World News* of September 4, 1984. The two-inch headline reads: EIGHTY-FOUR-YEAR-OLD WIFE PREGNANT AGAIN. The story from the Chansi Province of China tells of Chen-Loo, who discovered that she was pregnant again six months after having delivered her last baby. Her husband was 76. The 1989 *Guinness Book of World Records* lists 72-year-old Ellen Ellis of Wales as the oldest woman ever to give birth, but that was in 1776. These tales stretch one's credulity; but if accurate, they could lead to the development of a new specialty of geriatric obstetrics. Who knows what the future holds?

Despite social trends to delay childbearing, present medical understanding is that the older mother-to-be has a significantly higher likelihood of having an imperfect baby than does a younger woman. The risk of having a live child born with chromosomal abnormalities is 1 in every 526 births if the maternal age is 20, but 1 in every 7 births if the maternal age is 49. Although the statistics on the effect of paternal age on congenital malformations is less complete, it is again known that advancing age increases chromosomal abnormalities. The projection for an 84-year-old mother and a 76-year-old father would seem scary. Parenting seems chosen by nature to be better done by the young.

But reproductive ideal and full expression of sexuality are imperfectly correlated. Nature, vis-à-vis the asexual activities of lower species, and the animal husbandry labs at Purdue have taught us that reproduction doesn't absolutely require sex. Nonetheless, it's a lot more fun with it.

Furthermore, menopause and its induction of infertility does not connote the end of sexuality. Far from it. A number of extensive surveys have been conducted in the last few decades (beginning with Kinsey's groundbreaking work of 1940) which demonstrate clearly that older individuals are a lot sexier than we thought. Kinsey surveyed college students and discovered that their estimates of sexual activity of their parents were three times per month. The actual figure was seven times a month. One-quarter of the students guessed that their parents *never* had intercourse. I wonder what the estimate would be of their grandparents' or their great-grandparents' sexuality.

SEXUAL ATTITUDES OF OLDER PERSONS

In 1984 Edward Brecher edited a famous report for the Consumer's Union titled "Love, Sex and Aging." The study reported on 4,246 individuals ranging from ages 50 to 93. Brecher termed the findings concerning the quality and quantity of sexual activity in the group "astonishing."

Sixty-seven-year-old Brecher wrote, "Having successfully pretended for decades that we are non-sexual, my generation is now having second thoughts. We are increasingly realizing that denying our sexuality means denying an essential aspect of our common humanity. It cuts us off from communication with our children, our grandchildren, and our peers on a subject of great interest to us all—sexuality. The rejection of the aging and aged by some younger people has many roots, but surely the belief that we are no longer sexual beings, and therefore no longer fully human, is one of the roots of that rejection."

When discussing specific age groups, the report found that the following percentages of women were sexually active:

- 93 percent of women in their 50s
- 81 percent of women in their 60s
- 65 percent of women in their 70s

The corresponding figures for sexually active men were as follows:

- 98 percent of men in their 50s
- 91 percent of men in their 60s
- 79 percent of men in their 70s

For the purposes of this study, "sexually active" was defined as having sex at any time, including masturbation; but the number of women who reported having intercourse at least once per week were as follows:

- 73 percent of women in their 50s
- 63 percent of women in their 60s
- 50 percent of women in their 70s

The corresponding figures for men who reported having sexual intercourse at least once per week were:

- 90 percent of men in their 50s
- 73 percent of men in their 60s
- 58 percent of men in their 70s

Meanwhile, 24 of the 46 men over the age of 80 reported that they were still having intercourse; while 15 of the 38 women over age 80 reported still having intercourse.

In addition, 65 percent of those women in their 50s and 76 percent of the men in their 50s reported that their interest in sex was at least as strong as or stronger than it was when they were at age 40.

Another study, conducted in 1982 by Bernard D. Starr and Marcella Baker Weinerin, authors of *Sex and Sexuality in Mature Years,* involved a study of 800 adults aged 60 to 91. On average the subjects reported having sex 1.4 times per week. In another study (see below) of people 80 to 102 years of age, 47 percent replied that they still had intercourse, and 58 percent reported that they masturbated.

In 1986, Judy Bretschneider and Dr. Norma McCoy, of the Department of Psychology at San Francisco State University, published a paper entitled "Sexual Interest and Behavior in Healthy 80- to 102-Year-Olds" in the *Archives of Sexual Behavior.* Of their 202 subjects, 88 percent of the men and 71 percent of the women indicated that they still had intimate thoughts about the opposite sex, 72 percent of the men and 40 percent of the women masturbated, and 63 percent of the men and 30 percent of the women still had sexual intercourse. These authors remarked on the relative constancy of the reported frequency of sexual encounters among the various surveys that have been conducted, including others at Duke University, in Baltimore, and in Sweden. One age researcher reported being pursued amorously by a man in the Caucasus who was said to be 132 years of age. The studies all showed that marriage was clearly a major determinant of intercourse when women were surveyed, but that marriage was not a major determinant of male intercourse. Married men had lower sexual interest than did unmarried men, whereas the reverse was true for women.

Two points must be made about the reported incidence figures. The first is that the data were not validated. In other words, there were no checks on the accuracy of the answers. There is a strong suspicion that some of the responses may have been exaggerated, and that the samples represented more highly those individuals who would be more likely to give affirmative answers.

I recently sent out my own general questionnaire to the members of the Fifty Plus Running Association who are over the age of 70. In it I inquired about sexual activity. Twenty-five of the 32 respondents reported that sexual activity was still "fair" or "good." These preliminary results indicate that either physical fitness confirms the high likelihood of continued sexual interest and capacity (which I hope and believe is so) or that the respondents were "tooting their own horns." Maybe I should send out a separate questionnaire to their spouses.

The second point concerning the reports of sexual activity in older persons is that the researchers are surveying individuals who grew up and developed their sexual views before the "enlightenment." For most of these people, sex has been a closet issue; their willingness to respond to such a questioning reflects a new openness. Furthermore, if the statistics are so promising for the inhibited—what are they likely to be when the next generations come along? I hope that such data will not be described as "astonishing."

The consistency of all the surveys indicating the high degree of sexual interest and capacity in older persons is news that should be widely broadcast. If we can make it generally known that sex doesn't stop at age 40, or 50, or 70, or even 90—then much of the negative stereotyping of aging is offset. This is a major part of the new knowledge in redefining aging.

SEXUAL INCAPACITY

But this isn't all a "good news" story, for there is still much about our knowledge of sex and aging which is negative, incomplete, or just plain unsatisfactory. Despite the fact that all studies indicate that older people retain a very high interest in and desire for sex, there is still a gap between interest and performance. Until the past few years, sexual incapacity was almost universally labeled as psychologic in origin. "It's all in your head"— that's what an older person was likely to be told. Indeed, if someone offered me $10,000 to have an erection on command, I am sure I would fail.

Clearly, psychologic factors are involved in sexuality in a major way, but they are not nearly so universally responsible for failures as was previously preached. Medical approaches to sexual inadequacy are now achieving a substantial level of respectability as remediation becomes grounded in new understanding of the multiple complex aspects of our sexual machinery.

AGING AND MALE SEXUALITY

For men, impotence is the issue. It is generally estimated that 10 million Americans suffer from impotence, but that number may be far from actuality. Kinsey reported in a relatively small number of older men that 18 percent, 25 percent, 55 percent, and 75 percent of men 60, 65, 70, 75, and 80 years of age were impotent. In any case, the number is huge; and the problems of male impotence are being studied at many sites including the Impotence Foundation in Los Angeles.

Dr. Marvin B. Brooks of this organization says, "An erection in man is more than an outward indication of sexual arousal. It is a sign of being a man. Unfortunately, many men believe that when that sign is gone their manhood is gone."

In my practice I often see older men with cancer of the prostate. This cancer is unquestionably hormonally sensitive, and one of the hallmarks of treatment is castration. While urologists always labor to maintain potency when any surgery on the male sexual apparatus is involved, such a treatment option leads often to impotence. Thus it is no trivial matter that despite its potential life-saving quality, many men balk at or refuse this therapy.

The impotent male is only half of the problem, as the wife or other partner shares in the frustrations, disappointments, and depressions which often accompany it. For that reason, sexual counseling almost invariably involves two clients. And one of the things therapists have discovered is a behavior pattern associated with this condition. Masters and Johnson, in particular, have detailed six causes of failure in male sexual performance. They are as follows:

- boredom with repetitive sex
- preoccupation with career and money
- mental or physical fatigue

- excess food or alcohol
- mental or physical problems with wife or self
- fear of failure

With regard to the first factor, boredom with repetitive sex, there is an apocryphal story told by Frank Beach, eminent sex researcher. Beach recounted that one day President and Mrs. Calvin Coolidge were visiting a government poultry farm where they were taken on separate tours. When Mrs. Coolidge passed the chicken coops she asked the guide how often the rooster could be expected to perform his duty each day. On being told that the rooster could be expected to perform his duty dozens of times each day, Mrs. Coolidge was most impressed and said, "Please tell that to the president." When the president passed the chicken coops and was duly informed of the rooster's performance, he inquired as to whether this was with the same hen each time. "Oh no, Mr. President, a different one each time," was the reply. The president nodded slowly and said, "Tell that to Mrs. Coolidge."

This story has been codified into what is now known as the Coolidge Effect, an experimental model for sex research. For example, we know from laboratory studies that a rat will become exhausted after ten consecutive ejaculations, and will then enter a refractory period. However, when a "fresh" female rat is introduced to him, the refractory period is shortened.

Dr. Gabriel Lawry tells of a related incident in the November 1977 issue of *Medical Aspects of Human Sexuality:*

When a medical student, I trained for a while at a hospital where there lived a large geriatric population of patients with a majority of females. Each patient would receive a glass of wine with every meal. Some elderly ladies would collect their allotment of wine in milk bottles. On weekends, unknown to the hospital administration, they would invite the men for a "party" at which time the wine was served and sexual activities took place. By Friday, the patients would already be involved in petting activities and passionate kissing in expectation of the "party." One medical student asked one of the old men how well he was performing. The man, well in his 80s, proudly answered, "If I could have sex with the same girls as you, I would do as well as you. If you had sex with my present partners, you could not do as well as I do."

Preoccupation with career and money, as well as mental and physical fatigue, also impact adversely on male potency. The neuroticism and frenzied pace of our contemporary society are not the stuff on which sexual bliss feeds. In my travels I have seen the sexual frolicking and delightful robustness of the sherpas, the Masai, and the Dayaks; and it reminds me of how natural sex ought to be. When we consign sex to a staccato moment in the crowded rush of our lives, we lose a great deal. Dr. John Morley at UCLA Medical School points out that stress leads to the production of endorphins, which in turn lead to reduced testosterone levels. Even within the laboratory setting we see that stress leads to distraction and decreased sexual performance in animals. It would seem that "getting away from it all for a while" is good sex therapy for any of us.

Male potency is also negated by alcohol. In *Macbeth*, Shakespeare wrote, "Drink provokes the desire but unprovokes the performance." This most clearly addresses the numbing effect which alcohol induces. It widens the so-called libido-potency gap—the difference between desire and performance. Millions of romantic adventures have ended miserably after one or two too many drinks; and no physician treating the issue of impotence can overlook the advice to "lay off the booze."

It is, however, in addressing the pathologic causes of impotence that medical science has probably done its best job. For example, hardening of the arteries (arteriosclerosis), diabetes, other endocrine-gland abnormalities, and the pathologic effect of drugs were important topics at the recent Geriatric Grand Rounds Conference at UCLA.

Trouble with the arteries and veins is a common but not inevitable experience among older men. The penis, after all, is an inflatable device totally dependent on the pressures and volumes of the blood supply for adequate function. If the arteries are clogged or the veins are incompetent, the organ stays flaccid. Medical science is now able to measure these dynamics by way of the Doppler, a device using ultrasound waves, to tell if the blood vessels are open and working properly. Knowing this information can help the therapist design an appropriate treatment program.

Diabetes is also a common cause for impotence, by its effect on both the blood vessels and the nerves of the penis. This disease leads often to blocked arteries, and nerves which as a consequence do not transmit their sensual messages at full speed. Nerve function can be tested simply by the squeezing of the head of the penis and determining whether the muscles at the base of the penis contract reflexively. Unfortunately, if nerve damage is present, it is not subject to direct treatment.

Any one of the glands, when dysfunctional, can cause impotence; but obviously the ones most closely associated are the testicles. For centuries the testicles have been known as a crucial part of the erector set. Their extracts, as with the monkey gland business, have been utilized as restorative remedies. If a little is good, more must be better, and a lot terrific. But, like vitamins, more is not necessarily better.

The function of the testicles is to make sperm for reproduction, and to make testosterone, a hormone which has a number of purposes, among which is to build body muscle. The androgenic steroids, used too often by the muscle-building group, are an inappropriate and dangerous extension of this action. Because testosterone is necessary for good sexual function (potency), it has been the topic of much research; and a great number of studies have shown that many, but not all, older men have decreases in the amount of testosterone in their blood. It became easy, therefore, to presume that this decline was responsible for a lot of impotence. However, Stanford colleague and renowned sex researcher Julian Davidson casts heavy doubt on this correlation and feels that only a small proportion of impotent men are so because of diminished testosterone stores. Most impotent men have normal blood testosterone values. Nonetheless, a blood test for these hormone levels is one of the first examinations in the inquiry into a case of impotency. Unfortunately, far too much testosterone has been and is being prescribed inappropriately for impotence. Certainly it has much placebo value, but it can on occasion be dangerous. For example, testosterone can adversely affect the liver, can stimulate prostate growth, and can change blood cholesterol levels. The closely related anabolic steroids, the use of which was widely displayed during the 1988 Olympic Games, are heavily laden with major side effects.

SUCCESSFUL TREATMENT OF IMPOTENCE

I have probably done more good for my male patients' impotence problems by stopping medicines than by any other single maneuver. Drugs commonly used for hypertension and gastrointestinal conditions are the most frequent villains. But a whole host of other drugs (including self-prescribed alcohol) are sometimes culpable. The smile on the face of a patient who has recovered potency after the discontinuation of a medicine is a rich reward.

Treatment for impotence has more clearly defined procedures. First the physician must ascertain whether the impotence is constant or variable. Nocturnal penile tumescence (NPT) is the medical term for nighttime erections. In youth these average eight per night and occur simultaneously with rapid eye movement (REM) sleep. With age these episodes of NPT decrease, but any occurrence denotes that the machinery is intact. One way of determining whether NPT is occurring is the postage-stamp test. On retiring, the patient is requested to apply a band of four stamps around the base of his penis. If the perforations are ruptured in the morning, the chances are good that an erection occurred during the night. We may then presume that the pipes, pulleys, and cables are intact. Other, more sophisticated techniques are now available to detect NPT, but the therapeutic inference is that if you can have an erection when asleep, you can have one when awake. Which brings us to the psychologic component of impotence.

Erectile competence depends on a complex interaction of psychologic and physical factors. It is no good having the motor if you don't have the energy to run it. The sexual athleticism of our new age has spawned the "fear of failure" profile of impotence. Sexual liberation has created the imagery of the perpetual stud—ready, aimed, and prepared to fire anywhere, anytime, at anything in a skirt. This mythology is as unnatural as the impropriety of sex among older people.

On the other side of the coin, the widower syndrome is a well characterized clinical situation in which the older man who has not had a sexual partner for a period of time will actually lose his sexual capacity because of lack or practice or exposure. The situation is self-perpetuating as failure compounds failure. Sex therapists are very helpful at this time. Tincture of reassurance and confidence is a major therapy.

The July 1987 issue of *Medical Economics* carried this story by Dr. Arona Kagnoff:

> At the time of his annual checkup, I found the 87-year-old patient spry and alert, and in exceptionally good condition for his age. He told me his wife had recently died and then hesitatingly mentioned that he'd been impotent for many years. I asked him why he'd never brought that problem to my attention before. "Well," he said. "I was married then and it didn't matter, but now I'm single again."

Although impotence was thought to be permanent and intractable, our industrial age has come up with direct, if unromantic, remedies. Some remedies for impotence are mechanical. Penile implants are now commonplace. For that man who has failed at every other approach to correct erector failure, but who still has substantial libido, a variety of plastic surgical devices have been developed to enable intercourse. Some are inflatable, via pump; some are malleable; some are rigid; and each has its own particular and predictable disadvantage. Although I have had minimal professional experience with individuals in whom these devices have been implanted, it is my understanding that patient satisfaction is generally very high. In 1984, 25,000 such devices were implanted.

A similar example of a mechanical approach to impotence concerns the development of suction devices wherein the penis is inflated passively either by a condom device with a negative pressure inside which remains on during intercourse, or a negative pressure cylinder which causes blood to enter the penis, followed by the application of a clip at the base of the penis to prevent the draining out of the blood. It is reported that this new technique requires a great deal of manual dexterity, which may not be conducive to the act in question. It is comforting to know that some of the best engineering minds in this country are at work in the cause of treating impotence.

Another aggressive approach for a man whose impotence is the result of a vascular inadequacy concerns the self-injection of several drugs directly into the penis in anticipation of intercourse. These drugs serve to increase blood flow by dilating the arteries and veins, thus facilitating an erection. This approach, like those discussed previously, is obviously in the experimental stage and so we must wait for further developments. A recent letter to the editor of a medical journal reported scarring of the penis resulting from these injections.

The point emerges that impotence is no longer cloaked in ignorance and shame. Like the rest of sexuality, it is out in the open. An impotent man eagerly welcomes the suggestion that the problem may be addressed directly and programmatically, like all other valid problems. Medicine is just getting its act together. It has a long way to go, but it has at least made the quantum jump afforded it by the new knowledge and conceptual base which was provided by the sexual revolution.

AGING AND FEMALE SEXUALITY

Female sexual responsiveness similarly presents itself as a topic for inquiry and knowledge. It is a topic not only of legitimate scientific inquiry but of endless probing in popular magazines. The new feminism is equated with sexual liberation, new roles, and new assertiveness. The impact on our family structure is a topic for intense discussion; but that is a topic for other authors. My intent is simply to explore the older woman's interest and participation in sexual activity.

Women, like men, experience a gap between sexual interest and sexual performance; but the reasons for the gap are very different. The broad categories of lack of sexual performance in women are as follows:

- lack of interest (libido)
- lack of capacity
- lack of opportunity

Numerous studies attest that many women retain a high interest in sexual intimacy as they age, with self-image and pride being implicit in their continued sexuality. Menopause clearly does not cause a slackening of sexual interest, illustrating again the unique dissociation in humans between procreation and sexuality.

When still a medical student at Stanford (1980–82) Martha Morrell did a project in Julian Davidson's laboratory which involved a group of 29 women ranging from 22 to 71 years of age. The experiment included the insertion of a sensory bulb into the women's vaginas and the recording of impulses as the women watched an erotic movie. What emerged was the finding that psychologic arousal was undiminished with age despite the lack of sex organ responsiveness due to estrogen lack.

Martha was eager to discover whether the physiologic reality of sexual arousal was affected by the presence or the lack of the steroid estrogens which occur at the time of the menopause. Morrell termed this phenomenon "steroid starvation."

The issue of anatomic similarities between female and male responsiveness has also been studied in great detail by researchers Masters and Johnson. For example, at the menopause, women lose most of their estrogenic stimulation, which in turn leads to failure of lubrication and diminished labial response. Such atrophy leads often to the distressing condition of dyspareunia—painful intercourse. Several years ago I was attending a meeting where Dr. Theresa Crenshaw, eminent sex psychiatrist in San

Diego, was discussing this phenomenon. She discoursed on the immense misery that was brought about by this structural barrier to successful sexual function. She rhetorically asked the audience, "Can you imagine any other situation in which a person endures quietly for years and years a condition in which suffering and indignation are constantly admixed repetitively over and over." A quiet male voice from the back of the room piped up, "Golf," —a comment which served only to highlight the point which Theresa was establishing.

Happily, I believe the weight of scientific evidence today favors the use of estrogen replacement therapy after the menstrual periods stop. (This is not a simple matter, however, and it needs careful personal crafting.) While conjugal bliss is helped substantially by a little estrogen (either applied locally as a cream or taken orally in pill form)—this therapy has a great deal to recommend it above and beyond its ability to promote satisfactory sex. Estrogens also help prevent osteoporosis and retard hardening of the arteries.

It is neither lack of interest nor decreased capacity, however, that seems to stand in the way of female sexual fulfillment. It is a lack of opportunity. First of all, there are simply a lot more older women than there are older men, particularly unattached ones. In some institutional situations this ratio can reach eight or ten to one. The macho bumper sticker SO MANY WOMEN—SO LITTLE TIME actually seems to apply to these rare older gents who occupy a numerical advantage that most younger men would covet.

Wherein most older men blame themselves for the failure of adequate sexual relationships with their mates, women blame them too. When he was a researcher at Duke University, Eric Pfeiffer surveyed a group of older women as to the reasons behind their sexual desire/performance gap. Thirty-six percent blamed the death of a spouse as the primary reason behind their sexual inadequacy, 20 percent targeted their spouse's illness, 18 percent cited their spouse's impotence, and 12 percent blamed divorce. Thus, it appears that if we are to make a complete package of sustained sexual happiness over the full life span of women we will have to do a better job of providing more men to them as they age. We men are either going to have to stay alive longer or be prepared to take on the opportunities afforded to us by these senior sirens who are simply lonely. One will have to provide better partners, however, than the Archie Bunkers and Ralph Kramdens of the world. If fitness is the price we men have to pay in order to sustain our sexual capacities, the line forms to the rear.

SEX, AGING, AND THE HEALTH CARE PROFESSIONAL

I feel that one great problem for older citizens has to do with the sexual hangups of health care professionals. Many of my colleagues are unskilled, and frankly uncomfortable with the notion that their older patients need and want ongoing sexual experiences. I admit that as a practicing physician, I feel that I do a generally poor job when dealing with this topic. I do a fair job with my male patients; I do an abysmal job with my female patients. I feel that for myself and other professionals this is largely because—despite my knowledge of the scientific literature regarding sexual interest in all older patients—I am personally uneasy about raising the subject. I find it somewhat approachable under two situations in which sexual problems abound. The first is the use of prescribed medication. Beta blockers are commonly used for the treatment of hypertension. These drugs block adrenaline and are altogether honorable, useful, and widely used. However, they carry with their use a high incidence of impotence. I try to ask any patient on beta blocker drugs about his sex life.

The second situation often fraught with sexual problems is that of clinical depression. Any person who is feeling blue generally has little sexual appetite, or appetite for any of life's other pleasures. The juices do not run. A bruised self-image does not lend itself naturally to sexual exploration.

Many persons show enhanced sexuality when antidepressants are used, prompting some drug companies to suggest their use in individuals who are not depressed. However, until the magic elixir of eternal youth is concocted, the best formula would seem to be the pursuit of a lifelong habit of active sexuality.

When a condition of drug use or depression prevails, I generally begin my inquiry into sexual behavior by asking a leading question. At medical meetings I often ask experienced sex therapists about their techniques of gaining entrance into the cloaked intimacy. I've not learned any real tricks, but I'm still trying to do a better job. Hopefully there will be no more communication gaps about sexuality when the children of the "flower age" grow into their eighties.

For now I must rely upon something like, "Do you think that any of your medicines (or those of your mate) have any effect in your interest in or performance of sex?"

Not only is the patient often relieved to have been asked, but I feel relieved having gotten the question out of my mouth. I feel real restraint about venturing into an individual's sexuality. I fully acknowledge my hangups since, particularly in this day, sex practices are a substantial element in illness patterns. Nonetheless, I feel that my respected patient may feel that I am overstepping my realm or becoming too personally inquisitive. Freud would say that my reserve would have something to do with "long lost parental communication barriers," and I'm sure that he'd be right—but that awareness doesn't help me out of my embarrassment at doing such an incompetent job.

I have been the house physician of a lovely retirement home in Palo Alto called Channing House. For ten years I had the wonderful opportunity to care for a distinguished married couple. Each day after lunch, George and Norma would retire to their apartment for their time of intimacy, which was known to all the residents and was respected and admired. It was generally understood that one was never to call between one and three o'clock in the afternoon. This pattern persisted into their nineties. I did once ask about their sex lives. George smiled; Norma purred.

Rather than their love trysts representing a curiosity or bizarre excess, they were regarded as something wonderful, a marker of achievement worthy of envy, admiration, and respect. We were voyeurs of a sort, but the vicariousness which we all felt was warm and good, and served not only to bond us to the couple but to broaden our understanding of what we too might be.

EIGHT

NEW TRICKS AND OLD DOGS

We are only now on the threshold of knowing
the range of educability of man—
the perfectability of man. We have never
addressed ourselves to this problem before.

Jerome Bruner

PART 1

OUR MOST MIRACULOUS RESOURCE

T he brain, what a piece of work! No exaggeration can overstate the magnificence of the structure and function of our main organ. We, with easy logic, identify ourselves as *Homo sapiens*—roughly translated from the Latin, "thinking or knowing man." As far as we know, the brain is the finest construct in the entire universe. Many evolutionists maintain that the likelihood of anything like it anywhere else is so remote that it follows that our intelligence is absolutely unique.

Certainly we can find no such parallel throughout the plant kingdom. Nowhere can we identify a plant with a complex nervous system capable of processing information. In fact, a large nervous system requires a prodigious amount of energy to sustain itself, and plants simply aren't up to the task. In the animal kingdom, it is only within the vertebrates that an organized coordinating system develops; and it is only within a minute fraction of vertebrates that we may find the degree of complexity sufficient to be termed a brain.

Furthermore, anthropologist and evolutionist Owen Lovejoy notes that a big brain is actually a reproductive disadvantage both before and after birth. Big brains mean big heads and thereby limit the number of offspring which the female can carry at any one time. A big brain requires much more oxygen and nutrition, both in utero and after birth. A big brain also connotes the need for much training and learning after birth, lengthening the time of dependency on the mother and limiting her contribution to tasks other than child rearing. Lower animals with more limited behavioral repertoires develop self-sufficiency much earlier in life than does *Homo sapiens*. A large brain does not, of itself, confer a "selective survival edge" except under very rare conditions.

BRAIN SIZE

In evolutionary terms, no organ in the history of life has grown as rapidly as has the human brain. And this development has been most rapid within the last 4 million years.

Brain volume has increased 20 cubic centimeters each 100,000 years until our brains are now about 1,500 cc in volume (three times what they were during the time in which Don Johanssen's find, "Lucy," walked the earth). Meanwhile, the brains of our ape cousins are still 500 cc in size.

Most anthropologists concur that our spectacular brain development occurred during our hunter-gatherer era; and so it is natural to conjecture that such development had something to do with our lifestyle. In fact, Stephen J. Gould and Harry J. Jerison emphasize that brain size is a functional adaptation to modes of life. Gould points out that throughout evolution, the more active predators have had larger brains than herbivores and less-active creatures. For example, *Tyrannosaurus rex* had a larger brain than did brontosaurus; and sharks and the great cats have relatively larger brains than do their prey.

Furthermore, an examination of the animal kingdom as a whole discloses that the size of the brain correlates with longevity. The brain of the blue whale weighs 9,000 grams; that of the elephant weighs 5,000 grams. The dolphin, too, has an exceptionally large brain. All have notably long lives, thus suggesting a coevolutionary phenomenon.

Despite the fact that man's brain is large in comparison to overall body size, it is still only 2 percent of the total body weight. Nonetheless, it is deemed so important to our overall body function that it is deeded 20 percent of an individual's blood supply. During exercise, blood is shunted from our digestive, excretory, and reproductive systems to the muscles and bones; but the brain is spared this diversion. The hierarchical dominance of our brain is assured.

It's important, however, to recognize that these observations about brain size are relevant only when comparing one large species group to another. Stephen Jay Gould, in his book *The Mismeasure of Man,* discounts the efforts of early brain researchers who sought to predict individual human intelligence by measurement of head and brain size. It emerges that although the volume of our brain is critical to our potential intellectual capacity, there is so much overlap and imprecision when head or brain size alone is considered that it is valueless as an indicator of intellectual capacity within our family of man.

NEUROBIOLOGY: EXPLORING
THE NEW FRONTIERS

Until the last century the brain was the virtually exclusive province of poets and other spiritualists. Now the scientific method is catching up; and as we learn more about the physical nature of the brain, this fantastic structure emerges from its cloistered shelter. The whole exploding field of neurobiology is incredibly exciting and challenging. Our drive to "know ourselves" is in high gear. We are learning how the brain works: what goes on where, and, somewhat forbiddingly, how to control it. We leave the subjective era; we enter the objective era. The brain is no longer an "unknowable black box."

Our exploration of the brain began with surgical experiments on laboratory animals and with the study of accidental injury to humans. Both avenues led us to an understanding of which specific parts of the brain control (or are otherwise involved with) which specific functions. For example, our motor cortex has been fully mapped; we know that motor control of our legs and feet occurs in the top of the brain; control of our trunk occurs in the midbrain; control of our head and hands lies in the lower portion of the brain. We can be even more specific and pinpoint, for example, the exact spot which controls each hand.

Jerison asserts that there is a Principle of Proper Mass regarding brain tissue: ". . . the mass of nerve tissue controlling a particular function is appropriate to the amount of information processing involved in performing the function."

Form follows function, as other scientists, such as Carl Lashley, have proved with laboratory animals: the disruption of learned behavior correlates with the amount of brain tissue that has been removed. So too with humans—any major insult to a portion of the brain produces a predictable functional outcome according to which part has been injured. For example, an injury to the temporal lobe may produce amnesia; an injury to the parietal lobe may induce defective reasoning capacity.

Today, exploration of the brain has major new tools. No longer must we wait for the tragic and chance occurrence of a human trauma—we can study the brain without invasion, through technology such as computerized axial tomography (CAT), magnetic resonance imagery (MRI) and positive emission tomography (PET). The MRI and CAT scans are revolutionary X-ray techniques that allow us to see the structure of the brain to a degree that previously was not even vaguely guessed at. Before the CAT scanner was developed, brain detail was obtained by use of extremely uncomfortable and dangerous techniques often requiring the boring of holes into the skull. Even with this, diagnostic insight was not very precise. The PET scan is the next generation beyond CAT and MRI. Not only does the PET scanner allow a penetrating new insight into what the brain looks like, it also allows us to see which parts of the brain are really metabolizing (operational). The pictures are luminous and awe-inspiring. Unfortunately, the PET scanner, to date, is still largely a research tool due to its high cost and intricate technology.

A PRIMER IN NEUROBIOLOGY 101

The fundamental units of our brains are the neurons, or brain cells. Each of these units has its own cell body and nucleus; in addition, each unit possesses small filaments or branches which are vital to brain function. These filaments, called dendrites, are thousands in number and provide a connection to other brain cells. It is estimated that within our two-pound brain there are more than 1 *trillion* nerve cells—each with a thousand branches. Thus, the number of potential connections (synapses) between the cells becomes even more astronomical. It is through these connections that "thought" is accomplished; and only within the last two decades have we learned how our brain cells "speak" or connect with one another.

Science writer Lane Lenard describes this process eloquently:

> The brain is an ever changing kaleidoscope of electric peaks and valleys and chemical ebbs and flows in which about 10 billion neurons are constantly reaching out to one another across microdistances to deliver their molecular messages. The brain's functioning consists of the sum total of this steady and highly coordinated passage of information—in the form of a few molecules of a chemical transmitter substance—from one neuron to another. Neurotransmitter substances are stored in tiny packets called vesicles in the terminal of each nerve cell's axon (a kind of sending antenna). When a signal, in the form of a tiny electrical pulse, or action potential, reaches the terminal, a few vesicles spurt out their contents into the ultramicroscopic gap between the axon terminal and the surface of the next neuron.

Such beautiful exposition of the basic function of the brain was not even vaguely glimpsed when I was in medical school. My Stanford friend and respected neurobiologist Jack Barchas feels that our discovery of the neurotransmitters is a scientific moment of equal importance to Einstein's elaboration of the theory of general relativity. I would agree, and add only that it is also as primal as William Harvey's conclusions regarding circulation of the blood.

IS THE BRAIN A COMPUTER?

The cells and their branches are the hardware of your brain and mind —the cable system. The neurotransmitters are the sparks. Their connection is clear; but does this mean that your brain conforms to a mechanical model of wires and sparks? Is your brain a computer? Does it merely collect and retrieve random bits of information?

Carl Sagan illustrates the awesome power of the human brain when he notes that ". . . the most powerful computer has a storage capacity and information processing rate between 10 to 1,000 times less than the brain." While certainly the computer can be faster at the retrieval of stored information, when compared to the human brain its storage capacity is paltry.

Nevertheless, the computer has provided a wonderful system for the study of the brain; for despite our glorious new insights into brain anatomy and basic elements, we still lack a satisfactory conceptual model on such elemental questions as "How do we learn?" and "What is memory?" The computer allows us to play with such models. The entire new science of artificial intelligence enables our understanding of the mechanics of the brain. *Cybernetics,* the term coined by Norbert Wiener of MIT, describes the analytic process relating control and communication systems both in nature and in machines (automation). Suddenly we have a new vocabulary enriching our efforts to probe our sentinel organ.

As we learn more about the workings of the brain we will make better computers. As we make better computers we will learn more about the workings of the brain. Wiring diagrams and biochemical maps are vital to our unfolding understanding; but both the operational manual and the construction blueprint are still obscure. Is the brain (and ultimately the rest of us) merely a "printout" of genetic messages which were conformed at the moment of fertilization and subsequently destined to develop and emerge as a rigorously precise copy? Or is the brain moldable, responsive, plastic, and reactive to environmentally driven moments and influences? Nature or nurture? Hardware or software? Determinism or free will? Are traits such as territoriality, aggression, cooperation, hate, and love encoded? Or are they learned? Is the brain hard-wired from its beginning?

BRAIN GROWTH AND DEVELOPMENT

The wiring diagram of computer construction is complex enough, but the developmental mode of the human brain approaches miracle proportions. Early in embryonic development the brain makes its first appearance as a thin sheet of cells near the surface of the embryo. The sheet then folds on itself to form a hollow cylinder known as the neural tube, one end of which thickens to become the brain, the remainder elongating into the eventual spinal cord. The nerve cells during this phase reproduce hundreds of thousands of times a minute. Early on, the first nerve cells merely are present—they have no connections. Then migration starts. Groups of cells start to move slowly through the primitive nerve substance. (Progress will consist of perhaps 0.1 millimeter per day.) Eventually the nerve cells aggregate to form different nerve and brain structures. At this time the nerve cells commence to send out filaments which appear to seek out cousin neurons with which to establish synaptic connection. This nerve-filament-sending phenomenon is a wonderfully exciting area of current brain research.

The filaments continue to elongate by developing on their ends structures known as growth cones. These small protrusions "feel" their way over long distances within the developing nervous system.

Physicist Eric Barth, in his book *Windows on the Mind,* observes, "Movies of growth cones convey the startling impression of an intelligent search, a series of trials and errors, and decision making. They almost seem like bloodhounds sniffing their way through dense underbrush."

The growth cones haltingly but surely inch their way through the intricate latticework of the developing nervous system. The nature of their cues, prods, and blocks is unfolding as scientists now can watch developing nerve and brain cells grown in glass dishes—just like yeast. These efforts have produced a bountiful harvest. For example, we have identified a protein called "nerve growth factor," which serves to stimulate nerve growth. Moreover, we are learning of the delicate interplay that exists between elements such as hormones and nutrition, and environmental insults such as drug effects and maternal stresses. Each plays an important role in the development of the emerging brain cells.

A CONTINUING PROCESS

Unlike other animals, in which brain development is complete in utero or shortly thereafter, the human brain is not "complete" until the early 20s. A baby's brain is only one-third its eventual size. Even until death, most cells maintain the ability to divide and replenish. Not so our nerve cells. They stop dividing before birth—the *number* of individual brain cells being at its highest level. *But,* and this is the crucial "but," the bulk of the brain's *neurologic connections* still have not been made at the time of birth. As these connections develop, the growth of all important supportive cells eventually constitutes the remaining two-thirds of the brain's adult size. This potential—this delayed calendar of developmental events—has allowed us uniquely to heed the variety of environmental messages which early life provides.

The explosive networking growth of our emerging brains leads to that phenomenal organ of insight, love, fear, memory, creativity, and transcendence that gives our species its name—and its diversity. Sir Julian Huxley cites the brain's adaptability and diversity as the prime identifying characteristics of our being. Such diversity is awesome. The buzz word in brain research is *plasticity*— the brain's ability to respond; and the developmental capacity of the brain has produced some phenomenal specimens.

THE GENIUS

Every one of us probably can identify several people whose capabilities seem so far beyond what we reckon as ordinary abilities that we label them "genius." They are not just extrasmart; they are set apart—extraordinary. How can we explain this? Were Shakespeare, Mozart, and Einstein merely expressions of a freakish combination of genes? Or was the genetic inspiration tempered, expanded, and molded by environmental perspiration? Scholars teach us that Shakespeare was not an accident but rather an unusual but predictable product of his time. We know too that Mozart was born into music; his entire infancy and early childhood were spent in a home that reverberated with music most of the day and evening. In some ways, financially for example, Mozart was inept.

We know more about Einstein. As a child he didn't talk until he was 3. This unsettled his parents to the extent that they consulted a physician about their slow learner. In school Einstein was told he would never amount to anything. His teacher told him, "Your very presence spoils the respect of the class for me." He was eventually encouraged to drop out of high school; which he did in the 1890s. Einstein wandered through northern Italy, supporting himself by way of odd jobs, and eventually landed a post in the Swiss Patent Office in Zurich. While working there in 1905 (at the age of 26), he published four research papers—the latter two of which revealed his astonishing elaboration of the theory of relativity and its proclamation of the interconvertability of mass and energy.

After Einstein's death, Dr. Marian Diamond, about whom I will later report more, had the opportunity to study his brain. She found that while most of the brain was like any other, the parietal lobes (those areas involved particularly with associative thought) were markedly richer in dendritic branching. This, Diamond concluded, suggested increased usage.

In his book *Conceptual Blockbusting*, Stanford professor and friend James Adams wrote, "For most of us creativity is more of a dull glow than a divine spark. And the more fanning it receives, the brighter it will burn."

OTHER EXTREMITIES OF BRAIN DEVELOPMENT

We are all intrigued by genius accomplishment, but there is a rare situation in which the capacity of the human brain has developed to such a fantastic degree that it seems altogether impossible. Thus arises the phenomenon of the "idiot savant." Although he is profoundly impaired in every other aspect of thought and reasoning, a person with this syndrome will display a remarkable mental ability in one specific area. In the May 1988 issue of the *American Journal of Psychiatry*, Donald Treffert reports that this "juxtaposition of a severe mental handicap and prodigious mental ability" was first recorded about a century ago. Since that time there have been several hundred reported cases, with a sex ratio of six men to one woman. (The male/female ratio is as yet inexplicable. However, we know that testosterone can affect brain growth; and we can surmise that if affected at a critical time this could favor development of the kinds of right-brain skills observed among savants.) While a number of patterns may be displaced, several spectacular mental capacities seem to predominate. For example, common among idiot savants is an uncanny ability to calculate calendar dates. On what day of the week was September 11, 1411? In what months of the twenty-first century will the 15th fall on Thursday? Persons with this syndrome can successfully name both day and month in a matter of seconds. In another case, a young, blind Frenchman who had been placed in an asylum for profound mental retardation had two astonishing skills. He was able to calculate the cube root of any 6-figure number within 6 seconds, and within 44 seconds he could provide the sum of 64 progressive doublings of any number.

Other common patterns are mental retardation, blindness, and musical genius. Prominent in the medical literature is the case of Leslie Lemke, a boy from Milwaukee who was born mentally retarded and without eyes. In addition, Leslie was severely impaired with cerebral palsy. Abandoned by his birth parents, he was subsequently adopted by a nurse, May Lemke, a WW I war bride from England. May and her second husband, Joe, devoted their lives to caring for Leslie.

After 18 years of patient support and instruction, Leslie displayed his first response—he moved his finger while listening to some music. From that moment on, May filled the Lemke household with glorious music. She and Joe even bought a used piano, and May patiently pushed Leslie's fingers on the keys to show him that he too could make sound. Some years later the Lemkes were to learn that Leslie had been listening—and listening with remarkable concentration. As the story is told, they were awakened one night by the sound of a Tchaikovsky concerto being played—by Leslie—on the piano.

Another case exists which involves a 7-year-old boy with multiple handicaps. Extraordinary musical ability was obvious at age 3, but he could speak only single words or simple phrases. Nonetheless, he was able to duplicate complex pieces of classical or popular music after a single hearing. As with other musical geniuses, idiot savants appear to have an intrinsic knowledge of the mathematical nature of music; they have the ability to improvise and to change keys effortlessly.

How can this occur? It has been suggested that early life sensory deprivation and/or social isolation leads to this phenomenal intellectual capacity. Such individuals simply spend all of their time concentrating on this task.

Edward Hoffman wrote, ". . . the necessary if not sufficient conditions associated with idiot savantism appear to be a minimal cognitive level of functioning, intense practicing, motivation aided by a funneling of external stimuli and strong reinforcements to develop and maintain this unusual ability."

There are only four reported cases in which autopsy evidence has been provided of an idiot savant. These examinations, like that performed on the brain of Einstein, revealed extreme development of the portion of the brain concerned with the particular extraordinary faculty which was involved. The scientific world eagerly awaits reports of the use of the PET scanner with idiot savants.

Both extremes of the continuum, the genius and the idiot savant, give evidence of what the brain can do when channeled and developed in highly specific ways.

BRAIN DEVELOPMENT
AND EXTREME DEPRIVATION

There is still another developmental anomaly which intrigues and informs; this is the still rarer circumstance of feral man, the name and concept of which were proposed by the great taxonomist Linnaeus in 1758. Feral (Latin for "wild") is the term for extreme cases of isolation of infants who have been abandoned by their biologic parents and then adopted and suckled by animals; or of older children who have wandered away into forests and survived by their own efforts. The story of Romulus and Remus is apocryphal, but it probably represents a folk history of a she-wolf suckling a child. We have more modern examples. In 1966, the Reverend J.A.L. Singh of Bengal and Professor Robert M. Zingg of the University of Denver published the carefully documented account of Amala and Kamala, "the wolf children of Midnapore."

In October 1920 two young girls, estimated at 1 1/2 and 8 years of age, were found in a mountain den with four wolves: a male, a female, and two cubs. The children and the cubs huddled together and were guarded viciously by the mother wolf (who was eventually killed). The children ran on all fours with palms down and were mute except for guttural grunts. They were unable to stand or to grasp with their hands. While they liked the dark and were afraid of the light, each possessed an excellent sense of smell. They were aloof and scratched other children when they approached. They slept overlapping one another. They urinated and defecated anywhere. They ate their meat raw and drank their milk directly from the plate. Other foods were not acceptable to them.

Unfortunately the younger child died of intestinal worms a year after discovery. Her adoptive sister in this incredible experience crouched on all fours and sat forlornly in a corner for four days after the death. Eventually the older girl—now perhaps 9½ years old—approached other children. Exercise was used to help Kamala to straighten her legs; and after 2½ years of instruction, she was able to stand. She continued to eat like a wolf, ferociously, for 2 years. After 6 years of living in a Catholic mission, she knew thirty words and could express herself minimally. At age 16 she still ran on all fours and frequently lapsed back into primitive behavior patterns. In 1929, the Psychological Society of New York invited her to come to that city; but unfortunately she fell ill, and despite the efforts of numerous doctors, she died on November 14, 1929, without having been diagnosed.

INTELLECTUAL DEVELOPMENT: IS IT NATURE OR NURTURE?

What can we conclude from these examples of human beings reared in total deprivation? What do they tell us about those elements of the human intellect which are inherited and/or learned?

Professor R. Ruggles Gates, Chairman of the Human Hereditary Bureau in London, wrote:

From modern investigation of mental inheritance in man and animals, one must conclude that the fundamental bases of intelligence, ability, and character are inherited. The environmental effects, for better or worse, affect these inherited potentialities. This does not relieve the individual of moral responsibilities, because his decisions are the free expression of his own personality. At the same time, his character with the inherited basic element will in large measure determine the nature of his decisions.

The Reverend Singh of Bengal, the mentor of Amala and Kamala, concluded with a different emphasis:

If man is bound by heredity and predestination with only microscopic modification possible due to changes in environment, then all constant endeavor for social betterment would lose all significance. But if, on the other hand, it can be proved that the environment predominates in the molding of charac-

ter and habits, the laudable efforts of social workers could succeed into bringing into existence, if not the millennium, at
least the near vista of a better world, which could be realized if
we would only take the right path. The theory of social progress suggests that this view is more correct, and in the case of
Kamala it is clearly established that the influence of her wolf
environment was almost all-powerful, and even made her unable to develop those manifestations of the human body required for human life, as distinct from that of animals.

The moral overtones of this debate are not as important as the inevitable message of the dominance of the environment on brain development
in these cases. I believe that while we enter this world with certain basic,
"innate" intellectual capacities, these qualities can be literally overwhelmed by the influences of either an enriched or a deprived environment.

To me, these three—the genius, the idiot savant, and the feral child—
describe brilliantly the plasticity of our brains. This "moldability" of the
human mind is both wonderful and frightening. Whether by positive influences such as education, or negative influences such as deprivation or
formalized brainwashing, the potential for change has been demonstrated.
The challenge remains for us to master it. The brain—the mind—is born;
and it develops, largely in some unknown conformity to the input supplied
to it. The brain becomes what it does. The program is the message.

PART II:

THE AGING BRAIN

DOES AGING HALT
THE CAPACITY TO LEARN?

Clearly the extent of change, of development, and of potential alteration is greatest during the earliest months of life. The slate is clean then.
But as I have reported, birth does not imply that the formation and altera-
bility of the brain is complete. Far from it. Everyday observation illustrates
the rapid development of the newborn's intellectual curiosity and capacity.

It is the delight of every parent and grandparent. Boasting rights are loudly proclaimed. This development becomes institutionalized at school age, and our entire educational enterprise is consecrated to making maximal the power of our brains.

Then what? For myself, as with most doctors, my head seemed jammed with more facts per cubic inch at the conclusion of my formal training period than at any other moment in my life. In a sense this was certainly true, as college, medical school, and postdoctoral training were framed primarily in a learning mode. "Doing" wasn't so important; then suddenly, like a chicken hatching, a new role emerged. Suddenly, "doing" became the thing. Learning, in the formal sense at least, was sublimated. For me this hatching didn't happen until age 33. What if it happens at age 17 or 18—as it does for millions. Does learning stop?

The intelligence quotient (IQ) has been "credentialed" (by some) as a measure of innate thinking capacity. Fifty years ago there was a general consensus that our brains, reflecting parental capacities, could be rigorously tested in such objective fashion as to determine their horsepower (their "bits"), which then ordained how effective a thinking device we had. And yet the IQ has some notable detractors. For example, Stephen J. Gould interprets IQ testing as the logical successor to the discredited techniques of craniometry (head dimensions) and brain-size determinations as predictors of intelligence.

For most individuals, the IQ was found to vary some (but not much) during the educational years, and then to fall as we aged. "When the age is in—the wit is out," was Shakespeare's observation in *Much Ado About Nothing*. What goes up must inevitably come down? Maybe, or maybe not. We have many developmental models, including the ABA life model (discussed in chapter 5), which concludes that advanced years seem to mimic the earliest ones, particularly with reference to thinking ability. Yet, the admixture of Alzheimer's disease and other pathologies serves mightily to distort our presumptions of normal decline. The stereotype of aging has been shaped to a major extent by the notion that as we age our brains become more and more sieve-like—that after school at age 20, 30, or whatever, it's all downhill and falling fast.

Do our brains inevitably rot out? In 1958, Benedict D. Burns, professor of physiology at McGill University, estimated that during every day of our adult lives more than 100,000 neurons die. But where do all the exceptions fit in to this prediction? What about individuals such as Frank Lloyd Wright, Georgia O'Keeffe, George Bernard Shaw, Buckminster Fuller,

Golda Meir, Bernard Baruch, and thousands like them, whose wits and mental facilities were preserved until extremely late in life?

THE CASE FOR CONTINUOUS LEARNING

The issue has been forcibly addressed in a number of studies, with the newly acquired knowledge affirming and extending the concept of the plasticity of our brains even as we age. To me the most significant of these studies have been the research efforts occurring at the University of California at Berkeley. In the 1950s, Mark Rosenzweig and Marian Diamond initiated studies on laboratory rats designed to estimate the effect of early life environmental "enrichment" on intellectual functioning and brain size. The basic experimental model, still exploited presently by Diamond and her co-workers, consists of litter-mate rats raised differently in three environmental circumstances termed "enriched," "standard," and "impoverished." The enriched situation involves twelve animals to a cage with various toys and other stimulants; the standard situation has three rats in a cage; the impoverished situation involves isolation of solitary rats with a minimum of stimulation. Early on, the Berkeley researchers demonstrated that early life enrichment resulted in brighter rats. (They solved mazes faster.) More emphatically, enrichment actually led to bigger brains. When the bigger brains were analyzed under the microscope, it was seen that the enlargement was due to a stimulation of the dendritic branches—more and longer branches had been sent out.

This result was predicted in 1911 by the great neuroanatomist Raymon y Cajal when he wrote, "One might suppose that cerebral exercise, since it cannot produce new cells, carries further than usual protoplasmic expansions and neural collaterals, forcing the establishment of new and more extended intercortical connection." Moreover, Michele Malacarne, an Italian anatomist of the eighteenth century, found that there were more folds in the brain of a trained animal than in the brain of an untrained animal. These early results were soon confirmed in other laboratories and were among the first graphic demonstrations of the plasticity of the brain.

These experiments revealed chemical as well as physical changes. Specifically, it was found that the brains of enriched rats showed a higher content of the nerve compound noradrenaline, which is the strongest nerve stimulant identified to date. As noted before, when they are grown artificially in a glass dish, brain cells react to the addition of noradrenaline by extending the nerve branches—just as with enrichment.

Jack Barchas of Stanford wrote, "Behavioral events alter neurochemical function and altered neurochemical function can change behavior."

It is a positive feedback loop. Such enrichment required only eight days of stimulation in young rats to show marked differences. It is important to note that while the enrichment did not increase the number of cells (a factor which seemed to be fixed early on), it clearly affected the branching.

These results become more interesting still when we review data gathered with the PET scanner. Images showing the brain "in action" confirm that only certain portions of the brain are stimulated by a particular task. For example, the occipital lobes (located at the lower rear portion of the brain) "light up" when a visual task is undertaken; and the temporal lobes (located adjacent to the ears) "light up" when a memory chore is directed. Through such vivid images we see that thinking (or mental action) is directly related to increased metabolic activity. Blood supply with its extra oxygen and nutrients goes to the area being challenged—just as in a weightlifter's biceps. Energy flow is thus targeted. Form follows function.

Stroking a Siamese kitten makes it more active, attentive, brighter. Adopted children of bright people are often bright. Oldest children of families are usually the brightest. There are more firstborns listed in the *Encyclopedia Britannica* and in *Who's Who* than there are people of any other birth order. Our studies of these individuals reveal that as children they were most often afforded "extra stimulation" vis-à-vis more adult attention; and this seems to have made the difference. They had become like the enriched rats.

In further investigation of this phenomenon, Rick Heber, a psychologist at the University of Wisconsin, identified forty-four newborn children whose environmentally deprived mothers had IQs averaging 70 points (well below accepted rates of normal intelligence). For four years Heber and his associates provided the children with an intensely rich and stimulating intellectual life; at the end of that "enriched" time, he found the children's average IQ to be 130. A control group of similar children averaged 80 on the same IQ scale. Kindred to these results is the Pygmalion (or Halo) Effect in which teachers' expectations of a child's IQ (regardless of actual test scores) have been shown to increase both a child's in-class performance and subsequent standardized test scores.

George Bernard Shaw wrote in *Back to Methuselah*, "If the weight lifter, under the trivial stimulus of an athletic competition can 'put up a

muscle,' it seems reasonable to believe that an equally earnest and convinced philosopher could 'put up a brain.' Both are directive of vitality to a
certain end."

The established fact that the brain responds actively to stimulation
should not be surprising; but somehow we don't visualize the brain as a
muscle which, when exercised, gets bigger—or weakens with disuse. And
yet this is a recurring and consistent phenomenon throughout the animal
kingdom. Rabbits placed in the dark lose RNA from their retinas within
three hours; and somewhat later, RNA levels within the visual cerebral
cortex also decline. Darkness actually alters the chemical state of the rabbit's brain. This occurs because less amino acid is converted into protein
when light is withheld. When light is reinforced, protein synthesis is rapidly
reestablished.

And we have many human illustrations of this concept:

• Certain chemicals such as puromycin or cyclosporin block the synthesis of protein in the human brain. When they are employed, memory is
blocked.

• Add an active energy source (such as cyclic AMP, a chemical crucial to metabolism), to a dish of nerve cells, and within ten minutes the cells
will show sprouting and elongation of branches, which will last for six hours.
Is this, then, a stimulant that "makes you smarter for a little while"? Sounds
great, doesn't it? Then why isn't it on the market? Some hucksters have
tried doing such experiments, but clearly the material must be delivered to
just the right spot and in just the right amount and at just the right time to
be appropriate. Ingesting the testicles of exotic animals doesn't make you
sexier. Eating cyclic AMP doesn't make you smarter.

• A number of studies show that the mental reaction times of athletes are faster than those of nonathletes. We know from experiments with
laboratory rats that exercise will increase the amount of the stimulating
neurotransmitter, noradrenaline, in the animal's brain. The brains of exercised rats grow much like Marian Diamond's enriched rats. Our conclusions
are that this phenomenon is replicated in humans. When persons of low
fitness levels are trained, their reaction times improve. Such results have
led Warren Spirduso of the University of Texas to conclude, "As the evidence accumulates, exercise becomes a strong candidate as a contributor to
a general regulatory mechanism for high quality psychomotor function."

DOES BRAIN FUNCTION
DECLINE WITH AGE?

The enrichment work of Diamond and others has driven hard at the presumption that our brains wither as we age. But the presumption is a persistent one. Textbooks are filled with abundant evidences which detail the age-related decrements in the brain. Harold Brody, now with the Medical Center, University of Buffalo, estimates a 30 percent loss in neurons after the age of 20. Old brains weigh less. Multiple studies show that older people have lower IQs. Older brains have lower levels of the major transmitter dopamine and noradrenaline, which are involved with stimulation. The PET scanner shows that older people have lower utilization of glucose in their brains—thus lower metabolism. Blood flow goes down with age. That seems like a lot of damning evidence—but it's only a small part of the story.

The so-called evidences regarding the decline of the aging brain fail to answer some very critical questions. If it is "normal" for the brain to fail with age, why do *many* individuals show absolutely no intellectual decline with age? Why do most people have only selective areas of decline while other intellectual abilities hold up? Why do specific areas of the brain, such as the visual cortex of the occipital lobe (or visual brain), escape even the most minimal cellular deterioration?

These questions also troubled Marian Diamond; and so in a paper entitled "A Search for the Potential of the Aging Brain," she tells us of her experiments involving old rats. When older laboratory subjects (that's 600 days for a rat) were placed in enriched environments they, like their younger colony chums, were found also to demonstrate growth of the nerve branching and thicker cortical levels. Enriched older rats solve mazes faster than do their deprived controls. They are smarter.

Diamond's work challenged many prior studies which had recorded "decrements" in the anatomy of the brains of older rats. She concluded that these earlier works had been carried out largely on rats in socially isolated circumstances and that this lack of environmental "enrichment" led to the decreases. After the meticulous study of rat brains of all ages, she found that such declines actually occurred in rats when they were young. After 108 days, there was no further fall until extreme old age.

It seems likely that the reason why the visual cortex uniquely does not deteriorate with age is that, unlike other parts of the brain, it is in constant use. When I asked Marian Diamond how this conclusion relates to blind subjects, she told me that she suspects the visual cortex deteriorates in blind individuals and further that the auditory cortex exhibits hypertrophy —an increase in function. Further, the temporal lobes, usually involved with hearing, light up in a PET scanner whenever a deaf person engages in visual tasks. Again this illustrates the plasticity of the human brain.

We can extrapolate the results of animal experimentation to humans, but what of actual human studies? Generations of psychologists have linked age with a fall in IQ. The standard technique to demonstrate such a decline is to aggregate groups of individuals of different ages and administer a standard test. It was shown thirty years ago that different generations are smarter or at least test differently than do other generations. (College entrance scores are currently going down.) One such study was reported by Russell Green of the University of Rochester and involved 1,200 participants (the oldest of whom were age 65) from Puerto Rico. Green observed declines in the IQs of older subjects, but he attributed the entirety of the decline to educational differences between different age cohorts. For the individual he summarized, "Intelligence does not decline before age 65."

Because they use groups of differing ages, such studies are called cross-sectional, and they cannot therefore be used to demonstrate a change that occurs over time in a specific group. It is like comparing apples and oranges. To offset this, psychologists are required to follow the same group over time and to do longitudinal measurement. When this is done, the results get a great deal more scattered. Certain mental test capacities go down; others don't change; others even go up.

One such effort is an important ongoing longitudinal study of persons in Puget Sound, Washington. IQ tests taken by the same individuals in both 1956 and 1963 showed marked improvements. Those individuals in their 70s tested better than they had in their 60s. Television has been suggested as a possible agency of this improvement—just as it has been blamed for current decline in college entrance scores. Clearly, TV has the capacity to enrich one's awareness, reactivity, and intelligence; but when *Hollywood Squares, Magnum P.I.,* and soap operas are the standard fare, the brain is numbed and diminished.

In another exploration of the aging brain, Stanley Rapaport at the National Institute on Aging studied the intellectual functioning of 21 men between the ages of 21 and 83. Utilizing new and advanced technologic testing procedures, he concluded that when disease is excluded, older brains do not deteriorate with regard to blood flow, oxygen use, metabolism, and so forth. It is inevitable that when looking for age effects researchers find that such effects are intermixed with disease problems, some of which may not yet be apparent. For example, hardening of the arteries to the brain would be expected to impair brain performance; but this is a disease and not aging. Alzheimer's disease unquestionably impairs brain performance, but this too is a disease and not normal aging. Older persons fatigue more easily and this is also a factor in testing procedures.

The confounding effects of illness, depression, and fatigue, as well as less apparent issues such as motivation, complicate the question of intelligence change with age. Some researchers have suggested that older persons (whether living alone or in nursing homes) tend to have intellectually and socially impoverished environments (like Diamond's restricted rats). Further, older persons tend to seek immediate and idiosyncratic rewards rather than the delayed payoff which learning efforts hold for younger persons. Age differences in cognitive abilities are seen to reflect variations in the availability of concurrent environmental conditions which produce and maintain optimal levels of cognitive functioning. Decline in old age may reflect performance measurement rather than defects in competence. The studies suggest strongly that part of the previously observed declines may truly be attributable to disuse.

A common lament heard in my office is from the wife of a newly retired spouse. This man through his working lifetime was bright, involved, and on the front edge of decisions; but the wife now finds him to be tiresome, depressing, and a burden. Inactivity spawns inactivity.

As Charles Dickens noted so aptly in *Barnaby Rudge*, "Minds, like bodies, will often fall into a pimpled, ill-conditioned state from mere excess of comfort."

In summary, Stanford psychologist Dr. Laura Carstensen wrote, "It is an illusion that irremedial psychological deterioration is the modal course of old age."

NEW TRICKS FOR OLD DOGS

The belief that disuse contributes to intellectual decline naturally led to a series of studies in which new tricks were taught to old dogs. In a 1986 article entitled "Can Decline in Adult Intellectual Functioning Be Reversed?" K. Warner Schaie and Sherry Willis of Penn State University reported on 229 subjects from the Puget Sound, Washington, longitudinal study who ranged from 64 to 95 years of age, with an average age of 73. The effect of lifestyle on mental functioning was very important. Half of their subjects showed no decline between 1970 and 1984. Seventy-one subjects underwent five one-hour training sessions (in which a variety of mental chores were provided) and then were retested. Those individuals who showed declined intellectual ability between 1970 and 1984 responded more favorably to the training than did those who had shown no change over the fourteen years. This indicated to the researchers that the longitudinal decline was reversible to some extent.

The authors concluded:

> Although the improvement and reversal of decline demonstrated in this study are impressive, it should be understood that such results may be a rather conservative estimate of what could be achieved by more extensive programs of this kind. The training procedures employed with the massive educational interventions common earlier in the lifespan, and the breath of remediation possible with more extensive training effects has yet to be examined.
>
> Most importantly, our findings lend support to contentions regarding the plasticity of behavior into late adulthood. They suggest that for at least a substantial portion of the community-dwelling elderly, observed cognitive decline is not irreversible, is likely to be attributable to disuse, and can be subjected to environmental manipulation involving relatively simple and inexpensive educational training techniques.
>
> What our intervention procedures seem[ed] to accomplish was to reactivate behavior and skills that had remained in the subject's behavioral repertoire that had not been actively employed.

This observation is central to my daily clinical practice. I always search for new cues and interests that may respark and rekindle a life ember that has been allowed to cool and dwindle. A new pet, joining a seniors' club, taking adult education courses, traveling, or volunteering— the options are immense, if only we see to use them.

Another study from Penn State by Judy Plemons, Sherry Willis, and Paul Baltes looked at the degree of trainability of 15 experimental subjects, aged 59 to 85. Twice weekly for four weeks the subjects received one-hour training sessions. Following training the individuals were compared with a control group, and they had achieved a marked improvement.

MOTIVATION AND LEARNING

The element of motivation in learning is clearly important, and several studies have assessed the effects of providing incentives to older persons to check the effect on learning. Paul Baltes and co-workers found that they could improve the outcome for learning by giving older subjects redeemable "green stamps" during the training sessions. An experiment conducted in 1973, at the Morgantown, West Virginia, Senior Club showed that reinforcement by a nickel reward for each demonstrated cognitive improvement led to a more rapid training effect. Arnold and Madge Scheibel, of UCLA, reported that the tissue changes which they observed in the aging brain were better correlated to psychosocial impairment than to chronologic age. This accords with the work of Diamond. Stimulation leads to the release of noradrenaline, and noradrenaline stimulates nerve growth.

PHYSICAL EXERCISE AND INCREASED BRAIN FUNCTION

Several intensely interesting studies have looked into the effect of exercise on brain function. Not only would exercise be expected to improve circulation to the brain, but more important, it seems to stimulate the formation and release of noradrenaline. Four years ago Robert Dustman and his colleagues in Salt Lake City reported their work in a paper that knocked my socks off. They selected forty-three sedentary subjects from the community who were aged 55 to 70. They performed a host of baseline studies and then divided the group into three sections: one did aerobic exercises; one did flexibility exercises; and one group remained inactive. The aerobic exercise group improved in all the expected physical measurements over the other two groups—but what astonished me was that their cognitive abilities improved! Exercise, three hours a week for four months, led to "clear improvement" in intelligence. Theodore Bashore of the Medical College of Pennsylvania is extending these studies—with the same findings. *Wow!* I find it easy to understand reports such as those of Warren Spirduso, of the University of Texas, which show that racquet ball improves reaction times and coordination. But exercise improving intelligence—now that really is something.

There are other examples. A 1988 report from Ontario cited studies in which fit older subjects tested higher in intelligence tests than did sedentary control subjects. Fifteen subjects already involved in an exercise program were evaluated before and after a relatively modest forty-five-minute bout of exercise. They were compared with another group which only watched. The subjects were retested ten to thirty-five minutes after the exercise was completed. Even this short period of physical activity was found to be associated with improved mental functioning and memory skills. Dr. Richard Powell of the University of Maine conducted a study of 30-year-old patients confined to a mental institution. He instituted a program of brisk walking for one hour, five times a week, and found improved mental functioning. A study from the Netherlands recorded that the recall capabilities of forty nursing-home patients (average age, 83) improved after an exercise program.

It seems again that intellectual functioning (like sex, bone density, and other purported age changes) is secondary not so much to aging or disease as to disuse. All need to be wound up. The effect of physical exercise on brain function should not be so surprising when we recall that noradrenaline is a compound which is secreted during exercise, and that it serves to initiate and coordinate all of the diverse reactions and compensations which are necessary to support the increased demands placed on us by a workload. Brain stimulation, as with dexedrine and antidepressants, results when a higher level of noradrenaline bathes the brain. A friend, John Martinson, has coined a law: "A train of thought once set in motion tends to remain in motion. A mind at rest tends to remain at rest."

To illustrate this point we need look at only one experiment. Timothy Collier and his colleagues at the Department of Anatomy of Rochester Medical School transplanted fetal neurons with a high content of noradrenaline into the brains of old rats. He found that cognition improved. Such transplantation is akin to the current effort to correct Parkinson's disease by transplanting into the brain, cells which secrete dopamine. Collier was able also to improve cognition by simply infusing noradrenaline into the brains of older rats. He concluded, "These findings are consistent with the view that a decline in brain noradrenaline function during aging can be associated with behavioral changes contributing to impaired cognitive function."

In my view there is small likelihood of a "smart elixir" or "brain potion." There is no quick fix. But there does exist, for all of us, the chance to keep our batteries charged, our wires lively, and our neurotransmitter chemicals bubbling. Activity—both mental and physical—is the way to keep *sharp*!

So far in our review of the biology of the brain we've discussed several important points:

- The brain is an intensely complex and ever developing organism.
- People need not experience cognitive loss with age.
- Not every area of the intellect is involved when loss does occur.
- Such loss is very often the result of disuse and disease rather than aging.
- Exercise and use seems to influence brain function in a positive way.

Yet, cognitive decline is a very real concern for many people, and such decline is manifest primarily in one special area of the intellect—that of memory.

MEMORY LOSS AND AGING

One of the most common events in my practice of medicine occurs when a patient complains to me, either personally or through a family member, of a loss of memory. This encounter is poignant. It reflects a fear of the loss of self, the perishing of personal history. My initial approach is to pay attention. Some of these encounters are expressed in very offhand and casual fashions; but I recognize immediately that when the fear of memory loss is expressed, it is a profoundly held terror. The patients in my practice are all sophisticated enough to be asking, implicitly, "Do you think I have Alzheimer's disease?" This challenge is heavy enough; but beyond this is the question, "Am I losing my memory because I am growing old?"

Clearly, my principal responsibility is to address the concern rationally. I try to establish how severe the loss is and whether it is functionally disabling. I illustrate my own faulty memory, recounting my inability to name the last ten patients whom I have examined despite very personal experiences with each. I recount the day I lost my car and called the police to help retrieve it, when I had simply forgotten that I had left it at the bank and walked absentmindedly to the clinic. I illustrate that all of us forget most of what we experience. Your memory bank includes billions of pieces of information; but if you had to recall everything you've ever experienced, your brain would virtually explode. Each of us is, I am sure, exasperated by some useless pieces of memory that still exist and that are annoying by their pettiness or inconsequentiality. "If only I could remember the important things." Generally, people think their memories are worse than they really are.

Having sorted out whether the memory loss of a specific patient is real or imagined, I search for remediable causes. Alcohol and drugs are frequent offenders. Anxiety and depression commonly affect our abilities to recall. Any illness is damaging to memory. Hospitalization itself is enough to distort the orientation of older persons.

It is my job to assess whether any of the above elements are involved with memory change; and, as I discussed previously, whether I feel that Alzheimer's disease is starting to play its dreadful hand. Charles Colton said, "The body and mind, like husband and wife, do not always agree to die together." Some of the great tragedies of my medical experience have occurred when one or the other shows "terminal decline" while the other half of the self is still intact.

Thomas Jefferson wrote in a letter to John Adams, "Bodily decay is gloomy in prospect, but the most abhorrent of all human contemplation is body without mind."

It has been proposed that memory capacity decreases 20 to 40 percent with age, but this sort of assessment is fraught with all of the same reservations which have been made above. We know that the memory lives in the temporal regions of the brain. If you were to place your head in a PET scanner and then concentrate on something you had memorized, your temporal lobes would light up like a Christmas tree because of the intense metabolic activity connected with the task. The neurotransmitter acetylcholine is the specific chemical causing all of the activity.

HOW YOUR MEMORY WORKS

We divide memory into two types: short term and long term. Kenneth Higbee likens the short-term memory to the "in" box of an office desk, while the long-term memory is the file cabinet. Everything that gets into the file cabinet has had to come in through the "in" box, but not everything that gets to the "in" box winds up in the storage file.

Most of us were never taught how to remember. School may have used repetition as a driving force in the attempt, but we know there are better techniques. We tend to learn and remember easiest those things which please us to remember. Then remembering is effortless. The memory chain involves need or interest, attention, and organization. Forgetting occurs when any part of this process is impaired. Kathleen Gose and Gloria Levi, in their fine book *Dealing with Memory Changes as You Grow Older,* cite the three *R*'s of memory: registering, retaining, and retrieving.

The memory, like experience, is always changing. For full functioning, it needs to be in perpetual motion. It is a skill that needs to be practiced daily. Many nursing-home residents are demeaned because they don't know what day of the week it is, or who the president is; but for them, does it matter? Whether it is Thursday or Sunday or November or April, or whether it is Roosevelt or Bush, really doesn't matter.

What matters for them, I think, is whether the coffee is hot, whether the bed is clean, whether the telephone is close at hand. Immediate and basic needs predominate cognitive function. How these primal needs relate to ancillary information becomes pretty inconsequential.

In the Dark Ages, monks used to memorize *in toto* lengthy texts of scriptural or archival content. Now, memory, for all of us, is down-valued. Why remember when we have a machine to do it for us? Medical students now have much less emphasis applied to minute facts and more on analytic process—how to use information rather than how to store it. When we think of ourselves as a species, the eventual effect of this de-emphasis on memory need is not an idle thought. Maybe our temporal lobes will become vestigial.

So, memory is highly dedicated. It depends on energy inputs; and the most obvious cues to intact mental functioning are the senses of sight, hearing, and touch. Much effort must be extended to maintain these cues, including eye care, hearing aids, and simple touching, which keeps us whole and allows us direct contact with other human beings. In addition, we must maintain emotional energies which can very often be drained by physical illness, vicarious illness, grief, and feelings of aloneness. Maintenance of the senses, physical vitality, social and emotional involvement, and simple physical contact all work to keep the memory alive. The past is preserved; the present is assured.

As we age, energies diminish and memory becomes more and more passive. What once was automatic, dependent on gratification of many sorts, may become less so. We then search for external aids.

Several recent books, such as that of Gose and Levi, and *Don't Forget* by Danielle Lapp, can be major tools for helping a person with a faltering memory. Their strategy is clear. What was once automatic must switch to manual. Directed, programmatic efforts need to be applied to those areas of deficit that have become troublesome. If it bothers you that you can no longer remember all of the U.S. presidents in the order in which they served, then you can easily find a textbook which can show you how to retrieve that task. Just like a piano student playing scales or a chess player studying the board, memory is a skill to be practiced.

There are numerous experimental studies which demonstrate that all minds can be taught to remember, but it requires work. In 1979, Ellen Langer and her colleagues at Harvard evaluated the effects of reward on memory performance. Two groups of nursing-home residents were challenged by a set of questions of increasing difficulty (dealing with dates and names). Those who could not complete the tasks were asked to look up the answers and return for another session. Upon requestioning, those with the correct answers were given chips. For one group, the chips could be redeemed for free gifts; for the other, the chips were to be considered a memento of the visit. Three weeks later, both groups were retested and compared to a third, control group. Those who had experienced gift-redemption rewards scored better in tests of short-term memory and exhibited higher "alertness" ratings. Two and one-half years later, the experimenters revealed that the memory training had correlated positively with survival, as only 7 percent of the rewarded group had died, compared to 33 percent and 27 percent of the other two groups.

How successful the effort becomes depends on the ability to muster the conscious effort to do what originally was done by the unconscious. The memory needs its gymnastics, just as does the biceps. For example, until her death at age 94, my mother regularly worked crossword puzzles. She was as bright as a tack.

Six years ago the wire services jammed my office phones. It was the day after the first Reagan-Mondale debate; and the night before Reagan had done terribly, faltering and forgetting. The *Wall Street Journal* had run a morning headline: IS REAGAN TOO OLD TO BE PRESIDENT? My answer was easy and apolitical. I affirmed that some people are too old at 40 to be president, others can be president at 90—that age is irrelevant to intellectual purposes—if the circumstances are right. After all, Casey Stengel's wonderful contorted syntax of his 70s was the same as it had been for fifty years.

If a person is deprived sensually, or economically, or nutritionally, or socially, or emotionally, then that individual is at risk for harm. Order has been threatened; entropy is loose. If, however, a person can retain—maintaining vital function, energetic drive, and purpose; then the mind—the essence of life—goes on. Creativity, emotionality, and intellect are not the exclusive province of young people. The archives are full of old people whose works have enriched and inspired us all. This is the brain that we should all hope for. We should nourish the elements which seem to preserve it.

Our society provides such nourishment for the young. But should education be required only until the age of 18 or 22? I think not. Recent messages from biologic research teach us that the brain—throughout the life span—reacts enormously to challenge. It needs nourishment; it needs energy. Given the most basic encouragement, the organ about which we boast so mightily may really justify our sapient label. If we abort the full potential of our brains, we make less of ourselves. Carl Sagan asserts that understanding is a form of ecstasy.

Is the brain a computer? Is it hard-wired? Is it a mechanical system of wires and sparks? Such a scheme offends. The brain is both mind and soul. From it—in it—are the wellsprings of existence: the Sistine Chapel, Brahms's First, the Gettysburg address, a sense of dignity, dreams, rage, passion, and hope. The brain is all of these. It is a computer, but a wonderfully unique one. Its program is infinitely richer than any machine's; its opportunities and complexities, its past, present, and future are a magnificence. It is the ultimate treasure.

Use it, or lose it.

NINE

WHAT MAN LIVES BY: EXERCISE, DIET, AND SLEEP

It is meaningless and dangerous to encourage
the illusion that health is a birthright of man,
and that freedom from disease can be achieved
by use of drugs and by other medical procedures.
Like political freedom, freedom from disease
should not be regarded as a commodity to be
distributed by science or government. It cannot
be obtained passively from a physician or at
the corner drugstore. Goethe's words apply here,
"What you have inherited from your father you
must earn again or it will not be yours." Health
can be earned only by a disciplined way of life.

Rene Dubos

The pattern becomes clearer. The structure of the human body is glorious when it comes off the production line. The master design is a real prizewinner. Furthermore, during the early years, the body is stimulated, challenged, punished, rewarded, and shaped by the world into which it has been thrust. Additionally we see for the first time that this testing and shaping continues throughout the lifetime of the body. The ultimate effect of this molding process is more determinative of the effectiveness of the human organism than are the details contained within the original blueprint copy. A stream shapes its banks just as the body molds its contours. We become what we do.

Indeed, how long the organism lasts and how much work it can produce are much more dependent on operational activities than on the raw materials from which it was made. Certainly, there are improvements still to be found in original design. Noble and enlightened efforts are appropriate to assure that the stuff of which we are made is the best that our life course might demand. Yet for now, and the foreseeable future, the big gains in how well our bodies meet their world—both in extent and content—are to be found in how we tend this wonderful machine.

What kind of job are we doing? Not so hot.

Many of us run the machine too hard. Most of us don't run the machine hard enough. Many of us throw junk into the machine. Many of us put inappropriate fuel mixtures into the tank. Maintenance procedures by our repair mechanics have improved dramatically; but they are proving very expensive even when not used excessively. New parts cost dearly. Preventive care has been slow to respond. We seem not to give a damn.

Anne Somers, epidemiologist from Rutgers, and one of my real life heroines, has been a passionate proponent for positive health measures as we age. For decades she has championed the notion that we, individually and collectively, are basically in charge of our own health. Her prescription has three simple subcomponents:

1. Prolongation of the period of effective activity, an ability to live independently, and to avoid institutionalization if possible.
2. Minimization of inactivity and discomfort from chronic conditions.
3. Assurance of as little physical and mental distress as possible when illness is terminal.

Anne has no detractors, only admirers; but if we all know she is right, then why don't we do something about it?

I detailed the failures of preventive medicine in chapter 4. The failings fall on both the medical profession and the public. For example, the general physical exam, our periodic checkup, has been consistently maligned because of its cost ineffectiveness. Healthy persons without symptoms simply don't have enough undetected disease that a routine medical examination is likely to uncover. Blood tests, chest X-rays, sigmoidoscopy exams, and electrocardiograms (even those with exercise) have low yields of abnormalities when performed on symptom-free persons. But the detection of disease is not the principal reason for a periodic exam. Far more important is the opportunity to evaluate and counsel about lifestyle issues. The exam sets the agenda for the idealized life strategy. It is health—not disease—driven. How well can you be? Not, How sick are you? How do you function? Not, What illnesses do you have?

Such a viewpoint is not the standard fare of most doctor-patient relationships. It is more intense, and it essentially probes attitudes and behavioral outcomes, testing the physician as well as the patient. For example, how can a physician counsel a patient regarding the abuse of alcohol when the physician himself is an alcoholic?

The ability to influence another person's root behavior is one of the most challenging issues of humanity. And yet, perversely, we seem to adopt destructive modes much more easily than constructive ones. How do we encourage a person with advanced emphysema to stop smoking? How do we get the couch potato with angina to exercise? How do we get the diabetic to watch his diet? The answer to these and a host of kindred behavior-illness–linked situations is infinitely more vital than new insights into the technical details of the pathology of new pills.

I believe ten Nobel Prizes should await that person who can write the guidelines for how we all can help the deteriorating individual take care of himself. I feel personally inexpert, as do all my colleague physicians. But the periodic physical exam is at least the time to try. At this time, an inventory of health habits, emotional state, and reflective attitudes that may predictably bear upon future well-being is drawn up. The exam becomes more powerful when the assessment carries the conviction of confidence. When and if behavioral change is instituted, improvements are not merely likely but certain.

HOW CAN YOU BECOME HEALTHY?

The text is simple when we look for an evaluation of health. First is the implicit recognition that poisons and toxins—junk—cannot be thrown into the machine if it is to continue to work optimally. Beyond this is adherence to the three basic elements of health: exercise, diet, and sleep.

EXERCISE

Of the three tenets of good health, adequate exercise has primacy. First, this is true because most of us eat enough (many eat too much), and most of us get enough sleep. Second, when properly construed, exercise covers up a lot of sinning. Cicero wrote, "Exercise can preserve something of our early strength even into old age." Most of the body serves the purpose of movement.

It is a corollary of our development that each successive advance in one technology has been met by a concomitant decrease in our own energy expenditure. It is certain that early man was extensively active. Survival mandated it. The Agricultural Revolution allowed our ancestors to stay nearer home since the hunting range was compacted to the adjacent field, but farming still required full days of physical activity. The Industrial Age, our last millisecond, has demeaned active labor in productivity. Automation replaces muscle. A century ago, 40 to 50 percent of the energy required to run our factories and farms came from muscle power. Now less than 1 percent does. Over 40 percent of our adult population is completely sedentary; only 20 percent can be termed to be "active" in any substantial way. And a poll conducted by Lou Harris in 1978 found that 62 percent of Americans have no regular exercise. It's becoming worse. In 1986, the National Health Interview Study concluded that 32 percent of our population engaged in regular exercise and physical activity, while 68 percent responded that they were "inactive." The percentages are even worse for our older citizens.

America, particularly, seems infected by inactivity. Our obsessions with the automobile and with television assure our passivity. The vicarious nature of TV sports is numbing and addictive. I sheepishly confess to Thanksgiving and New Year's Day at our home being orgies of TV football games, interrupted only temporarily by other visceral self-indulgences. During my year at the Max Planck Institute in Munich, twenty-five years ago, we lived in the wonderful little suburban town of Grafelfing, where our kids attended the local *volkschule.* Our home was over a mile from the school, and each morning our children joined their schoolmates in a fun-filled walk to school. They clearly enjoyed that part of the day, even during the winter, which was a particularly bitter one in Europe. In the afternoon they hiked home, and occasionally at midday they came home for a brief while. When we returned to America and Bryn Mawr after my fellowship year was up, we were not reestablished more than ten days before our kids were expecting to be driven everywhere—even two blocks.

There has developed a cultural bias against physical work and exercise. Manual labor connotes a low level of enlightened activity. Use of the body and use of the intellect appear mutually exclusive. The battle cry of the sluggards is the one used by Churchill: "Whenever I get the urge to exercise I lie down until it passes away." Even efforts such as the President's Council on Physical Fitness and Sports have been scarcely visible.

After the death of Jim Fixx, Dr. Henry Solomon of New York wrote the book *The Exercise Myth*, in which he proposed that exercise was both an unnatural and dangerous act. He asserted, "Exercise will get you nowhere," and went on to cite the horror stories of runners like Fixx, who died while running. Denial of the manifold benefits of exercise is similar to cigarette companies' refusal to acknowledge anything harmful about smoking. Solomon's most basic assertions simply don't stand up under careful review. For example, Paul Thompson, M.D., good friend and former Stanford colleague, now at Brown University, surveyed the jogging deaths in Rhode Island from 1975 to 1980. Thompson found that there were twelve jogging-related deaths during this time, eleven of which were found to be due to a heart event. Furthermore, he calculated that this translates into one death for 396,000 man hours of jogging. It is true that even this incidence may be higher than those deaths which occur "at rest," but the vast amount of benefit jogging accrues is certainly not offset by these rare and tragic incidents. Focusing attention on these events is like faulting eating, sleeping, or having sex as "dangerous" because so many people die while engaged in these activities.

Others attempting to certify inactivity as the desired state, point to studies of former college and professional athletes in which longevity is not assured—in fact, it seems to be foreshortened in these early-life exercisers. Nevertheless, follow-up of these groups reveals that physical activity has rarely been sustained through midlife, and that bad health habits often accumulate more readily with ensuing inactivity. What we can learn from this example is that early life activity confers no immunity to later life problems.

Darwin wasn't wrong. The fittest will survive. I am willing to bet Dr. Solomon, whatever amount he wishes, that I can choose a group of a hundred "fit" persons who will outlive and outperform any group of "unfit" persons he may select. Any time. Any place.

However, chest thumping isn't enough. It is both startling and embarrassing to the scientific community that to this day we don't have the ultimate, conclusively proven program for the idealized lifelong exercise program—just as we don't have all the answers regarding nutrition and sleep. Science, particularly American science, has been slow to inquire into the nuts and bolts of exercise. Europeans, particularly Scandinavians, have had it all over us in their research efforts into the nature of this vital component of our lives. For example, I learned nothing about exercise in medical school. It is not mentioned in most of the leading medical textbooks today. Unquestionably one of the major reasons why the East Germans have done so remarkably well in Olympic competition has been their strenuous embrace of a rigidly scientific approach to physical performance characteristics. Their master exercise laboratory in Leipzig maintains exhaustive inventories on performance characteristics of thousands of their athletes. When talent is identified in a youngster, he or she is nurtured, trained, and tested, like an astronaut. Our American programs, by contrast, are a collection of individual systems with little cooperative development or communication.

Does Exercise Extend Life?

The answer to such a question is far from simple. When Charles Goodrick, of the National Institute on Aging, took a group of laboratory rats and allowed them *at libitum* exercise, they outlived their sedentary mates by 15 percent. How can we explain such an increase? Was it because the inactive rats were artificially constrained from activity, and so were, in effect, "zoo animals"? Or was the life extension real? The problems encountered when answering these basic questions become much more complex when we extrapolate the model to humans. And yet, many still try.

Ralph Paffenbarger, another Stanford colleague and outstanding ultramarathoner, is the major worker in an ongoing study of 16,936 Harvard alumni men, aged 37 to 76, which is examining the effects of exercise on longevity in humans. In the March 6, 1986, issue of the *Journal of the American Medical Association* he reported that those graduates who spent over 2,000 calories per week in active activity could be expected to live 2.15 years longer than those without this exertion. Thus, it appears that for every hour spent exercising, two to three hours of life were gained. The benefits were most apparent after the age of 70.

For the Paffenbarger study, caloric expenditure on exercise was determined by asking how many flights of stairs were climbed per day, how many blocks were walked, and what other activities were pursued (including type, duration, and intensity). Numerous other variables were assessed as well, including heredity. When the data were disentangled by elaborate statistical maneuvers, the JAMA report concluded, "Death rates were 1/4 to 1/3 lower among alumni expending 2,000 or more calories during exercise per week than among those less active." Most of the protection seemed to derive from circulatory and respiratory benefits.

In 1989, Steven Blair and his colleagues at the Cooper Aerobics Institute in Dallas reported a very important finding. They reviewed over 13,000 persons who had visited their institute for a health inventory. They followed the group for 8 years. When they divided the 13,000 according to their fitness rank they observed a straight line relationship between "all cause mortality" and fitness state when first evaluated. Two other central points were made. First, the greatest proportional longevity gain seemed to be between those who did nothing (the least fit) and those who did a little. Progressively better fitness led to progressively increasing life spans, but at a lesser increment than that between "none" and "a little."

Second, Blair observed that the protective effect of physical fitness on mortality rates become steadily greater the older the groups. In other words, fitness becomes more important to survival the older we become. This should be intuitively apparent since mortality in the 30's and 40's is generally from catastrophic events and little related to fitness state, but as we age physical conditioning becomes increasingly predictive of survival.

In 1965 the Human Population Laboratory in Berkeley initiated a major ongoing study of 6,928 adults in Alameda, California. Dr. Lester Breslow, dean of UCLA's School of Public Health, has been a major worker in this study which focuses on the following seven health habits: no smoking, regular physical exercise, moderate or no alcohol consumption, seven to eight hours of sleep per day, proper weight, regular breakfast, and no midmeal snacking. The results have been most interesting.

For example, on average, a man aged 45 who practiced zero to three of the seven beneficial health habits could expect to live 21.6 more years, where a similar man practicing six or seven of the habits could expect 39.1 more years of life. The category "often active in sports" was the single best predictor of longevity of study participants. The biggest percentage gain, again, was between those who did nothing and those who had a little exercise. It would appear that inactivity is lethal, and that even a little bit of physical exercise is a strong enough potion to ward off the multiple deteriorations that accompany a life sluggishly lived.

Another study conducted by the American Cancer Society and involving 1,064,000 subjects (4,600 of whom were over the age of 85) showed that physical exercise was powerfully correlated with longevity. And a major study by the National Institutes of Health, the Multiple Risk Factor Intervention Trial (MRFIT), looked at 12,138 middle-aged men and found that leisure time activity not only cut down on coronary disease but reduced overall mortality as well. Inactivity was labeled as a major risk factor for premature mortality in a study of 2,779 middle-aged Los Angeles firemen and policemen. Additional studies from Holland and eastern Finland confirm the protective effects of physical exercise.

Exercise physiologist William Haskell has conducted an extensive search of the medical literature and concluded that 150 exercise calories per day (a 15-minute jog) is the lowest amount which can be shown to provide some benefit. There is a step-wise progression of benefit up to 400 calories per day (a 40-minute jog), above which further benefits are not obvious.

It seems likely, therefore, that there now emerges the first verifiable evidence that a life actively lived will be longer. But longer is not enough. We must ask ourselves, "how" is the longer? Sidney Katz of Providence, Rhode Island, coined the term "active life expectancy" to denote the years of quality life—the years in which we are free-living, functionally effective, and autonomous. He has estimated that individuals aged 65 to 70 have an additional 10 years of active life expectancy—or 60 percent of the total life expectancy. At 85 years of age, however, there are only 2.9 years of active life expectancy, compared with 7.3 years of total life remaining, equaling 40 percent. It appears, therefore, that as we age, the proportion of active life expectancy—the good life—diminishes. However, the "inactive" life expectancy increases as we age. This is not a design for which we would wish. Nevertheless, it seems that this is precisely what we are getting.

The good news is that we also have evidence that an exercise program *expands* our active and decreases our inactive life expectancy. Thus, exercise extends not only your life but its quality as well.

Earlier I discussed the hosts of evidences that physical exercise exerts beneficial effects on virtually every bodily function. The list of credits which exercise exhibits is great: body weight, blood pressure, HDL cholesterol (the beneficial kind), blood clotting, respiratory function, heart muscle strength, muscle mass, bone density, obesity, intestinal function, sexual capacity, glucose tolerance, immunologic capacity, and behavioral characteristics such as mood, cognition, and memory.

A recent survey showed 11,000 articles on the effect of exercise on mental health alone. One study showed that in a group of older subjects, a fifteen-minute walk was "a more effective tranquilizer than meprobamate" (a commonly used "downer" drug). Exercise confers a quality of sangfroid —imperturbability, equanimity, and lack of urgency. Action allays anxiety. Exercise is the balance wheel to tension.

Exercise and Cancer

The issue remains: Does exercise protect a person from cancer? When I ask my colleague Ralph Paffenbarger about this, he dodges the question. He is unsure. And yet, there are reasons to think that maybe exercise *ought* to prevent this, our most dread disease. There are a number of suggestive works which indicate that physical activity activates the immune system, and it is certain that the immune system is intimately connected with resistance to cancer. But maybe exercise protects against cancer merely by the associated behavior characteristics. Certainly joggers' incidence of lung cancer is very low; but this is due to the fact that virtually no joggers smoke, and not to any intrinsic resistance afforded by the exercise.

We have other evidences. Steven Blair reviewed the death reports of 248,000 veterans and found that deaths from cancer of the colon and kidney, brain tumors, and leukemia were less in those who were physically active. Brian Henderson, professor of preventive medicine at the University of Southern California, and Ray Frisch, associate professor of public health at Harvard, separately published reports which indicated that young women who had engaged in active sports suffered less from cancer of the breast and reproductive organs later in life than did their inactive schoolmates. This effect could possibly be explained by the depressant effect of heavy exercise on estrogen production in early life, and a consequent hypothetical protective effect thereby. Similarly, cancer of the colon may be retarded by the salutary effect that exercise has on bowel function, not necessarily by a direct protective effect of exercise on malignant predisposition. But by whatever mechanism, by whatever association, physical exercise is found to lessen the chance of developing cancer. As with the textbook collection of other benefits noted above, the list of credentials which accrues to an active lifestyle lengthens steadily and impressively. The cynics and nay-sayers have less of a platform upon which to stand.

Exercise and Heart Disease

Several years ago Paul Dudley White, eminent cardiologist from Boston, was labeled a kook when he embraced exercise as a major therapy for heart disease. I recall recoiling with worry when I heard that White had urged then President Eisenhower to resume golf after the leader's much publicized heart attack. The medical dogma, just twenty-five years ago, was that heart trouble mandated weeks, to months, to a lifetime of inactivity. That myth is now securely exploded. Each day I exhort my cardiac patients to work their hearts, sweat, ventilate, percolate. Don't sit. The heart is a muscle, it needs to squeeze. A heart patient when in bed is at high risk.

My experience with Frank is typical. Frank is a 56-year-old executive who approached me two years ago for a physical exam. Although he felt fine, his wife had been after him to have a checkup, as he hadn't had one in nearly ten years. The history taking and physical examination revealed nothing of startling relevance; but when Frank took the exercise electrocardiogram on the treadmill, the technician stopped him at a very low workload because of a markedly abnormal pattern in the EKG tracing. The pattern was so alarming that I referred him to one of my colleagues in the cardiology department. Within the week Frank had open-heart surgery and his badly corroded coronary arteries were bypassed.

Now that might be the end of the story, but it isn't. Within a few weeks after discharge from the hospital, Frank joined the exercise class at our nearby YMCA and began a walking/jogging program. He had previously done no physical exercise. None. His conditioning improved over the months until now he is running 10K races with his children. He probably would have saved himself and the medical system a great deal of money and anxiety had he seen this light thirty years before. My Stanford colleague Dr. Thomas Raffin has coined the term "The Bruce Jenner Protocol" for patients in the intensive care unit. By invoking this activist set of orders, these sickest of patients are constantly primed toward recovery.

It used to be that if a patient died while jogging, the physician was held culpable for being overly zealous in prescribing activity. I hope that the day is not far off when a physician will be held for malpractice for allowing a patient to die in bed. We should develop a rating system for physicians whose patients die on their feet rather than in bed. I know whom I would patronize.

What Kind of Exercise?

If the standards are shifting, as they certainly are, in all realms of medical endeavor, we look for guidelines as to the types of exercise to be prescribed, as well as to the amount and the intensity. What does an exercise prescription look like? What is the Recommended Daily Allowance (RDA) for exercise? During the initial visit with any patient, I ask whether he or she exercises. Frequently a look of consternation appears on the face, followed by an appearance of relief and an answer like, "Oh yes, Doc, I bowl." Bowling is picking up a ball, taking four steps, and rolling that ball down an alley. How often do bowlers sweat? I exert virtually the same amount of energy when scrubbing my teeth, but I don't consider that exercise. Such activity, while commendable in many respects, is not real exercise. It is recreative, and as such is the first of three purposes for which exercise is generally considered:

1. recreation
2. vanity
3. cardiovascular conditioning

1. Recreation. Recreation is wonderful, to be pursued as a break in the mainstream activity of a busy life. However, many recreational exercises have become totally mechanized. The prime example is golf. This hurts me personally, as I love the game. Now after a couple of practice swings, and the first one that counts, a golfer walks a few steps to the golf cart, drives down the macadam path toward the next shot, takes a couple more pivots, swings, goes back to the cart, and on and on around the course. Often one is not even allowed to walk! You can't even rent the cart and leave it at the first tee! I know; I've tried! This technique serves to speed up the process, which is to the discredit of the game. For me, the joy of golf is in the opportunity to leave machines and time behind in a lovely setting of grass and water—played while carrying my own bag, and feeling a pleasant fatigue at the end of the round. The faster tempo of the game—the higher costs involved—would be abhorrent to the original Scot; but it is an expression of contemporary exercise, a relic of the real.

2. Vanity. The second way to consider exercise is as a body-building vanity. In this group are the weight lifters and body builders. Their aim is to make muscle and build strength. To me, such bodies are grotesque—as unsettling as the opposite extreme. Strength and health are not synonymous. I delight in stories such as that involving Mr. Santa Cruz, California, who won the local body-building championship, applied for a job as a fireman, and flunked the physical examination. Such a "muscle man" may be able to pick up the city block, but he can't run around it. A person may be as strong as a bull and yet be in poor physical condition.

3. *Cardiovascular conditioning.* The third, and to me correct, purpose of exercise is cardiovascular conditioning. In this type of activity, the heart, lungs, blood vessels, blood cells, muscles, tendons, and bones are meshed to their highest working efficiency. Oxygen transport is augmented, waste elimination is facilitated, and nutrient supply is maximized. Such an idealized exercise program is best seen in the endurance athlete, the cross country skier, the marathoner, or the long distance swimmer. In each of these activities the body can go on and on, at high performance levels for long periods without failing.

How Much Exercise?

Endurance exercise that confers cardiovascular conditioning, that is the basic prescription—but how much? Per Olaf Astrand of the Karolinska Institute in Stockholm established that in order to obtain a conditioning effect, a person must exercise three times a week for half an hour per session at a consistent intensity. One session is better than none, two is better than one, and three is still better than two. After three times a week, the gain in cardiovascular benefit, while still increasing, becomes progressively less. Additionally, when we start to exercise five, six, or seven times a week, orthopedic injuries become more of a problem. Therefore, there is a window of optimal frequency—three or four times each week, at which time the gain is near maximal while the injury risk is minor. More often becomes a threat to well-being—we wind ourselves too tightly.

It is intriguing to observe this three-times-per-week optimal frequency for physical conditioning and wonder why it is imprinted on our biology. I propose that it is more than coincidence that the optimal hunting frequency for hunter-gatherer populations is also three times per week. Such a schedule makes sense in terms of chase and reward. For millions of years we probably hunted three times a week, and this activity pattern has come down to us as a functionally ideal exercise habit.

Intensity of Exercise

If we clearly know the frequency, what of the optimal intensity of exercise? Once again Astrand teaches us that in order for the exercise to benefit us, we must exert ourselves—stretch ourselves, work ourselves. The textbooks state that in order for us to attain fitness we need to exercise at 70 percent of our maximum. What does this mean? How is it determined? One handle is to use your pulse rate. Like other vital functions, there is a maximum number of times your heart can beat per minute. If I run around the block once, my pulse rate goes up from 60 to 110 beats per minute. One more time and it is 130; another time around and it moves up to 160 beats per minute. After that, my pulse will remain virtually constant—no matter how many times I circle the block. This is the maximum pulse rate. It is linked to age, and it falls progressively as we age. An indirect predictor of maximum pulse rate is 220 minus your age. For example:

Age 60 Max. Pulse Rate = 220–60 or 160 beats per min.
Age 75 Max. Pulse Rate = 220–75 or 145 beats per min.

The exercise prescription then aims at 70 percent of the predicted maximums. So, for the 60-year-old, 160 beats per minute × 70 percent equals a pulse rate of 112, while exercise for a 75-year-old should bring about a pulse rate of 101 beats per minute (145 × 70 percent = 101).

Exercise should be enough to put a stretch on the organism, but not so much as to overburden. In the clinical sense this can be seen when you can provoke a sweat in a cool environment—and still be able to talk while doing it. It used to be that our work experiences provided this necessary exertion. We came home to rest. Now, we must come home to exercise.

What Types of Exercise Are Best?

The types of exercise which are best suited for aerobic training are those which are characterized by two words: rhythmic and sustained. Remember, three half-hour periods per week of a little sweat and a little conversation. What forms of exercise come to mind? Jogging, rapid walking, swimming, bicycling, rowing, calisthenics, square dancing, and (if you do it right) sex. In fact, sex is usually accompanied by pulse rates around 120, similar to climbing several flights of stairs or arguing. At orgasm, the pulse may reach 150. Keep this in mind: you should be in good shape to have sex. Foreplay is encouraged.

Other forms of exercise such as tennis, basketball, softball, and squash qualify if they are played in a rhythmic, sustained fashion. Some persons play tennis in a bouncing, flowing fashion; others play abruptly with sudden dashes.

The benefit from the activity spills over each domain of living. The documentation of this fitness is harder to prove. The blood pressure and the cholesterol levels are remote markers of physical conditioning. The determination of the VO_2 max (discussed in chapter six) is the best test, but it is expensive, rarely available except in research labs, and simply inappropriate for a general fitness guide. Instead, one may use the resting pulse rate on first waking in the morning as a pretty good fitness estimate. Fit persons often have resting pulse rates below 50, indicating a very efficient heart pump.

Certainly performance declines as we age, and this can be seen as an end product of entropic decay. Marathon age records lengthen over time. In 1971, Lars Bottiger published a paper in *Acta Medica Scandinavica* in which he assessed the age performance of 7,625 competitors in the extremely tough 85k cross-country ski race, Vasaloppet. The best performance, Bottiger reported, was at age 31 with a linear drop-off until age 66 (that of the oldest athlete to finish the race). Interestingly, he found that this drop-off in performance corresponded exactly with that of maximal oxygen consumption (a biologic measurement), just as did the earnings of Swedish lumberjacks who were paid per piece of wood cut (a financial estimate.) A central point to be asserted again is that it is never too late to start. An unfit person of 70, 80, 90, or whatever, is wonderfully served by starting. The first step is the hardest—and the most important.

Such an inevitable decline in performance is daunting if a person is possessed by competitive nature. I am a friend and immense admirer of Dr. George Sheehan, the spiritual guru of us runners. George writes beautifully of the spiritual message which physical fitness carries; but he does so always with the message of the winner, and being faster. This is understandable when one recognizes that he once was a high school half-mile runner and was driven by the competitive edge which still occupies him fifty years later. Vince Lombardi said, "Winning may not be everything, but losing is nothing." To me this is wrong. I feel that exercise should be done for the simple joy and health yields which it provides.

The Olympic creed of *"Altius. Citius. Fortius.*—Highest. Fastest. Strongest.*"*—impels us to compete, to risk at the outermost margin of performance. Setting such a standard is intimidating and inhibiting for most of us. We are not talking about the Olympics or even organized competition; we're talking about basic human needs.

I feel that exercise should be divorced from time. My own life's work is organized into fifteen-minute increments; and so when I run, I don't want to perform with reference to what a watch tells me. Rather, I want to exercise in response to what my body feels. Some days I feel like a gazelle and want to kick up my heels. Other days I feel like I have on army boots. I don't want a watch to dictate what I should do. Who cares anyway? Whether it takes fifteen, twenty, twenty-five, or forty-five minutes to travel three miles will not be written on any cosmic scroll. Records are not the issue. Not winning is not un-American. Who cares?

How does all of this translate into my daily activities as a practicing doctor? Virtually all of us can and should be more active. The question then arises, How to do it? It is commonly stated, "Start to exercise; but before you do, see your doctor." It is hard to quarrel with the folk wisdom that seems intrinsic to this platitude, but the necessity of seeing a doctor before starting exercise poses a barrier that I feel is unnecessary. The Canadian government has addressed this dilemma with a Fit-Kit containing a simple questionnaire which one may consult before entering any fitness program. The Canadian model suggests that you should consult a physician if you have any of the following elements in your medical history: heart trouble, chest pain, dizziness, high blood pressure, joint pain, or if you are age 65 or older. I am not at all convinced of the last qualification. Innumerable research reports indicate the general safety of a program of physical exercise in older persons. A resting electrocardiogram is of virtually no screening benefit, and even an exercise electrocardiogram has only a 1:10,000 chance of identifying a potential problem in an asymptomatic person. Therefore, I do not insist on a complete physical examination before prescribing exercise.

The exact prescription must be tailored to fit the individual. Certainly jogging isn't for everybody, nor is swimming, nor biking, and so on. Walking comes closest to the most available form of exercise. It is cheap, safe, and requires no equipment. I frequently encourage patients to purchase Dr. Kenneth Cooper's simple paperback book *Aerobics*, which gives a cookbook approach to initiating an exercise program. Step by step the reader is introduced to exercises (such as walking, jogging, and others) and told how to progress as conditioning is conferred.

But some persons say, "I don't want to lose it, but it hurts too much to use it." This reality must be confronted. The ability to exercise depends to a great extent on the structural and functional integrity of the bone and muscle system devoted to that exercise. I have a friend with pronounced bow legs; despite his desire to run, he simply can't. Other persons have foot problems, or vision problems. Clearly, some alternative form of exercise must be found which fits. But the exercise cannot be only a momentary exuberance; it must be a committed lifestyle, as much a part of the day as is brushing your teeth or going to the bathroom. If a Wednesday, a Friday, or a Sunday goes by without my having run, I feel like I have a hangover, or like I am incompletely dressed. I am way out of sorts. Thus, I have been trained and conditioned by years of committed exercise.

Such remarks are not intended as a boast, for I am in no way a gifted athlete. In high school, college, and medical school I was an eager player of basketball, squash, softball, golf, and touch football (my favorite). I never ran for the sake of running. When I was 40, my dad died and I was devastated—an only child of a wonderful dreamer physician father who was alpha and omega to me. In my grief I started to run, almost as a reflex; and it was healing. Within a few months I was running long distances and even aspired to run the Boston Marathon.

I am enough of a Walter Mitty type to indulge my sports fantasies. George Plimpton makes me jealous. Twenty years ago the only world-class sporting event open to the public at large was the Boston Marathon. I set my cap for this goal; and just as I had committed myself to it, the Boston Athletic Association, sponsors of the event, decreed that only "genuine runners" of proven athletic ability were to be granted entrance. This certainly wasn't I. I was crestfallen. Wondrously, there was born at the same moment a new organization, the American Medical Joggers Association. Their annual meeting was and is held yearly in Boston just before the Boston Marathon, and *their* marathon is run over the same course at the same time as the main event. I hastened to enlist and to attend the scientific session.

The thrill of being part of the congregation in the Hopkinton gym on Patriot's Day was immense. Two thousand runners and a few odd doctors on their way to Boston. My run was torture—in preparing for this race, I had only run 22 miles maximum. The marathon took me 5 hours. At 2 hours and 15 minutes into my run, I was in Wellesley—the winner had already finished in downtown Boston. Through most of the race I was cursing myself for having ever gotten involved in such an unlikely adventure; but when I saw Commonwealth Avenue, I felt an incredible surge of spirit. I sprinted down the last incline—in rapture. The fact that the grandstands had already been dismantled and the crowds were long gone was irrelevant. Further, 5 minutes after the race was run, I was committed to returning the next year. Much like having a baby, I am told.

I have run a marathon a year for 20 years—in Honolulu, Athens, and Boston six times, but mostly around San Francisco. Last April, I finished the San Francisco Marathon in 4 hours and 15 minutes—45 minutes faster than my first one, 20 years earlier. I figure that if I can improve my time 45 minutes every 20 years, by the time I am 90 I will be Olympic caliber.

I now run 3 miles Wednesday and Friday mornings at 6 o'clock and 15 miles on Sunday. I probably am in the best shape of my life.

My running is now an integral part of me. It is a good feeling to know that I am capable of running a long distance, having a glass of juice, and then going to work. I like to run by myself, as a time of creativity—a time to be alone and think freely. It also holds occasional moments of transcendence, like the time in Yosemite Valley when I took a right and headed directly toward El Capitan, framed by the dark pines and brilliantly lit by the morning sun. I felt for a while like I was running right into the pearly gates themselves—what a high! My endorphins were streaming.

For me, exercise is the sacrament of the commitment to living life fully. Dr. Richard Cabot, of Harvard Medical School, wrote in his book *What Men Live By*, "We are, many of us, creatures who can be purified only by motion, as the running stream drops out its pollutants, when its currents grow swift, but get defiled as soon as it stagnates in the shallow end."

DIET

The industrial consultant is convinced; our machine will run longer and better if it is used and not left to idle. Yet, if the machine is self-destructing at too early a time, could it be because of a bad fuel mix, or too little, or too much? This is, of course, the question placed to nutritional scientists. Despite the thousands of volumes and billions of dollars, francs, and yen which have been dedicated to finding out the best fuel mix in amount and type—the simple truth is that our insights are still fragmentary; and many of our practices are clearly wrong.

The science of nutrition is biochemistry. The elaborate maps of biochemical reactions detail the myriad syntheses and combustions which characterize the operation of our engines. Despite its brilliant advances, biochemistry is still an infant science. The maps still have many obscure spots which invite future exploration.

I realized early in my training how central biochemistry was to become in my own medical career. I wrote my honors thesis at Williams College on arteriosclerosis, which at that time (and still today) is felt by many experts to be a condition due basically to faulty nutrition. After medical school and house officership, I took three additional years of fellowship training in biochemistry at Berkeley and at Munich. In the latter, I had the opportunity to work in the laboratory with Professor Feodor Lynen, who was to win the Nobel Prize the year after I left. These were years of great intellectual excitement and growth. My researches were devoted largely to the control mechanisms of fat and cholesterol synthesis. The clinical relevance was, of course, immediate to our two major nutritional disorders, obesity and elevated body cholesterol levels.

My sense of wonder at the beauty of our body's ability to take the foodstuffs from our dining room tables and shape them to our complex purposes is profound. A grape helps me frame a new idea. Amazing! A lamb chop fuels the morning jog. Wonderful! A glass of milk becomes part of my femur. Terrific! These phenomena become even more wonderful when one considers the diversity of diets available to populations throughout our world, and the many uses we ask our food to fulfill.

Through Father's friendship with Clive McCay I was aware early of the startling effect which nutritional alteration had on aging in rats. This set of experiments done at Ithaca forty years ago remains one of the cornerstones of age research.

In 1965 my research training helped me obtain a National Institutes of Health grant, the title of which was, "The Effect of Diet on Metabolism of Fat in Man." Over the next ten years our research group detailed the results of our investigations in more than a hundred scientific papers in the best journals. The rigor demanded of such testing required the questioning of much dietary dogma. "Eat a good breakfast," "three square meals a day," "never snack," "starvation is harmful." These and other folk wisdoms were reviewed and found wanting. The mythology of nutrition is immense, and confounded by culturally acquired eating habits and prejudices. Our hunter-gatherer ancestors certainly didn't live by these rules; they survived —marginally, true, but survived—on erratic rations of whatever their ingenuity could conceive and their legs could catch. Nutritional supply, survival, and mobility were tightly linked. Today we have uncoupled this relationship.

What Is the Right Diet?

What is the RDA for everything we put into our mouths? The totally confounding variable in giving the correct answer to this question is, "For what state of activity?" The correct, best, appropriate, full diet for a person who is physically active is much different from that which is best, appropriate, etc., for the inactive twentieth-century person. Zoo animals must be fed very carefully. Therefore, any simple, flat assertion about the "proper diet," without this qualification, has an inappropriate illusion of certainty about it. We are not only what we eat—but what we do.

As noted earlier, the two malnutritions of our time are obesity and elevated blood cholesterol values. As Denis Diderot wrote, "Doctors are always working to preserve our health and the cooks to destroy it, but the latter are more often successful." The central role of calorie ingestion on the control of body weight is unchallenged. The ridiculous book *Calories Don't Count* of twenty years ago was hooted down within months. Of course calories count, just as gas in the fuel tank counts. Calories build and run our machines. Insufficient calories cause us to run down; that observation has been vividly demonstrated. But what of excess calories? Our machine doesn't reject them as would an automobile; instead, we store them, to use during periods of caloric lack as were common during our aboriginal days. Twenty years ago I wrote a paper for the *Annals of Internal Medicine* entitled "Metabolic Consequences of Obesity," which pointed out the interesting (to me, at least) parallel between the fed, fat person and the lean, starving person. It appears that the fat person is poised and ready for starvation—probably as an evolutionary relic.

Were a fat person and I shipwrecked without food for several months, he or she would outlive me by a substantial margin. This is because—all other things being equal—obesity provides an onboard energy reserve. However, being fat is a survival advantage *only* under such extraordinary circumstances. By and large, extra weight is a burden and a liability.

While obesity certainly represents caloric excess, it can also be regarded as precocious aging in that a fat person falls heir to the multiple degenerative conditions seen as we age—but at an earlier time in life. For example, hypertension, arthritis, and diabetes are accompaniments of obesity. Most studies show that fat people don't live as long. Still, some authorities, most notably Ruben Andres, dispute the simplicity of this contention. If a fat person can avoid, with good luck, the morbid accompaniment of obesity, then he or she may do all right. Until her death my own mother was forty pounds overweight. Her constant bark to me was, "How come I'm doing so well if I haven't done all the good things you advocate?"

My personal insight is that her obesity served her well. She somehow escaped the common side effects of excess weight. Unfortunately, we don't understand this phenomenon—most fat persons have a collection of ailments. To assume that you will be one of the "lucky surviving obese" is a foolish risk. Furthermore, the fact that my mother was able to keep her mobility intact (for example, she could climb stairs quickly until the end) means that, despite the lack of a real identified exercise program, she had been doing a lot of exercise merely by moving her bulk around. Early on in our researches we found that many fat people are really quite fit, able to move a lot of oxygen due to the extra burden which any physical activity holds for them. Obviously, if they retreat to the couch, as is the usual case, all bets are off. For the lean among us, many seek to augment the benefits of physical exercise by carrying lead weights in our hands, or tying them on our legs to increase the workload.

Obesity results from extra calories, but is this the result of too much intake or insufficient expenditure? In chapter 6 I cited the central experiments done by Jean Mayer in which he confined mice to small quarters and found that they became obese as their "appestat" did not reset downward to reflect their inactivity. In another work, Mayer took movies of fat and lean children while they played tennis at summer camp. During each hour of tennis, the lean kids were in motion half of the time, whereas the fat youngsters moved only a third as much. In other words, if a ball were hit several yards to either side of the thin child, he or she would sprint for it, whereas the fat child would watch it sail by. This movement deficit could be calculated to hundreds of calories and was of sufficient degree to account for the obesity.

How Much Is Just Enough?

Now we may ask, How many calories do we need? The response must be, For what exercise state? If we are inactive, then calories must be curtailed; if we are active, the body weight self-corrects.

How much should you weigh? The common answer is, "What you weighed when you were 25 years old." This leaves too much room for error. More precisely, you are often referred to a set of height-weight charts; but I find these equally unhelpful. My response to the "How much should I weigh?" question is simple: "You should weigh what you *know* you should weigh." The place to look at "how much" is in the mirror—not in a book. A proper weight is intuitive. It doesn't need a lot of fancy guidelines. You ought to weigh what you ought to weigh, and no one need tell you when you're over the mark.

Cholesterol

The cholesterol story, although separate from obesity, nonetheless emerges with a similar conclusion. Cholesterol has become a theme of our age, memorialized from Nobel awards to *New Yorker* cartoons. It dominates cocktail party talk and bestseller lists. How did we ever get along before we knew there was such a thing?

What is cholesterol anyway? For most of us it is a waxy goo that clogs up our pipes and chokes them off. When the pipes shut, the machine stops. One gets the impression that if only cholesterol would go away, we could all live happily ever after on our fried eggs and bacon.

But wait a minute. Cholesterol is good for you. You need it. It contributes greatly to your good functioning, and nearly every tissue in your body has the capacity to make cholesterol from simpler materials.

Fundamentally, cholesterol serves you by acting as a facilitator of fat transport. Although cholesterol itself is a form of fat, it is a special sort—the chemistry of which allows it to solubilize the other fats which you need for energy purposes. Cholesterol acts as a transport vehicle for the other fats by coupling with them both in the bloodstream and across cell boundaries. Fat is, after all, water insoluble. And as you are a watery machine, so fat needs help working its way through your body. This is why cholesterol facilitates.

Cholesterol also serves as the parent compound from which bile is manufactured. The liver, your main cholesterol factory, sits beneath the diaphragm and in its hollow contains the sac called the gallbladder—the purpose of which is to store bile. As you eat a fatty meal, the gallbladder receives that message and squirts some bile down its tube into the intestine, where the bile helps to emulsify fat. Thus you are able to absorb it. The more fat you eat—the more bile you need to solubilize it—the more cholesterol your liver makes. As your body has more fat to move, it synthesizes more cholesterol to help move it. And so the cycle continues.

This device, which provides cholesterol to carry fat, works wonderfully throughout the animal kingdom. It starts to cause mischief only when there is too much to do. When there is too much fat, then too much cholesterol is made for the body to handle. This is particularly true, it seems, in the human body. Other animals are much more resistant than are we to heavy fat and cholesterol burdens. They get rid of it, much more efficiently; but our disposal mechanisms aren't very efficient. Hence the problems.

Too Much Cholesterol? What To Do?

Call the doctor. The machine is broken. Bag in hand, the doc sees the problem, but what to do? Pills, or diet, or replace either the pipe or the pump? But what if the whole system is plugged up? Or what if the replacement pipe falls heir to the same problems as did the original? The docs haven't been very effective; and in my opinion, we never will be. This is because we don't do well when confronted with total system failure. Our patch-and-mend repair capacity is pretty well confined to localized problems. But hardening of the arteries applies to the whole system.

Yet, deaths from clogged pipes are going down. Is this due to medicine's efforts or to preventive care? Living within their own environments, primitive people don't have clogged pipes; when they move to the big city, they do. Is this because of too much fat in the diet? Partly. But there are three very different population groups which have been rigorously studied and which have taught us a lot on this subject. They are: the Swiss farmer, who eats primarily cheese; the Masai of East Africa, who eat milk and cattle; and the American Marine recruit, who seems to eat whatever fatty foods present themselves. Individuals in each of these groups have a lot of fat in their diets; but they all have low amounts of cholesterol in their blood. How can this be? Simple. As soon as these groups eat the fat, it is burned for energy purposes and consequently doesn't get laid down for storage. When the inactive person eats fat, it sediments—and clogs.

"Good" Cholesterol

Recently we have learned that one part of the blood cholesterol is not bad for us. This is the HDL (high density lipoprotein) cholesterol. The higher it is, the *less* are our chances of a heart attack. My old friend Dr. Peter Wood discovered that running exercise raises the "good" HDL cholesterol. It is likely that the HDL portion of the cholesterol is packaged in such a way that it is easily excreted—it is on its way out of the system, so it cannot plug anything up.

So, again, like the obesity story, we conclude that exercise covers up a lot of sinning. The body harmonics work again when the machine is run at its originally programmed speed and not allowed to rest in idle.

Both body fat and body cholesterol levels go up as we age, until a point at which most older persons have less. This is probably due to the fact that those with high levels die off before they can get old! But does aging, of itself, provoke nutritional change? Is there a different set of RDAs for older persons?

What Should You Eat
When You Are Old?

How many calories an older person needs depends upon how much fuel is needed to run the machine and tend its repair. If the body shrinks, it needs less fuel; but if kept fully vigorous, caloric need will remain largely unchanged with the passage of time. The types of food similarly mimic those of younger persons—a balanced diet for an older person is the same as a balanced diet for a younger person.

Having laid such groundwork, I must state that certainly there are a host of changes in older persons which may conspire to cause fuel problems. Every survey of elderly people's nutritional status has concluded that their incidence of deficiencies is much higher than are those in younger persons. Rarely are the deficiencies so profound as to cause outright disease; but they are usually subliminal, of sufficient severity as to cause diminished immune responses, slower wound healing, and more fragile tissues.

The question of what to eat must first consider the question of taste and smell. Both capacities are different in older persons. As acuity of aroma and pungency of taste are dulled, appetite and food appeal may decrease.

Additionally, dental problems abound. It is hard to eat what we cannot chew. Intestinal absorbing abilities change. Depression has real nutritional cost. A good appetite is inconsistent with "the blues." Immobility limits food choices, as do economic constraints. Social isolation and institutionalization both provoke dietary challenges. It therefore grows more difficult to maintain the adequacy of diet (fuel supply) as we age. We are more at risk for system failure.

I recently had the following experience with a patient I'll call Nancy.

She and her husband had been married for sixty-one years. He fell and broke his hip and died shortly thereafter. Nancy was devastated. Her children noted that she had virtually stopped eating and was losing a lot of weight. One of her grandchildren had the inspired idea to buy Nancy a dog. The puppy gave renewed companionship and meaning to her life. Nancy started to eat again and her frailty eased off.

Very often, intestinal intolerance and distaste lead to decreased dairy product intake—and the resultant calcium lack. The careful doctor will ask his older patient with diarrhea whether the loose bowels accompany milk or its derivatives. If they do, it is then wise to go on a milk-free diet for two weeks to see if the diarrhea arrests. If milk intolerance is indicated, there are products available which can substitute for the enzymes which are deficient in the intestines, so that the treated milk does not cause diarrhea. More convenient, concentrated foodstuffs and immobility both lead to constipation, the partial response to which should be increased dietary fiber. The Kalahari bushmen have amazingly good bowel habits; but they also eat roots and berries and run around all day.

Vitamin Supplements

What of vitamins? Do older persons need more? This is one of the most commonly asked questions in geriatrics. Vitamins are critical to your machine's operation. They catalyze and facilitate your metabolism. But they are not fuels. They aren't burned for energy. They are constantly regenerated, consequently we need only a relatively small amount of them. Taking more than we need isn't necessary, and may be dangerous. Vitamins A and D, specifically, when taken in high amounts can lead to substantial medical problems. The other vitamins, too, when taken promiscuously can irritate the intestines merely by their excessive presence.

Vitamins are like light switches. As we build a house, we need only so many electric light switches. Twenty or thirty will usually do; supplying three hundred or three thousand doesn't make the house work any better. And thus, the extra switches are thereby discarded. Someone once observed that Americans pass the most expensive urine in the world, as we simply slough off extra vitamins that we don't need. But vitamins are a testimonial to our obsession with cures that come in bottles. The quick fix. Their placebo effect is enormous; but like other placebos, the benefit is to the belief—and not necessarily to the physical—system.

Still the fad continues. The megavitamin group pushes to stamp out aging, and everything else, by consuming handfuls of vitamins each day. The problem is that no one has ever shown that it makes any difference. Vitamin E, vitamin B_6, and other pseudonutrients have been proposed as age extenders by their antioxidant, free-radical–scavenging modes of action. Some animal studies have shown that chemical attempts to lengthen life have extended average life span, but not the maximum life span.

The educator Eberhard Kronhausen, Ed.D., has become the new Ponce de León—reincarnated from death by Indian arrow in 1521, and now fully in search of eternal life. Kronhausen's recent book, *Formula for Life: The Anti-Oxidant, Free-Radical Detoxification Program,* provides the formula for extended youth amid which the herb thyme is said to relieve low back pain. Defined by Kronhausen, free radicals are "unstable molecules that chemically break down almost any compound with which they come into contact." In addition to thyme, other "free-radical–retarding agents" such as dill and sea vegetables are alleged to provide relief for ailments from cancer to unseemly fat deposits. Meanwhile, Roy Walford's book, *The 120 Year Diet,* states, "no vitamins, anti-oxidants, or other supplement has been shown to 'retard aging.' " Later Walford ambiguously argues that "although there is no compelling reason for believing that Vitamin E will slow down the basic aging process, . . . amounts quite a bit larger than the RDA's may render you less susceptible to several diseases and to chemical pollutants, and *may* slightly improve your general health to whatever number of years you have to live." (This sounds to me like "damnation by faint praise.")

What are we to make of such conflicting claims?

A summary article in the 1985 *New England Journal of Medicine* by Drs. Schneider and Reed, entitled "Life Extension," concludes that although a number of dietary "antioxidants" have been shown to extend animal life expectancy, in only one study has it been shown to extend life span. Further, the weight loss that accompanied the administration of the antioxidants may confound the overall findings. Schneider and Reed state, "The available evidence at this time does not support recommending diet supplementation for either life extension or the prevention of cancer."

Aligned to the vitamin E/antioxidant game is the promulgation of an enzyme "superoxide dismutase," which promotes the removal of free radicals. Schneider and Reed advise further, "Superoxide dismutase tablets are promoted for oral consumption as an anti-aging remedy—a practice that may simply reflect the entrepreneurial zeal of the sellers of these products since oral intake of this enzyme will not result in augmentation of its levels in blood or tissue." It is therefore difficult to develop much enthusiasm for such theoretically hopeful, but unproven, approaches to decreasing the metabolic havoc due to free-radical generation with aging.

Diet Restriction

Obviously, implementation of Clive McCay's basic life-lengthening diet of caloric restriction, proven repeatedly in rats, is hard to do in humans —although, as you will recall, Roy Walford himself is trying personally, and advocates its extension for the rest of us. "Controlled undernutrition" is the key, part of the problem being that we don't know how little is enough, let alone whether it will work at all. My hunch is that in order for anything to lengthen life it must have an effect on how hard our machine runs. For example, if we could cool our core temperatures from 98.6 to 88.6 degrees, we could live a lot longer. I feel sure of this. By slowing our machines by undernutrition, we theoretically will live longer, but at what price? I am not sure life would be recognizable at 88.6 degrees. When on occasion someone is fished out of a frozen lake still alive and the body temperature is below 90 degrees, the person is in a coma and all body processes are markedly slowed. The gears would grind so slowly that effective living would be impossible. I don't know what underfed living would be like, either.

It looks therefore as if the old machine needs pretty much the same amount and type of food that the younger machine does, providing it is well maintained and fit.

However, if breakdowns and inertia accompany aging, then these specific elements will require specific counteractive strategies—but these are not caused by age per se, but generally by disuse. A disused body needs a much more structured diet than does a used one, which is marvelously adaptable and forgiving of temporary excesses. Attitudinal pathology is the cause of most malnutrition in older people. Nutrition is ultimately a "self-service" action. Decisions made and not made about our dietary patterns are highly determinative of overall life quality. Eating is and should be a delight, but it should also be smart.

SLEEP

Sleep is the last of the three constituent shaping forces of our basic design. Use, fuel, and rest contribute separately but are interdependent. Exercise and nutrition are interrelated. Exercise affects nutrition. Nutrition affects exercise. Exercise and sleep, as well as sleep and nutrition, each interplay; but if we are apologetic about our general ignorance concerning the bases of exercise and nutrition, our knowledge base about sleep is even slimmer. During medical school thirty years ago, I recall having learned only two salient facts about sleep—that the brain has a sleep center and a wakefulness center.

Fortunately, this ignorance is being addressed through the combined research work at a number of sleep centers around the country, one of the best being here at Stanford, under the direction of Dr. Dement.

What Is the Function of Sleep?

What have we learned from Dr. Dement and others? First we must consider that a 75-year-old person has spent twenty-five years of his or her life asleep, in a state the reason for which and the nature of which didn't intrigue us very much until the last several decades. Freud et al. have proposed that the reason we sleep is that it provides us a chance to dream. James Horne of the Department of Human Sciences at Loughborough University called dreams "a cinema of the mind, the brain's great entertainer to while away the nighttime hours." Hamlet's "Perchance to dream" was an effort for insight. Most of the time my dreams are a nuisance as they are filled with anxious, urgent, neurotic minicrises the value of which totally eludes me. Thus, if dreams are the reason for me to sleep, I would just as soon forget it.

In the first paragraph of his 1988 book, *Why We Sleep,* Horne wrote, "Of course, I do not have the answer to why we sleep." Later he continued, "Despite fifty years of research all we can conclude about the function of sleep is that it overcomes sleepiness, and that the only reliable finding from sleep deprivation experiments is that sleep loss makes us sleepy."

Animals and infants without a cerebral cortex still sleep, thus indicating the very deep roots which sleep has in our evolutionary development. In animals and man, lack of sleep prompts sleepiness.

Folk wisdom intuits that sleep provides a respite from the challenges of the day—recovery after exertion. Confucius said, "Big night, small day." There is some evidence that we grow more at night, and cell growth and tissue repair occur most rapidly during sleep; but it appears that this is the result of lower levels of cortisol and noradrenaline during sleep. These compounds inhibit most tissue repair; but it is they, rather than the sleep itself, which affect the recovery processes.

Activity such as physical exercise has two beneficial effects on sleep:

1. It promotes wakefulness (I recall being bushed at the end of a long work day, but becoming refreshed after playing ball with the kids after dinner.)
2. It improves the quality of sleep (more deep sleep).

Body temperature and energy flow are intimately involved with sleep. I recall pictures of the iguanas in the Galapagos snoozing on the rocks until the sun had been up long enough to raise the temperature of the rock and provide the lizard with enough heat to get its metabolism going.

In humans, exercise has been found to provide high-quality sleep only in fit persons. Professor Horne has conjectured that this is due to a threshold effect. Only fit persons are able to work hard enough to raise the temperature of the brain enough to trigger sleep. However, merely warming unfit persons—in a sauna, for example—provokes deeper sleep. Body temperature has been termed the master control oscillations cue. This is like the iguana. Light, food, and physical exercise obviously interplay.

Your Biologic Clock

Another human phenomenon which has fascinated us for centuries is the biologic clock. Eighteenth-century astronomer Jean de Mairan was the first person to describe a time-driven clock in biology. He noted that the heliotrope plant opened and closed its leaves even when kept in the dark. Several years ago I was late in planting, and found that my tuberous begonias were starting to erupt in the paper bag in my closet. In a classic experiment, oysters removed from the shore in Connecticut and flown to Evanston, Illinois, continued to open their shells coincident with high tides on the East Coast. The significant element of the experiment, however, is that this was only a *temporary* happening. Within two weeks, all of the oysters had reset their clocks to Central Standard Time!

For ten years I (and hundreds of others for longer) conducted experiments on cholesterol formation in the livers of rats. To accommodate standard laboratory convenience, virtually all of these rats were killed at or near 9:00 A.M. each day. The reason is simple, and exceedingly human. Nine o'clock was when we opened the lab. Then a German biochemist at my old lab, Max Planck in Munich, found that the rat makes almost all of its cholesterol from 12:00 A.M. to 4:00 A.M. and very little between the hour of 9:00 A.M. and 10:00 A.M. It conformed strikingly with the rat's feeding period. This basic revelation literally shook the cholesterol research empire. We recovered quickly by simply shifting the lighting schedule in the animal colony so that our "9:00 A.M." became midnight to the rat.

The rhythmic oscillatory behavior (known as the biologic clock) of hosts of living events is obvious. While some cue on daylight, some on lunar, and some on seasonal times, we see that various time periods are in operation. Certain biochemical reactions have oscillations which last only a fraction of a second; while other rhythms, such as predator/prey interrelationships, take years to appear. For example, the numbers of wolves and rabbits have closely related cyclic patterns. As the number of wolves increases, the rabbits will decrease to a certain low level. Then the number of wolves will decrease, allowing the rabbit level to increase, and so on. The point is that oscillatory behavior is a universal constant. It is part of the universal energy flow.

Physicist Harold Morowitz points out that whenever an object intervenes between an energy source and a sink (as in space), that object causes the energy which it has received to undergo at least one oscillatory cycle before eventually being shed into the sink. Geophysical, magnetic, electrostatic, and metabolic forces and reactions are some of the forms which these oscillations take. They certainly are not confined to living creatures, as there are a number of experiments which can be carried out in test tubes in which the participating chemicals change from one form to another and back again. Oscillations (rhythmic variations) then are commonplace in any system undergoing energy flow.

Exactly what purpose the cycle serves (if it serves any) is unknown; but if we ever understand this phenomenon, then it is my prediction that we will understand why we sleep.

Jet lag and shift work provide the two major encounters with phase resetting. Westward travel is easier, as we condition easier in that direction. We, like the clam, may have deeply seated rhythms which cue off of sunlight, and we do better when we *follow* the sun, rather than run into it. However, this is only my conjecture. Both travel through time zones and changing work shifts require that we reset our clocks and resynchronize our biologic rhythms. Such discordant time cues can have serious physical effects over the long term, as witnessed by the higher incidence of ulcers in those individuals whose jobs entail constant shifting of work schedules.

What Is the Anatomy of Sleep?

Although the function of sleep, if there is one, is only vaguely glimpsed, the anatomy of sleep has come clearer with the observations made with the utilization of the electroencephalograph (EEG). This tool can record the electrical activity of your brain—your sparks. The human brain demonstrates rhythm patterns awake and asleep, but it is during sleep that clear distinctions can be made. Sleep laboratories observe four different stages of sleep, plus REM (rapid eye movement) sleep, each characterized by a distinctive EEG pattern. During an eight-hour sleep there may be as many as thirty-five stage changes, with each cycle taking approximately ninety minutes. Eighty percent of dreaming occurs during REM sleep and is accompanied by increased heartbeat, increased temperature, and (in males) an increased number of erections. Bed-wetting and sleepwalking occur during the depth of sleep stage IV. Individuals who have been experimentally deprived of either REM or stage IV sleep are found to reclaim their losses when unrestricted sleep is allowed.

There are chemical components of sleep as well. For example, the neurotransmitter serotonin has been found to be sleep-inducing. Tryptophan, an amino acid found in high amounts in milk, has been called "sleep juice." (Tryptophan supplements were prescribed as a sleep aid until the recent discovery that they occasionally cause major side effects halted their use.) When the cerebrospinal fluid from a sleep-deprived animal is injected into a well-rested one, the rested one falls asleep.

What is the average human sleep pattern? As with many things, it depends upon the ages and activity levels of the persons reviewed. For example, research tells us that newborns sleep 17 of the 24 hours; premature babies sleep even more. Six-month-old infants sleep 14 hours per day. Sixteen-year-olds sleep an average of 10 hours; while college-age students sleep 8 hours. Pregnant women sleep 2 additional hours per day. On average, women sleep the same number of hours as do men. American children sleep longer than do British or German children.

Regarding famous individuals, we know that Napoleon and Edison were reported to have slept very little. Einstein slept a lot. The Sleep

Center at Boston State Hospital reported that those who slept less tended to be efficient, ambitious, and highly programmed individuals; whereas those who slept long tended to be more nonconforming and neurotic. Short and long sleepers all appear to have the same amount of deep stage IV sleep.

Sleep Deprivation

One week of sleeplessness will kill a puppy; two weeks will kill a dog. New York disc jockey Peter Tripp stayed awake for 200 hours in order to raise money for the March of Dimes. Toward the end of the experience, he became episodically psychotic. In 1965, a high school student in San Diego, Sandy Gardner, conducted a science project in which he stayed awake for 264 hours and 12 minutes. Gardner remained rational for the entire time. He then slept 14 hours and 20 minutes. William Dement, of Stanford, credits Gardner's intactness through this ordeal to his high degree of physical fitness. As mentioned earlier, fitness and movement facilitate wakefulness. A bed is constructed to encourage inactivity. Sleep is thus facilitated by decreasing the cues from all of our senses.

Prohibition from sleep (often called "sleep deprivation") has been incorporated as a classic tool in "brainwashing." Prolonged wakefulness leads to emotional liability, but there is no evidence of permanent damage after prolonged wakefulness. The marathon dance craze of the 1930s coerced couples to stay on their feet for months on end with only brief respites of a few minutes allowed. Such extremes appeal to our morbid curiosity, but the mean of eight hours sleep per night has been certified as being conducive to general health and to longevity.

However, many of us tend to feel we would do better with some extra sleep. Twenty years ago I had the wonderful opportunity to address, with my father, the plebes at West Point on the elements of health promotion. What a terrific audience! One of the first questions that came out of the audience in the Q & A period was, "How much sleep do we need?" Rather than giving a discursive scientific answer, I replied, "More!" My response was met with a howl of approval from all, as that was what they were hoping to hear.

Age-Related Sleep Disorders

Sleep problems are big business. It has been estimated that 15 percent of Americans—30 million people—are insomniacs. In 1979, there
were 38 million prescriptions for sleeping pills and tranquilizers. (Women
take more than do men.) That's 1 billion prescription pills, plus another 2
billion nonprescription or over-the-counter sleeping pills for a total consumption of 3 billion pills! Twenty sleeping pills for every American citizen.

Sleeping pills are dangerous. They are widely abused. They are ad-
dicting. They alter the stages and anatomy of sleep. Several studies have
concluded that people taking sleeping pills on a regular basis have a 1.5
times higher death rate than those who don't. In my own practice I am
constantly fighting off patients whose lament is that they have an inability
to sleep. Very often this complaint is unfounded. Sleep clinics are always
confronted by persons claiming not to sleep at all; yet who, when observed
under rigid conditions, are found to sleep like babes.

Sleep does change with age, but again we are confronted with the
recurring question of whether it is age or inactivity which is the villain. The
"sundowning syndrome" seen commonly in nursing homes results from
older persons' napping through the day, arousing at dinnertime, and being
awake much of the night. Much of this is due to what is known as the "phase
advancement" of their biologic clocks. Most adults demonstrate a natural
cycle which conforms to a 24-hour periodicity. (Biologists have long referred to this as the circadian clock.) Young people have a slightly longer
cycle of 25 to 26 hours, while older people have a shorter cycle of 20 to 22
hours. The circadian clock, like the owner, runs faster with age. This ex-
plains why teenagers are great at midnight, but not so good at 8:00 A.M.;
whereas, old folks crump out at 6:00 P.M., only to waken at 1:00 A.M. and
then want a pill that will keep them asleep all night. Older people nap
more, have lighter sleeps, and are more easily aroused. Even their sleep
efficiency deteriorates as they spend more time in bed to get the same
amount of sleep.

True to other life elements, older persons demonstrate increased
variability in sleep patterns. This includes higher proportions of older individuals who sleep more than younger individuals, as well as higher proportions of those who sleep less. They have less REM and stage IV sleep. It
takes longer for older persons to change their sleep patterns. Older shift
workers adjust less easily than do younger shift workers. Older rats synchro-

nize to time shifts more slowly than do younger rats; and before death, all circadian rhythms disappear completely.

One element of sleep in older persons that has aroused a great deal of interest recently is the documented increase in episodes of sleep apnea. Sleep apnea denotes the frequently observed periods of nonbreathing. True apnea lasts for at least ten seconds, with some episodes lasting much longer. Loud snoring is the best diagnostic clue, for after a period of no breathing, the next breath is a loud and disturbing one. It is estimated that 25 percent of all persons over the age of 65 exhibit sleep apnea to some degree. Forty percent of persons in nursing homes have it. Obesity also correlates with sleep apnea. These episodes may occur dozens of times each night; and because of the failure to breathe, they are accompanied by a decrease in the oxygen content of the blood.

Some of our data regarding sleep apnea came from the Scripps Research Institute study which looked at the death certificates from the New York City Bureau of Vital Statistics. Of 4,920 deaths surveyed, it was found that there was a 60 percent higher death rate from 2:00 A.M. to 8:00 A.M., and this was found only in those over age 65. These deaths, often coded as "natural causes," can be logically attributed to sleep pathology and are not "natural" at all.

Donald Bliwise, of the Stanford Sleep Center, reported recently on 198 subjects with sleep apnea, average age 67, who had been followed for twelve years. Those with severe forms had much higher death rates. Sleep apnea occurs most often during REM sleep, and that seems to cluster particularly in the early morning hours—a time when most deaths occur. (It is interesting that births, too, have a diurnal rhythm, being 35 percent more common between 3:00 A.M. and 5:00 A.M.)

I generally deduce the condition of sleep apnea in one of my patients when his or her spouse complains of very loud snoring. Deeper questioning will reveal that the unruly sleep pattern is most evident after the spouse has not taken a breath for a moment or two. Then a number of outlandish snorts emit.

Loud snoring is not a common complaint heard in my office, but when it does come I pay attention to it. Several years ago a patient came in accompanied by his wife, who maintained that her husband's snoring caused the pictures on the wall to rattle at night. He was oblivious to it. But the presentation was enough for me to refer the couple on for a more thorough evaluation.

Sleep apnea leads to dullness during the day and possible changes in cognition. This pattern has prompted some persons to suggest that this state may predispose one to Alzheimer's disease, because sleep apnea is found in a high percentage of persons with this disease. (In addition, REM is decreased with Alzheimer's disease.)

In my mind this is only interesting conjecture. We await much needed sleep studies of older people, well and otherwise.

Where does this leave my older patient with his insomnia? Writing a prescription for a sleeping pill is the last option. Before that, I exhort my patient to do the following:

1. be fit
2. learn to relax
3. be on a schedule (going to bed and getting up at regular intervals)
4. limit the time in bed to only the "sleep time"
5. schedule "worry time" for earlier in the day
6. avoid stimulants and try a little warm milk instead
7. take a warm bath before bed
8. control the sleep environment with quiet, darkness, and a comfortable temperature

Finally, and perhaps most important, I advise my patients with insomnia to find a bed mate. Countless studies show that bed mates invite better sleep patterns.

If none of these steps work, I tell my patient that he has two other choices: either to count sheep, or to stay up one whole night and prove to himself that it really won't kill him. Besides, as my mother used to say, "You are going to be asleep a long time someday."

Exercise, rest, and nutrition represent the operational plan for our machine. It seems simple, but we seem wonderfully able to mess up even our most basic instruction. We are the product of millions of years of evolutionary forces which have operated in such a way so as to provide a magnificent carriage vehicle for hope, courage, and creativity. If we lack the intellect or "will" to tend our heredity, then our characterization as "sapient" is problematic.

T E N

SELF-EFFICACY

You are as young as your hope,
and as old as your despair.

Anonymous

I can't give you a recipe to live
long—life is how you live, how you
sleep, how you eat, how you drink,
how you work—life is what you are.

Dora Zins, age 104, at the
100th celebration of the founding of
the National Institutes of Health

H ealth is necessary but insufficient.
A machine is more than wires, pulleys, rotors, and switches. A home
is more than sidings, pipes, and windows.

A year ago I was attending a lecture at Stanford, the topic for which
was the ideal medical management strategy for the patient with severe
arthritis. The speaker concluded with the statement that for a person with
advanced arthritis to live well, he or she must have a well developed sense
of self-efficacy. As soon as the phrase was uttered I seized upon it and in
effect said, "That's it! That's really what aging is ultimately all about—
maintaining a well-developed sense of *self-efficacy*."

Other words and phrases have been used in an effort to capture that
extra dimension which goes beyond the basic elements of good health.
Words such as control, autonomy, independence, mastery, élan vital, intactness, and completeness have all been used to identify the outstanding older

person. And yet none of these capture the real essence of successful aging as well as does "self-efficacy."

THE SEARCH FOR THE
FORMULA OF LONGEVITY

Twenty years ago, Dr. Henry Page, a colleague of my father's at the Lankenau Hospital in Philadelphia, identified a group of older persons who were, as any interested observer would clearly agree, "superior older people." Dr. Page sought by questionnaire, physical examination, and interview to discover that "extra something" which allowed these persons to stand out from their less notable peers. It became clear early that physical health was not the decisive factor; many had disease conditions. Furthermore, no single characteristic such as money, social class, race, education, heredity, or sex could be found that would fit everyone in the group. For the group as a whole, certain characteristics were found; specifically, family support, work participation, and a sense of commitment were general qualities which seemed commonly present. Even so, no probe or question was found to provide a single, simple key to the central question, "What makes a superior older person?"

Subsequently a number of longitudinal studies have been undertaken in the hope that some identifying scheme could be uncovered which could account for a long and full life of both quality and quantity. In a longitudinal study of 268 subjects, researchers at Duke University hypothesized the elements of successful aging as:

1. work satisfaction (a sense of usefulness and the ability to play a meaningful social role)
2. happiness
3. good health
4. not smoking

Virginia Stone and Erdman Palmore reported, from the ongoing work at the Institute for Population Studies in Alameda, that physical mobility was most highly correlated with superior aging. Following this factor, researchers listed: education, occupation (professors seem particularly successful), and having a job. Currently the MacArthur Foundation of Chicago is funding a number of population studies, under the general direction of John Rowe, the purpose for which is to develop a template for "Successful Aging." Researchers are being asked to address questions such as: "What is aging?," "What are its components?," and "What can we do to encourage its implementation throughout our society?"

Forty years ago Erik and Joan Erikson proposed a model of human development based upon eight separately defined stages of life. They included: infancy, early childhood, play age, school age, adolescence, young adult, adulthood, and mature age. Since being suggested, this model has proven a standard of psychologic theory. In 1986, this esteemed couple, together with Helen Kivnick, published a book entitled *Vital Involvement in Old Age*. In constructing this work they interviewed twenty-nine octogenarians—people who like themselves were members of the omega generation (the oldest generation of any family kindred). Their book is a treasure house of insights into the dynamics of the coping strategies of persons in their eighth stage of life.

Wallace Stegner, noted author, enters his ninth decade as a local treasure. He is a vital civic leader; he champions our open space; he is a caring neighbor; he is fully involved; he is perpetually creative. Clara Snow (not her real name) sits with her husband, Herb, in their trailer home, having been brought here from the east by their children. Clara is 83; Herb is 85. Both are fairly healthy, but they are constantly on the phone to their children complaining about what's wrong with them. I must have checked Clara twenty times for a supposed bladder infection due to her incessant complaining about having to urinate all the time. As yet, I have been unable to document a disorder. These two individuals are preoccupied with their constricted existences and draw energy from everyone with whom they come in contact. One or the other is on the phone to my office daily. My staff dread them; and I must admit it is very tough to be civil to them through their whining, self-serving behavior. Our collective idealism is stretched to its tolerance.

These three are all survivors into old age—the third, new age. One has entered triumphantly; two have entered without grace or understanding. What's more, they don't give a damn about anything but themselves. One gives energy; the other two take energy.

The Eriksons state:

> The last stage, old age, challenges the individual to rework the
> tensions and rebalance the resulting strengths of all the earlier
> stages in an effort to establish an integrity of self that, while

drawing sustenance from the past, remains vitally involved in
the present. . . . In old age, as one's physical abilities wane, a
lifelong sense of effectiveness is a critical resource.

The Eriksons propose that these "collectors of time and preservers of
memory" have developed a conviction of their own completeness which
has allowed them to ward off the disintegrations of aging. In a *New York
Times* review of her 1988 book, *Wisdom of the Senses* Joan Erikson is
quoted as stating, "Lots of old people don't become wise, but you don't get
wise unless you age."

This is similar to the saying of the elder to the kid, "I have the
advantage over you, because I have known what it is to be young; but you
don't know what it's like to be old."

In their 1986 work the Eriksons and Kivnick emphasize the term
generativity as the life goal of the main, adult stage of life. By this they
mean: "taking care of what is being procreated, produced, and created."
"Adulthood's generative responsibility for the 'maintenance of the world' is
the responsibility of each generation of adults to bear, nurture, and guide
those people who will succeed them as adults."

Surrender of the official postures of responsibility, as we age, con-
fronts our elder selves with unwelcome feelings of stagnation. The authors
expand this point when they say, "Old age may impose its own, unique
demands, and it may offer its own unique opportunities for integrating
inevitable stagnations with new and modified involvement in the lifelong
capacity for generative caring." They emphasize that amid the threat of
deteriorating physical vigor lies the opportunity for growth.

Finally, the reconciling of generativity and stagnation provides the
elder with what the Eriksons and Kivnick term a "grand-generativity."
Prominent among these roles is grandparenting, which is seen as a "second
chance" at generativity, in that it presents "the possibility of caring for the
newest generation more robustly, and less ambivalently than they did for
their own young children in their years of active parenthood." The in-
tergenerationality provides the opportunity for assistance and advice to be
extended both up and down the generations. The years of our earlier life
stages and our own parenting are reexperienced vicariously.

My wife and I are now in the delicious life stage of grandparenting.
We have, by latest, up-to-the-minute count, seven grandchildren. Six years
ago we were in Honolulu at the home of dearest friends for a party with
other close friends, all of whom had already reached grandparenthood.
Over dessert we posed the fact that we were shortly to become grandpar-

ents for the first time, and asked what this moment would do to our lives. We were immediately overwhelmed by a cascade of highly emotional reactions from the group. "It's like reincarnation." "It is as though an entire new domain of existence has opened up." "It is the entry into an entire, higher level of existence." To us, at the time, this spontaneous outpouring seemed excessive and inappropriate; but now that we are in that stage we would answer similarly.

Now when we have a new opportunity, we vicariously extend it to our grandchildren as adeptly as we can. Classical music, skiing, new tastes—these are all things we have ourselves, but now we must extend this pleasure and knowledge to the new generation.

We feel privileged to have lived long enough now to have learned this part of living. They are our future. I can't help but feel that this is a major asset in creating a successful aging.

I feel a pang for friends who for one reason or another don't, or won't, have grandchildren. It seems like a spoiled design. Certainly we are all broad enough creatures to have meaningful lives without them. They only make it easier. Life as it presents to us is so gloriously rich in its opportunities for adventure and learning and creativity that we don't require descendents to leave our personal signature on tomorrow's world. I believe, my basic faith system reads, that the reason for my life is to make this world a better place—in all that this means. It can be as major as writing a book that I hope will help a reader, or by scratching the ears of our neighbor's dog, or going to seniors' centers board meetings, or dealing gently with Clara and Herb.

Upon review of the twenty-nine octogenarians they studied, the Eriksons concluded that old age—successful old age—is characterized by a reworking of and reinvolvement with the basic mechanisms of being alive. It is an active process. All twenty-nine had a "near religious faith in industriousness and competence." Vital involvement in life is the central control.

HOW WILL YOU COPE WITH AGE?

Another word for the reworking and reinvolvement defined by the Eriksons is *coping.* And much has been done to analyze the ways in which people cope, and the adverse consequences when they do not.

The inability to cope is most dramatic in the helpless-hopeless syndrome proposed by Seligman. Earlier I discussed the laboratory observations that when certain animals are exposed to situations in which they were powerless to resist, they consequently "give up." This also happens to humans, with the most clear example being the reactions of some individuals to illness and/or bereavement. Conversely, animals that are taught to offset a noxious stimulus through a conditioned behavior pattern develop survival capabilities, including improved immune responsiveness.

It appears that animals, like ourselves, develop an armor that diverts the slings and sorrows of our world in a self-protectiveness. This is not a conscious act—it is a survival mechanism; the fittest make it. Coping is what Darwin was all about. Those among us—people and creatures and plants—which cope survive, nourish, and are nourished. The remainder don't.

Norman Cousins spoke brilliantly of his own personal fight against the "helpless-hopeless" experience in the book *Anatomy of an Illness* (first published as a paper in the *New England Journal of Medicine*). Cousins told how his body deteriorated from illness (possibly rheumatic) while under the care of a team of expert physicians, each of whom was taking samples of him off to be analyzed, to no apparent benefit. His story of how he reestablished his sense of self-efficacy—largely through the benefit of laughter—is compelling.

One major effort at defining coping strategies has been undertaken by Albert Bandura, of the Department of Psychology at Stanford. He proposed that coping capacity could be quantitated by a series of questions relevant to the issue at hand. For example, he investigated the common fear of snakes and developed a questionnaire which ordered a series of reactions to that particular phobia. Bandura's measures were highly predictive of a person's ability to deal with snakes. Like the Eriksons, Bandura found that past mastery of experiences affect self-efficacy, while continuous failure weakens self-efficacy.

Dore Abler and Bruce Fretz, of the Department of Psychology at the University of Maryland, used Bandura's model to design a questionnaire dealing with self-efficacy and competence in a group of persons over 85 years of age. Their set of twelve questions assessed the perceived ability of these "oldest old" to cope. Sample questions were as follows:

1. If walking down the sidewalk some late afternoon I am jostled and harassed by a group of young, male teenagers, I will contact the police when I return home and will still try to get outside every day for exercise and fresh air.

2. If I make a careless mistake related to my finances and end up

having a problem with the bank, I'll be able to forgive myself for the mistake and continue to trust myself with my own financial matters in the future.

3. If I am lonesome for a member of my family with whom I have not spoken in quite a while, I will call him or her up on the telephone for a chat.

This study is an effort to show those strengths which the "successfully aged" older person has in full measure. This number has much more relevance to the well-being of persons than does the cholesterol level or the blood pressure or the other common remote markers of effective aging.

Measurement of self-efficacy is a potent predictor of an old person's ability to create and recover from the new challenges of failure and loss. This should concur with an individual's own estimate of his or her ability to deal with complex, ambiguous, and pressure-filled situations.

MIND OVER MATTER

There is growing evidence that the sense of control (sometimes called the "mind-set") has manifold effects on physical health. Judith Rodin, a psychologist at Yale, wrote, "Control is more likely to affect health than health is to affect control." The ability to cope has been shown to help master phobias and to control pain. For example, when pregnant women who had been taught relaxation techniques to facilitate childbirth were rated according to their sense of control, it was found that those who perceived a greater coping capacity tolerated labor pain for longer periods before requesting medication, and overall required less pain relief. Similar experiments need to be conceived and extended to older persons. There is a rich experimental world awaiting exploration.

Until recently the medical establishment has had trouble accepting proposals that mind-set can affect outcomes. Now there are enough clear demonstrations of biologic mechanisms which interconnect the central nervous system with the rest of the body. Emotions clearly affect the endrocrine glands. Anxiety, rage, fear, and love—each has its own biochemical profile. Stress, in particular, provokes the outpouring of excessive amounts of cortisone from the adrenal gland and the multiple adverse effects therefrom.

Whenever task demands seem to exceed our capacity to solve them, a chain of reactions ensues. Not only does self-efficacy have direct effects on health; but, perhaps more important, it has a potent effect on our health behavior. For example, when we feel in charge we are much more likely to pursue health-promoting activities; and when we languish into dependency, recidivism from previously established good practices is likely. This is the probable explanation for why the death of a spouse is so commonly followed by the death of the mate. "What is there to live for?" "Why keep going?" But if we can survive this acute phase of grief, regroup, and reidentify reasons for living, then new opportunities open up. To paraphrase the motto of Suicide Prevention: "Dying may be the permanent answer to a temporary situation."

Bandura wrote, "Judgment of self-efficacy determines how much effort people will expend and how long they will persist in the face of obstacles or aversive experience."

If in doubt about how to manage, many people give up.

This whole area of probing transports my imagination back to the Serengeti 2 million years ago. Our great- . . . great ancestors were faced with the ultimate decision—to move on and seek food, or to settle at the home site and see if tomorrow's hunger would somehow be relieved by a deus ex machina device. Our ancestors moved on. Those who waited died. Energetics decreed survival. It is no less so now.

Moreover, Bandura concluded, "Efficiency in dealing with one's environment is not a fixed act or simply a matter of knowing what to do. Rather it involves a generative capability in which component cognitive, social, and behavioral skills must be organized into an integrated course of action to serve innumerable purposes."

Self-efficacy is ordering. It requires energy.

WHY IS CONTROL SO IMPORTANT?

The importance of a sense of control to overall health increases as we age, because advancing age, despite all counteractive strategies, inevitably involves deteriorations and threatening change. Yale's Judith Rodin remarked that it is not the aging process itself that is accountable for the diminution in one's sense of self-efficacy, but rather it is changes in environmental factors and a loss of self-image. Rodin, together with fellow psychologist Ellen Langer of Harvard, concluded that as we age, "Our prospects for avoidance or even reversal of functional loss with aging are vastly improved, and thus the risk of adverse health outcomes reduced by an active program of involvement."

Is a loss of self-efficacy an inevitable accompaniment of aging? Certainly not all older persons evidence a loss of control. (A point illustrated at length further in this chapter.)

The Eriksons characterize aging as the stage of life in which "physical disabilities infringe on freedom and self-determination of activity," breeding too often a new sense of invalidness. "It does not seem to be the particular capacity of incapacitation itself that most strongly affects the old age integration of feelings of autonomy with those of shame and doubt. Rather it is the *meaning* of an experienced disability—and such meaning varies widely from person to person."

Once again the concept of the "plasticity" of aging appears. Old age is a life stage to be managed, worked at, and created—not one to be languished in and complained about. To this end Bandura has written a prescription for self-efficacy, much as I write prescriptions for headaches and heart attacks. The prescription has four components:

1. the creation of a set of mastery experiences ("Successes build a robust sense of efficacy.")
2. display of a set of relevant and successful role models
3. social persuasion
4. conditioned alteration of the physiologic response to how people perceive their inadequacies

At the present time there is fragile evidence that the filling and taking of this prescription will add years to life and life to years; but it is my firm conviction that this area—maintenance and extension of self-efficacy as we age—is a prime target not only for medical and psychologic research but for national policy as a whole. Let's look at the prescription step by step.

STEP 1.
CREATING MASTERY EXPERIENCES

Validation of Bandura's first premise comes primarily from work done with persons living in controlled environments such as nursing homes and other group-living accommodations. Such facilities provide an opportunity for testing the concept, as well as illustration of what can go wrong when older individuals are not involved in the decisions affecting their daily existence.

A number of studies have been performed in nursing homes where a whole host of aversive strategies are employed for the convenience of patient management. Such strategies include dining, socialization, and recreational activities which are conducted en masse for "convenience' sake." Independent actions are labeled "unruly." The staff in such nursing-home facilities tend to reinforce dependent behavior because it facilitates manpower utilization. Patient compliance is strongly sought. Sadly, often "active" nursing-home residents are sedated, not necessarily for their own best interests but in order to make their nursing care more convenient. The benefactors of such sedations are the institutions and their staffs, not the patients.

Daily I receive a phone call from a harried nurse at a nursing home. "Dr. Bortz, Mrs. Simpson was on the buzzer all night. She disrupted the whole floor. Can't you do something for her?" The nurse is really asking for something to be done for herself. In the ideal situation, she or someone else would have gone to be with Mrs. Simpson and touched and stroked and fed and listened and interrelated to whatever degree was required. But that is not the real world. This same nurse also had sixty other patients and charts to attend. Therefore, the call. The system works when everyone is quiet from seven at night until seven in the morning. The tight staffing relies on this. "Disruptive behavior" is not tolerated. Conformity, abandonment of self-ness, is the rule. "Don't break it, or I'll call the doctor." I sense echoes of *One Flew Over the Cuckoo's Nest.*

In a key study by Langer and Rodin, the nursing staff of a nursing home encouraged one group of residents to assume their own activities of daily living, including dressing, eating, toileting, and maintaining their own environments. At the same time, on another floor of the same nursing home, a second group of residents was told that the staff would take care of all of their needs. After three weeks the groups were compared. Those residents franchised for their own care were more alert, more active, and happier. Eighteen months later these findings were sustained. Further, in the interim, only 15 percent of those in the self-management group had died; while 30 percent of those in the control group had died. Langer and Rodin have shown in other studies that developing a sense of control also improves memory.

Richard Schulz of the Carnegie Mellon University performed a study in a nursing home in which visits from local college students were variously scheduled and controlled by the residents. Again, control improved activity, satisfaction, and health after the intervention; but long-term benefits were highly dependent on the ability to sustain the control. Termination of the visits seemed to increase the sense of loss, leading to an increased debilitation.

In another study, residents of a retirement home with many restrictions were compared to those living in a home with few constraints. Health outcome seemed improved as autonomy was encouraged.

A small but interesting experiment was designed by Jerry Avorn and Ellen Langer of Harvard. Seventy-two residents of a nursing home in Boston were asked to complete a jigsaw puzzle. Each person had four twenty-minute practice sessions. One-third of the group received direct assistance during this practice; another third received verbal encouragement; the rest received neither. Those who were encouraged did much better; those with no intervention remained the same; and those who were assisted did worse. In her book *Mindfulness* Langer wrote, "The opportunity to make choices increases our motivation."

This experiment was designed as a proxy for the actual events in the lives of older persons and illustrates what Maggie Kuhn of the Gray Panthers means when she castigates the medical profession, social workers, counselors, and educators for the paternalism and treating of old folks "like children and wrinkled babies." The often well-intentioned solicitousness has major downside effects. "Take my seat." "I'll do it for you." "I'll drive you." All mean well, but all accelerate decline and helplessness. Most older people—even old, old people—are well. All old people are improvable.

This is not easily accomplished. The good intentions of others often block the self-efficacy of the old. I was vividly reminded of this concept several years ago when I served as chairman of the Palo Alto Task Force on Aging. This group had been selected by the city council and charged with the task of surveying our community and making recommendations regarding the needs of our older citizens. One of the most important principles that I maintained was that the old participants be encouraged in every way possible to see the purposes and activities as their very own—for the old, of the old, and *by* the old. This was finally accomplished over the reservations of the members of the city staff, who, in my opinion, seemed motivated primarily by their own needs to feel that they were doing something for someone else. The major recommendation of our task force was that a senior center be created to have a number of educational, nutritional, social, cultural, and volunteer activities. The city staff wanted the decision-making responsibility for the task to rest with themselves. Our task force objected strongly to this paternalism.

Each of us has within us a sense of obligation, of taking care, and of doing right. But sometimes this gets in the way of allowing other persons to exist. Any new parent comes to the moment in which the air beneath the wings must be supplied by the offspring. Nurturing becomes an onboard activity and responsibility. Such recognition applies equally to older persons. The city staff should have realized that the greater good was to be served by the provision of self-management of the senior center by the seniors themselves, and not by even the most well-intended shepherding. The risk of failure must be sustained, if life is to go on effectively. I concur with Langer that "the more help older people are given, the more help they will come to need. . . . Well meant protectiveness generally undermines any autonomy."

Thoreau observed, "If I knew that a man were coming to my house with a conscious design of doing me good, I should run for my life."

For all of us there is a tension point between security and independence; but when the balance beam shifts to the security end, our coping capacity becomes at risk. When does concern become condescension? When does support become solicitousness? When does caring become patronizing? Who is at risk? The elder or ourselves?

More recently I joined the board of directors of the East Palo Alto Senior Center, a facility serving the city's black community. I held my tongue through early sessions as other board members made wonderful plans for the residents. Finally, I restated my conviction that older persons need to be encouraged to run their own lives, their own senior center.

My colleagues on the board heard me out but then counseled, "Dr. Bortz, we appreciate your comments; but you just don't understand. Our older folks don't want to be in charge; they are tired; they want to be taken care of."

Several months ago I visited the outstanding geriatrics training program at the University of Washington in Seattle. While there I met with the members of the geriatrics assessment unit. They were evaluating the care of a moderately disabled Chinese gentleman. The physical and occupational therapists, the dietitian, the social worker, and the nurses and doctors were all aligned to encourage and facilitate the recovery and rehabilitation of this patient. Yet, he was largely uninvolved in the program. The family asked, "What are you doing to our father? He doesn't have to feed and dress himself. We are here to do it for him."

Situations such as the preceding spawned an awakening in me—an indication of my naïveté and sorrowing. These culturally embedded attitudes, totally understandable once I thought about them, make the Bandura prescription harder to fill. Maggie Kuhn calls this attitude "the disengagement approach": "I deserve to take it easy." "I don't want any responsibility." "I earned it." If this approach plays out, we will have major intergenerational problems. If older citizens are seen by younger generations as liabilities requiring major societal resource allocation, this conflict is assured.

Conversely, when a person clinging to an autonomous existence is denied that opportunity, decay quickly happens. Last week I made a house call to an older lady prompted by a request from her concerned brother. It took my patient five minutes to respond to the doorbell. I could hear crashing noises behind the door. When the woman eventually answered, she was clad only in a slip. The temperature in the room must have been around forty degrees. She was blue with cold. She had broken two chairs in trying to answer my call and was so weak she could scarcely walk. For days all she had had by mouth was coffee. She is now in Stanford Hospital. She is so depressed that she barely speaks. I hope to help her recapture her sense of independence; but she is highly at risk, because her space, her freedom, is no longer available.

Retirement and Self-Efficacy
When Living Independently

I am convinced that mastery is a prime determinant for those who are elite elders—wherever they live. For those who live independently, a host of factors impact upon their completeness (or lack thereof) of aging. Perhaps prime among these is work. The revered physician Sir William Osler termed work "the master therapy." Old age is a habit that a busy person doesn't have time for. Retirement—a relatively new mode of life made possible by both Social Security and generous pension plans—has been widely suggested as having negative effects on well-being. And yet the studies looking into this invariably get confounded with other variables —most notably, health. Adolf Zukor, Chairman Emeritus of Paramount Studios, at age 98 asserted, "Infirmity is a state of mind." Do people retire because of poor health? Or does poor health follow retirement? In any case, for most of us, retirement is a major life passage.

The Eriksons have described this passage in the following manner:

> With retirement from salaried employment most elders lose, or at least undergo major change in the areas in which they express and experience primary competence. In addition they forfeit the sense of accomplishment that often accompanies the bringing home of a regular paycheck. . . . We noted that the separation from the work setting often removes the individual from those circumstances in which he or she learned to demonstrate competence and initiative. Thus, retirement may leave the elder without the structure that has come to be essential, or at least customary, in behaving with skillfulness and creativity. . . . With the advent of technology and the impact of the values it represents, not only do elders no longer provide continuity, but they also find themselves out of step within their social milieu. The experiential knowledge they could convey seems outdated and even quaint. . . . Decline in lifelong skillfulness poses a major challenge to the sense of mastery in old age.

A recent Lou Harris poll found that 81 percent of persons 65 to 69 years of age do not look forward to retirement with pleasure. For them work connotes what life is about. "Statutory senility" doesn't apply. The search for meaning in aging finds close identification with continued activities, whether these be gainful, salaried employment or in other active pursuits.

The message of this to all of us is clear. Those primitive societies which exhibit exemplary cultures for the older members do so largely through keeping the elders involved in the daily fabric of existence. We should do no less. Resist the gold watch! The important question is not, "What are you retiring from?"; it is, "What are you returning to?"

Simone de Beauvoir, in *The Coming of Age,* catalogs newfound creativity that has been allowed to develop in the later years of many artists and writers. My father, in his book *Creative Aging,* emphasized how we all should pursue creative outlets, be they connected with work or not. Such efforts give impetus to order and a sense of mastery. Educational opportunities augment this renewal effort and should logically be extended to every life stage. Learning is not just for the young. As the Eriksons have said, "For those who are enjoying retirement, the primary satisfaction does not seem to come from open-ended relaxation and permissible laziness, instead from new expressions of skillfulness and perseverance."

The increased mobility of our society leads to disruptive living arrangements. Widowhood and dispersion of families threatens family continuity. It has been noted, sadly, that "old age is often a time lived among strangers." The autonomy of independent living is threatened by a lack of familiarity and established routine. The Eriksons remind us that "residential continuity provides supportive rootedness."

Physical Mobility

One of my personal insights into superior aging comes from the conviction that mobility and survival are tightly linked. It is my repeated observation that successful aging occurs when the older individual can move.

When a person is physically confined because of immobility, a host of deteriorative effects follow. These can be social and psychological as well as physical. Movement confers freedom and independence. Lack of movement confers helplessness and passivity. As with other decrements, it is often not merely the specific effect of immobility that is assaulting, but the meaning of this loss. For example, I am frequently confronted with the decision as to whether an older person should still be allowed to drive. This issue mixes what is safe for the particular individual with what is safe for the rest of us. The issue is never simple. It is more than taking the car keys away so Pop will be safe; it is more what it will mean to Pop if he can't drive anymore. It is more than vision, or alertness, or reaction time. It is judgment. It is habit. But it is also a strong part of self-efficacy. To remove this is a major amputation.

I feel very sad when I take on the role of denying driving privileges to a patient. My reasoning is that such a distasteful role is better served by me, for I have less emotional investment than would the spouse or children of the "at risk" driver. At the moment when driving is no longer appropriate, I try to construct a surrogate support device that makes sense and is acceptable to the denied person. This is analogous to the parent whose child unreasonably demands an expensive bike or dress. Accommodation—acceptable accommodation—must be accomplished. Maybe a favored grand-child will show up twice a week to drive the patient to the Elks Club. Or maybe Maria, a not so secret flame, may be enticed to take Pop to the movies once a week.

By whatever contrivance this privilege is withdrawn, it is nonetheless a rite of passage—downward. Real, necessary, but sad. This is a daily part of the practice of geriatric medicine.

In the effort to maintain the mobility of faltering older people, various aids such as wheelchairs, canes, and walkers enable safety, but their use may connote a sense of infirmity which is threatening. Many should use canes, but they are often resisted.

How all of these elements of self-efficacy (work, transportation, housing, and the rest) interact to maintain our autonomy is almost a blank slate. Intuitions and folk wisdom abound, but it is my firm sense that a greatly expanded research base needs to be provided if we are to implement the first part of Bandura's prescription with intelligence and confidence.

STEP 2.
SUCCESSFUL ROLE MODELS

How do they do it? The individuals who achieve self-efficacy. As we strive to analyze the process, we must pause to celebrate the end result.

Naturalists, professors, and symphony conductors, in particular, are renowned for their productively long lives. Dr. Donald Atlas, of the University of California, San Diego Medical School, found that maestros live five years longer than the average American male. Toscanini, at age 90; Bruno Walter, age 85; Walter Damrosch, age 88; and Leopold Stokowski, age 95, are prime examples. Atlas concludes that they, like William Steinberg, lived lives of incredible richness and a sense of fulfillment. When Andrés Segovia died at age 90, "there was silence." Segovia, who had fathered a child at age 77, was prodigious until his death. It was said of him that the reason Bach, Beethoven, et al. had not written for the guitar was that Segovia had yet to be born.

Two additional groups which I feel are great role models are the centenarians and the master athletes.

Living Five Score

The best collection of information concerning centenarians is the result of interviews carried out by the Social Security Administration during the years 1963 to 1972. Twelve hundred responses were recorded (637 males and 563 females) and summarized in the book *Living To Be 100,* by Osborne Segerberg. Of the 1,200, 118 were still married, 2 for over 80 years. One respondent was married on his 100th birthday. Bravo! The most famous of this group was Grandma Moses; but other dignitaries were represented, including Nellie Taylor Ross, the first woman to be both governor of her state and director of the U.S. Mint.

Thirteen percent of the group reported excellent health and 69 percent reported good health, for a total of 82 percent. Two-thirds reported no diseases; 42 percent had no need of a physician; and 30 percent were still doing some work. Sixteen percent attributed their longevity to not seeing doctors (I like that), and a few said that the medical profession had helped. Twenty-nine percent had faulty vision, but 104 used no glasses. Twenty-six percent had decreased hearing. Five percent were bedridden; 8 percent were in wheelchairs; 12 percent used walkers; and 75 percent were fully mobile! Segerberg estimated that 5 percent were still sexually active. Only 16 individuals exercised specifically for its own sake. (This only emphasizes the point that formal exercise was not an activity persued by the members of this generation. Possibly the next cohort of centenarians will contain many more exercisers. I hope so!) Heredity was not an important factor; their parents were not exceptional as to their longevity.

As Segerberg assessed the results of the questionnaires for a Rosetta stone that would identify the cause of this phenomenon, he recorded, "The first pattern to emerge clearly from the questionnaire was orderliness." (Obviously shades of the Second Law of Thermodynamics!) Ninety-six percent of the responses reflected a high degree of order in their lives. Sixty-two percent of the respondents had lived on farms, with the ordering influences thereof, and thus reflected the prime cultural mode of the era. Eighty-nine percent of the group reported working hard during life—26 percent were still working, 70 individuals for wages, 10 as farmers. Next in the list of characteristics was stability—these people didn't often move their households; and the third characteristic was a strong family fabric. Sixty percent of the centenarians were living with a family member. (It should be noted that Hawaii and Minnesota are the two states that lead our country in average length of life. Seemingly dissimilar in most gross measurements, both states evidence cultures which emphasize strong family bonding.)

Twenty years ago, Dr. Belle Boone Beard, a sociologist at the University of Georgia, conducted a survey of one hundred centenarians and concluded that their central identifying feature was "an exceptional ability to make social adjustment." Their sense of harmony and absence of frustration were notable. Segerberg also concluded in this study, "Will is not simply another trait in the centenarians' repertoire, but the centerpiece." It appears therefore that these extraordinary people survive long and well. They sustain meaning, and serve powerfully as examples for us all.

In my medical practice I estimate six to eight centenarians at any one time. Just last week I was referred a breezy 103-year-old as a new patient. Over half of these patients are healthy; the rest are frail. I look to all of them as to what my life might be, what I might learn. We all should.

A year or so ago, I was making rounds at a local nursing home when I heard the social director announce the day's activities over the intercom. At the end she announced, "And today is Maude Smith's one-hundredth birthday. Let's all wish her a wonderful day!" I inquired of the floor nurse where Mrs. Smith's room was; I sought it out and ventured in.

"Mrs. Smith, my name is Dr. Walter Bortz. I've just heard that today is a big day for you, so I stopped in to add my voice to those of others in wishing you a very happy birthday."

My decorum was rattled when she replied, "Give me a smooch."

A favorite 101-year-old patient, LuLu Pinard, still plays duets on the piano with her family members. All the centenarians pride their birthday greetings from the president.

The Census Bureau projects that in the year 2080, there will be 1,870,000 centenarians in the United States. Our grandchildren will be approaching 100.

Master Athletes

As a family we are keenly interested in sports—nearly all sports. The reasons for this are the same as everyone else's, but with the added dimension of seeking the limits of human endurance, particularly as we age. It is a part of defining who we are. As a part of this, our family has become involved with the Western States 100 Mile Endurance Run over an old gold mining trail from Squaw Valley to Auburn, California. It has been billed as the world's toughest endurance test. My son, Walter, and my wife, Ruth Anne, have both gloriously completed it twice in recent years. We annually give the awards to the oldest "finishers." (Any kid can run 100 miles, but for how long can he or she keep it up?) Our real heroes and usual winners are Ed Fishman, age 67, from Honolulu, and Helen Klein, age 66, from Auburn, California. At a time when Social Security and Medicare apply, these two are running 100 miles. That makes an emphatic point. Their marks are glorious, but surely are there to be broken. Eighty-one-year-old Willie Hayward recently completed the famous 61-mile Comrades Run in South Africa. He first won it in 1930, 59 years ago. Anabel Marsh, 61, ran across the United States, 3,261 miles in 113 days. Presently, there are marathon records held by individuals who are up to and including 98 years of age! Ruth Rothfarb ran the 1987 New York Marathon at age 86—in 8 hours and 7 minutes! She started her running career at age 72. At age 67, Eula Weaver suffered from angina. At age 75 she experienced a heart attack and developed hypertension. Then she started running; and by age 82 she was asymptomatic and off all of her medicines. Ed Benham of Ocean City, New Jersey, ran a 3:43 marathon at the age of 80—30 minutes faster than my own "personal best"! Ed ran 10 miles in 75 minutes. I couldn't run 1 mile in 7 1/2 minutes!

In 1987, John Gilmour entered the Western Australia 10 Mile Championships. At 69 years of age he ran a 58-minute time. Forty-one years earlier he had recorded a time of 47 minutes, thus losing only 11 minutes' speed in 41 years. Terrific! A local star in my home community of San Francisco is Ivor Welsh. Ivor, now 92, started to run as a result of grief when his wife of 57 years had just died of cancer. At age 83 he started to run and shortly thereafter ran his first marathon. He is still running. Larry Wilson, a waiter in San Francisco, was still jogging until he died a couple of years ago at the age of 106. My father's Harvard medical schoolmate Dr. Paul Spangler is training for a world record for 90-year-olds in next year's New York Marathon.

A good friend and constant amazement is Walt Stack, a legend in San Francisco. Over 80, Walt still swims and runs prodigiously. It is his life, and by it he has inspired tens of thousands to explore and expand themselves. He did it to us. He started to exercise at age 58. One year, at age 61, he ran the Pike's Peak Marathon, beginning at 6,500 feet and climbing 14 miles to the 14,110-foot summit seven times in the nine days preceding the run—just for practice! Walt's advice to us all, "Just keep breathing." He observed, "Unfitness is the disease that precedes other diseases."

The idea of exercise and aging meshes most completely in the tournaments and championships which include, along with the winners, recognition of performance based on age. I have a number of patients who participate actively in these events. "I can't wait to get older" is a familiar refrain, as they enter an older, and hopefully easier, age group. To them I warn, "Don't be sure!"

The *Running Times* issue of May 1988 heralded the most outstanding performances of the Seventh World Veterans Games held in December 1987 in Australia. Almost 5,000 athletes from 51 nations participated. Ninety-seven-year-old Azad Singh Prithvi of India ran the 100- and 200-meter dashes, but was beaten by 94-year-old Jin-Chang of Thailand in the 200 meters in a world record time of 48 seconds.

Among my heroes was Duncan MacLean. Duncan, who died recently at the age of 96, was known as the Tartan Flash and competed in the dashes in the first two World Masters Championships. At the age of 93 he ran 21.7 seconds for the 100-meter sprint. After he died, I wrote his physician in Great Britain and learned that he had stayed physically active almost until his death.

Other sports reveal their old heroes and heroines as well. A recent issue of *Sports Illustrated* congratulated Pearl Miller, who, at age 90, had just won a 50-yard backstroke championship. In 1985, Ella Peckham set nine world swimming records at the age of 86. Luella Tyra, 92, entered all swimming events open to her at the 1984 U.S. Masters Championships. Ludwig Magenes, 93, a champion many times, still swims daily at the Olympic Club in San Francisco.

I recently heard of a rugby league in the United Kingdom called the Puckered Ruckers, which color-codes their players by age. How much mayhem you are allowed to commit on an opponent is dictated by his color jersey. A Japanese player, over 70, wears purple and is virtually untouchable. I think of rugger Rudy Schultz, age 85, of San Francisco—I wonder what color they would give him.

Jim Cain, of Saint Louis, joined a health club at age 99.

To indulge his own fantasies, Charles Schultz, of *Peanuts* fame, organized an ice hockey league for players over age 60. In Colorado, the Over the Hill Gang Ski Club is flourishing. It is comprised of individuals who do not see age as a disqualification for anything—particularly skiing. The 70+Ski Club in New York has over 700 members, 38 of whom are over the age of 80. The late Lowell Thomas belonged to the club; their 1983 roster listed Joe Ross, age 89, as the oldest member. Ross started skiing at age 52 and ski racing at age 89, got married at age 92, and began roller skating at 93. That's living life at the edge.

Tesicki Igarashi first climbed Mount Fuji at the age of 90 and returned to climb it again at the age of 100. Helen Klein, 67, in her 66th year ran five 100-mile mountain trail races—in the same summer. Eighty-year-old Lyman Frain bicycled from New York to San Francisco, 3,244 miles in 86 days. Harness racer Morris Nixon celebrated his 90th birthday by winning a trotting-horse race. At age 100, Henry Miller scored a 99 for eighteen holes of golf. Willie Shoemaker won the Kentucky Derby at the age of 54. During one week in his 90th year, Larry Thackwell climbed the three highest mountain peaks in Great Britain.

Etta Clark's book *Growing Old Is Not for Sissies* offers a wonderful series of portraits of senior athletes which includes some of those individuals mentioned above. Also present is 81-year-old Helen Zechmeister, champion weight lifter who jogs once and swims four times daily to help her conditioning. The conditioning apparently works—she recently "deadlifted" 245 pounds. Eric de Reynier, an 81-year-old hang glider, is included in the compendium, as well as 80-year-old karate expert Eleanor Hyndam. These and tens of thousands like them are exploring both their own and our limits. They are reservoirs of durable energy. In Dr. Richard Selzer's words, "they reject the erosion of longevity."

In late July 1989, my wife and I drove to Eugene, Oregon, to participate in the Eighth World Veterans Track and Field Championships. Five thousand competitors from 58 nations had come to the largest track meet ever, anywhere. The opening ceremonies were awesome as we marched in behind banners depicting our ascending ages in 5-year increments. The stands were packed. The bagpipes piped us in to great acclaim. The cheers grew and grew as the ages mounted. The oldest competitor was 97-year-old Otto Porath, of Germany. An Indian sprinter, age 102, was scheduled to compete but he had some visa problems which held him up at the Delhi airport. As we paraded in we looked behind to see our future selves, and we liked what we saw.

The twilight in which I ran my 10K race was gorgeous. There were runners from New Zealand, Norway, Japan, and elsewhere. There was a loud cheer as I passed the stands at the fourth or fifth lap, but the ovation was not for me. It was for the 97-year-old who had just broken the world shot-put record for persons 95 to 100.

The highlight race of the meet was the 200-meter dash for those aged 90 to 95. Ninety-four-year-old Wang Ching-Chang of Taiwan bolted to an early lead; but 90-year-old Herbert Kirk of Bosland, Montana, caught him with 40 meters to go. Wang charged again to win by a foot; but the competitors didn't see the finish line, so they kept dueling for another 70 meters.

Recognizing that the race was at an end, they turned and trotted back to a delirious crowd.

Al Oerter, ex-Olympian, age 52, observed that this meet was more like the Olympics than were the Olympics. Somehow, being older was liberating.

STEP 3.
SOCIAL PERSUASION

Bandura's third component of self-efficacy involves social persuasion. That is what this book is about. I hope it is a lesson in self-efficacy—the aggregation and synthesis of hundreds of bits of evidence that aging can be good, and that its goodness depends upon each of us.

STEP 4.
CHANGING PHYSIOLOGIC RESPONSES
TO PERCEIVED INADEQUACIES

The fourth and last part of Bandura's compound prescription is the alteration of physiologic cues associated with failed performance. His principal example of this technique derives from his research with Dr. Robert Debusk of the Cardiology Division at Stanford. Patients who had had heart attacks were taught, preferably with the spouse in participation, to regain their vigor rapidly after this insult. The tool used to do this was the treadmill. Under careful watching, these post-heart-attack patients were instructed in a gradually increasing work intensity and encouraged to avoid panic. Physical cues such as breathlessness, fatigue, and so forth were aborted by assurance and guidance. Thus, through such training, the patients were able to rejoin an active lifestyle much quicker than they would have through an unguided and thereby uncertain recovery period. Gentle coaching helps us all cope with life's assaults. Norman Cousins tells of how he failed the standard exercise electrocardiogram conducted under strictly controlled rules, but passed it without a concern when he was allowed to manage the pace and the environment.

Not only is self-efficacy approachable—it is also "treatable," just like a strep throat. Taking charge of our own lives is a central thread of our existence. Its presence and importance becomes more evident as we grow older. But mastery of the practice does not come out of a bottle, nor is it something that can be painted on or delivered in a monthly envelope. As Oscar and Hammerstein wrote, "It's got to be carefully taught."

For all of his good qualities, I am personally peeved with former President Reagan because he failed consciously to allow us to use him as a role model. He denied his age—apparently as a specific political strategy. In effect he said, "I will be more popular as a younger leader than I would be as one who is pushing 80." In 20 years or so from now, I hope he will allow us to admire him for this magnificent accomplishment.

Lying about one's age is absurd. I heard about one woman who kept defraying acknowledgment of her age until she had children who were older than she said she was.

Mastery of self-efficacy does not come all of a sudden—but it is never too late to start. You can't run a marathon without first running one or two miles. You can't walk if you are in an armchair. You can't smile when you are frowning. The first step is the hardest. And yet limits broken become new expectations. After Hillary climbed "unclimbable" Mount Everest, hundreds of others now have. After Roger Bannister broke the unbreakable four-minute mile barrier, hundreds of others now have. After we have broken the stereotypes of what older people cannot do, there is a floodgate of opportunity opening for us all.

ELEVEN

THE LAST PASSAGE

Dying is not popular. It has never caught on.
That's understandable; it's bad for the complexion.
It also upsets your daily routine and leaves
you with too much time on your hands.

George Burns

When we are familiar with death
we accept each week, each day, as a gift.
Only if we are able thus to accept life—
bit by bit—does it become precious.

Albert Schweitzer

A certain characteristic of the perfect machine is that when it wears out, it does so all at once. A design engineer would not have many repeat customers if he continued to plan devices that sputtered, fumed, stalled, and overheated before their terminal disruption. We want machines that run until they stop. Nothing is worse than the car that dies in $200 increments. The generator, the fuel pump, the transmission—here and there, exasperating and impoverishing. But how does the human machine wear out? Too often we die incrementally—not by $200 bits, but by many thousands of dollars of progressive decrements.

I used to be very upset when my patients, knowing my enthusiasm for jogging, would fling down a newspaper clipping onto my desk which described the death while jogging of some individual—most prominently and lamentably, Jim Fixx. But now I turn the proposition around, and reply that I hope that I too die while jogging, or making love, or climbing a mountain, or in some other active, pleasurable pursuit, and not in the dreary company of protracted decay. Rene Dubos's characterization of "medicated survival" is not for me. I want to die in full stride, hopefully pursuing rather than being pursued. The American Indian found it dishonorable to die in bed, and we must not forget that death was Patrick Henry's *second* choice.

THE FACE OF DEATH

How do we die, individually and collectively? What does the end of life look like? What is our trajectory? Is it a sharp edge, active, useful, well until the last moment—or a slow, downward spiral wherein each day is paler and gloomier than the one before? Death does not seem to be quite the arch-villain that dying does.

In warlike primitive societies, physical weakness was regarded with contempt. The elders often suffered disdain, and this prompted many of them to request burial—while still alive. The family council made a major ceremony out of it. Among the Indians of Gran Chaco, it was the custom for an old man to require his son, out of love, to strike him dead as soon as he became a burden to the nomadic tribe. Only vigorous life could sustain or be sustained.

The Romans had a similar attitude toward age. *"Ad pontem"*—"to the bridge"—was the cry surrounding the summary drowning of old and worn-out people. Yet, it was observed by historian Heinrich Schwartz that age alone was not the issue which drew on the older person the antipathy of his fellows. Rather it was his weakness and helplessness. As long as the elder was robust and active, and capable of working and fighting, there was no issue drawn.

Norman Cousins wrote, "Death isn't the ultimate tragedy, rather it is that which dies within us while we are still alive."

Life expectancy isn't enough. Active, productive, resourceful life expectancy is what we seek.

Protracted dying is a new phenomenon; we are not prepared for it. Animals in the wild don't linger long in an ailing state. So too, primitive humans, when ailing, have not generally survived for long. Until the present day, medical science has not had the tools to retard the moment of death. Now it does. Multiple evidences abound in the anthropologic literature as to how our aboriginal ancestors dealt with death. American Indians, Eskimos, and other native cultures from around the world exhibit residual practices and lore regarding their age-old customs associated with death. For example, our January 1988 trip to Borneo taught us firsthand how the hunter-gatherer Punans, nomads of the rain forest, still ritualize death. When an elder can no longer move and keep up, a week-long ritual is held with the end moment being the leave-taking of the individual on a platform in the jungle. Death would not be far behind. And a fascinating report in the *Journal of the American Anthropologist* related how in the 1920s an Eskimo son was prosecuted for killing his father; the reason for which was that his honored father could no longer hunt. The son was found not guilty.

The driving element behind this widely observed abandonment and/or actual killing of a tribe's most frail was that it was necessary due to energetic considerations. For the highly mobile tribe to survive, movement was essential. If a person could no longer move, someone else would have to carry the disabled one, or the person would be left behind. There is nothing cruel, barbaric, or "inhuman" about this. It was simply a matter of survival of the tribe as a whole.

It is my contention that the nursing home represents a contemporary expression of the abandonment motif of aboriginal people. In our highly mobile, disconnected society, old people live within the framework until they can no longer keep up. *We* have conceived of the nursing home as a repository of the unable; there are few nursing homes in primitive countries. Furthermore, I believe the nursing home can be considered an example of a failure of our successes. When we had no capacity to extend lives, there were no such "facilities." Now they burgeon. Richard Lamm asks provocatively whether our technology prolongs living or prolongs dying.

DEFINING DEATH

Technically—now with mechanical support devices and organ transplants—we have the capacity to sustain vital functions (heartbeat, breathing, filtering of poisons, etc.) for decades after cessation of natural function. The anomalies that this can and does create are fearsome. Death has historically been heralded by the stopping of the heart. Groucho Marx as Dr. Quackenbush taking his patient's pulse quipped, "Either this man is dead, or my watch has stopped." But if we have the capacity to keep the heart beating, semi-indefinitely, then what is death?

Bearing this in mind, we have turned more recently to another organ, a more important organ, to define death—the brain. When the brain has lost all sensate, cognizant function, the person is declared "brain dead," and sustaining efforts are discontinued. Pope Pius XII affirmed this recognition in 1957 in a speech titled "Prolongation of Life." This consensus that life in any reasonable sense is over when the brain stops working—this profound acknowledgment—argues that life quality is the essence, and not mere breathing or heartbeat. Flesh alone is not enough to define life. This assertion is of immense significance to our species and represents one of the most important philosophic decisions of our age.

But having agreed that heartbeat alone is not enough for life, what is? In April 1987 I arrived in Howrah railway station, my wife and I having ridden the train up the eastern coast of India from Madras through Bubeneschwar. We had come to Calcutta for three reasons. First, we wanted to see this magnificent city to determine for ourselves if its despairing reputation was deserved. It isn't. (A point which is beautifully punctuated by Dominique Lapierre in *The City of Joy.*) Second, Calcutta was the takeoff point for our next voyage in Bhutan; and last because I wanted to meet with Mother Teresa.

It was Palm Sunday morning. Within half an hour of arriving at the hotel, I have voyaged to the Mother House and met with the almond-faced gentle lady whom we all revere. I opened, "Mother, I am an American physician devoutly concerned and daily involved with the issues of how do we decide how much to do for old and dying persons."

Mother Teresa answered, "Dr. Bortz, don't worry about that. Just love them."

Her response was a total surprise for me. I couldn't imagine being disinterested or passive in addressing the issue which I had posed. But I did as Mother Teresa urged. I visited the Home for the Dying in the south part of Calcutta the next morning and spent most of the day there. I was self-conscious and ill at ease. I felt I was intruding on a covenantal happening. I visited with the staff and eventually donned a green apron to help out. My clumsiness as a bedside nurse was immensely humbling. I left at the end of the afternoon challenged and very uneasy. I then understood Mother Teresa's words, "Dr. Bortz, don't worry about that. Just love them." The majority of the people at the home died—the men from tuberculosis, the women from sepsis. They were given only token medical care; a minimal amount of antibiotics could have saved most. And yet, if they had been saved that day only to be discharged back into the streets of Calcutta, they would have likely been back in the next week. In the meantime, there were 300,000 others waiting to get in. When seen that way, it was a technically unapproachable problem; and Mother Teresa's answer to it was "love."

In my life, in the life of any Western physician, such recourse is no longer relevant. For better or worse, medical science has provided us with tools which can cure sometimes and comfort always. Their employ is the curriculum of medical school and postgraduate training. We can do good, and we do good. I hope we have not simultaneously lost the beckon to love.

Edna St. Vincent Millay wrote,

> Love cannot fill the thickened lung with breath
> Nor clear the blood, not set the fractured bone.
> Yet many a man is making friends with death
> Even as I speak, for lack of love alone.

Clearly, technologic immortality is not a goal which any of us would advocate. Yet, our rationality in dealing with dying and death is erratic and uncertain. Modern medicine too often sees death as a disease, a pathology, to be therapized and cured.

In 1965, Sir Geoffrey Gorer wrote, "Pornography would appear to be a concomitant of prudery—pornography has been concerned with sexuality, copulation and birth were the unmentionables. Now in the twentieth century, however, death has become more and more unmentionable as a natural process—preoccupation with such processes is morbid and unhealthy, to be discouraged by all and proscribed in the young. If we dislike the modern pornography of death, then we must give back to death, natural death, its parade and publicity, readmit grief and mourning."

E. Mansell Patterson, in his book *The Experience of Dying*, portrays death as a taboo. He observed that since 1900 we have had no wars on our soil, no public executions, no plagues of childhood death, and we have eliminated frontier deaths. Death has become a closet experience.

Ivan Illich in *Medical Nemesis* wrote, "The modernization of society has brought the epic of natural death to an end. Western man has lost the right to preside at his act of dying. Death or the autonomous power to age, has been expropriated down to the last breath."

We have no comfort zone with death. Our alienation from our own terminus pretends that our death is somebody else's job to preside over—like Woody Allen's fabulous quote, "I am not afraid of dying—I just don't want to be there when it happens."

Subsequently, the hospital has become a place to die. But in medical

school I didn't have any courses on how to die or how to let patients die—
that goal was not part of my job description. That was a clear and glaring
error. I feel deeply that playing steward at the end of life is one of the most
precious roles which a physician can play. I take it very seriously.

For a research project I kept a record of all my patients who died in
1987. There were ninety-seven. I recorded from what they died, where and
how, what medicines were involved, presence and compliance with advanced directives concerning medical interventions, functional state of the
person in the year before death, and the "appropriateness" of the death. In
one sense, none was appropriate because each person could have lived
longer under idealized situations; but in another sense, at the time of dying,
all of the good had seemingly been squeezed out of my patients' lives. With
three exceptions, those who died in the hospital did so because of the
presence of a potential benefit for them. The exceptions were patients who
had been hospitalized against their will and against my instructions because
the nursing home in which they were living was terrified of penal review.
Quite simply put, the administrators of the specific nursing homes feared
the appearance that these individuals had been "allowed to die" while in
their charge. I am still furious about this callousness.

Montaigne wrote, "Death is the moment when dying ends." It is our
job to shorten the interval between the start of dying and death. I hope that
all of my patients' dyings are appropriately brief. Jim Fries has written
extensively about "the compression of morbidity"—to be healthy until the
end. That is our highest ideal.

THE COST OF DYING

Unfortunately, the growing debate about how much treatment we
should offer a dying person is not confined only to issues of best interest and
technical capacity. Money rears its ugly head. The "high cost of dying" is
asserted. Someone calculated that 1 percent of our gross national product is
spent on dying—more than on all of research, or on all private education, or
on all mental illness. A 1984 analysis conducted by James Lubitz and Ronald
Prihoda showed that the 6 percent of Medicare enrollees who die each year
use up 28 percent of the budget. Dying costs a lot of money.

In 1987, Ann Scitovsky, noted medical economist at the Palo Alto

Medical Foundation, performed a study for the Hartford Foundation in which she detailed the medical expenditures of the last twelve months of life of 513 patients here at my clinic. Eighty-two percent of those who died were over 65 years of age. Forty-eight percent died in the hospital; 26 percent died at home. At the time of the study the average cost per person was $23,000. Importantly, Ann found that we physicians spent three times as much money on patients who were functionally intact than we did on those who weren't.

For example several years ago an 88-year-old patient of mine was brought to the Stanford Hospital emergency room by the paramedics in what is called "respiratory arrest"—she wasn't breathing. I was called instantly and asked how to proceed. "Full code" was my response. This activist assertion was easy. I knew my patient and her husband well. I had made several house calls to their lovely apartment nearby. They lived a bounteous life full of the cheers of their family and selves. My patient had a minor degree of high blood pressure, which was easily controlled, and was otherwise well. Therefore, the decision for "full code," mindless of her age, was easy.

To sustain her we broke all of her ribs in artificial resuscitation. This produced the condition known as flail chest, where when she breathed in, her chest sagged instead of expanded. Her life was sustained by numerous machines and drugs; we had tubes into virtually every orifice of her body. She received exquisite care in the intensive care unit. Each morning on rounds I was asked by the nurses and junior physicians whether we should continue our efforts. I said "yes," over and over again.

My patient lived. After six weeks of heroic work on her part and on the part of her regular attendees, she went home directly to her apartment and her husband. She lived a fully active, happy, symptom-free life for one year. Then she died suddenly in her bed. The point of this story is that each day I had made an affirmative decision that resulted in the salvaging of one year of an 88-year-old woman's life—a very good year. But the cost of the six weeks in the hospital was $125,000. This huge expense was paid exclusively by Medicare—which means that we, the taxpayers, paid for it. We bought one year of life for an 88-year-old woman; but it cost us $125,000. For me this was clearly a correct decision, one not sanctioned by Mother Teresa's approach; but one created and demanded by our technical competence and by our wealth as a nation. In reaching the decision to go on, I acted specifically as my patient's advocate. I could not, did not, act simultaneously as a social arbiter, arguing with myself as the gatekeeper of these life-determinative decisions that this money could be better spent on school nutrition projects, or housing developments, or the stealth bomber. Colleagues in academia argue that social conscience must permeate these tough decisions, because they are too expensive and the high cost of dying is debilitating our country.

The State of Oregon is now causing waves by making rationing of medical care explicit rather than implicit. Treatment of meningitis is at the top of the list of expenditure "allowables," liver and bone marrow transplants and hernia repairs are at the bottom." Dr. Paul Kirk, Health Services Commissioner, estimated that Oregon spends up to half of its medical funds inappropriately for crisis rather than for preventive care. The prioritizing of medical services is intended to increase accountability. Representative Ron Wyden of Oregon observed "Medicaid is such a Byzantine crazy quilt, all Oregon is trying to do is to make some sense out of it."

This issue was captured in a recent book by friend and esteemed ethicist Daniel Callahan, head of the Hastings Center in New York. Dan's book *Setting Limits* has been widely reviewed and serves wonderfully as a focal point for debate on the matter of allocation of resources. *Rationing* is not a word with which physicians can identify. We don't take to the limiting proposition at all. Aside from a battlefield experience in which only one bottle of blood is available to two bleeding patients, we do not see ourselves confronted with who gets what. This position of generosity of capacity, spirit, effort, and expenditure is now ending. Clearly we cannot afford ever increasingly expensive maneuvers to increasingly smaller yields. The debate is entered.

I find much that is laudable in Dan's book. He emphasizes that the answer to this will not be found in cutting the fat out of the system—i.e., in controlling unnecessary tests, etc. And yet, the issue is much bigger than this. So, too, we need to develop the sensitivity and sensibility to spend money in the right places as we age—more for home care and prevention, less on high-tech miracles. But the point—the critical point—at which Dan and I diverge is the use of age, per se, as the criterion on which health resources will be allocated. Some 40-year-olds are too old (i.e. dysfunctional) to receive precious help; some 80-year-olds aren't too old. Dan sees the "late 70's or early 80's" as the cutoff point. Age rationing is thus advocated.

I feel strongly that such reasoning is false. It leads to dangerous and ominous projections, and it defaults a rational approach to what has clearly become a matter of immense national importance. There is much good life to be lived at the age at which Dan advocates pulling back. I would project that there probably is some age at which chronology itself would be an appropriate consideration for the denial of sustaining care; but this decades further out, maybe at 119 years, 364 days.

Having negated the use of age as a factor in making these tough claims makes the job itself tougher. Time is an easy handle, but convenience is not an excuse for error. Jerry Avorn, of Harvard, and many others argue too against age being a determinant for clinical decisions. In fact, Jerry is against any effort which seeks to systematize this decision-making. He feels that any guidance scheme would be so inherently faulted that it would be useless or, worse, dangerous. Again, I disagree. I feel that we are at a time of sufficient awareness and competence and sensitivity that we can propose guidelines which will help us all confront our dying with a confidence and mutual respect.

"COST" IS MORE THAN MONEY

The cost of dying must be expressed in terms which transcend mere commerce. I feel that there are two basic principles which underlie whether a life is worth saving—one extrinsic and one intrinsic. The extrinsic principle that serves to help define "quality of life" is function—how well do we work. For this determination we have now developed very clear measurements which detail explicitly not just how various miniature parts of our bodies work, but how we work as a whole. For example, we know that life is threatened when the oxygen content of blood is below a critical level, or when the poisons in blood exceed a threshold level. By combining some of the most critical of these we can develop a very real predictive estimate of the outcome for any particular intervention.

The intrinsic side of one's quality of life is harder to quantitate—but it is no less real or, I feel, less approachable. All of us obviously have different estimates as to what makes our individual lives livable and worthy. Although the intrinsic definitions of life qualities are infinite, I suggest that the term *joy* comes close to embracing a universally acceptable tenet. If a person possesses the potential for joy, then life still has quality. Without this, life loses meaning. Others hold up terms such as *cognitive competence* as the intrinsic benchmark, and by this they mean one's ability to react and interreact. For me, however, joy is a more penetrating and decisive term. If, for example, a person fails to experience joy on a Christmas morning when the grandchildren first see the nighttime's exuberant bounty, then that person's intrinsic quality of life is gone.

The derivation of a set of principles or guidelines with which to help us all approach nontreatment decisions is, to me, not even optional. Rather, it is mandatory. Such guidelines, which for me are logically derived out of cool assessment of extrinsic (functional) and intrinsic (joy) observations, must be tempered by the dimension of time. We can be very dysfunctional or despairing, temporarily; but the illness or injury or depression passes. Efforts at restitution should be abandoned only when the situation has been clearly analyzed and observed over time and only when such observation indicates that the determinants of life quality are irreversible.

This was the philosophic and intellectual background that gave me confidence when dealing with my 88-year-old patient who had stopped breathing. She was wonderfully functional and full of joy. She would have flunked Dan Callahan's limit test; she passed mine.

Clearly we need to do an immense amount of further work to define better our predictors of good life. Prognostication now is still very crude and uncertain. But unless we collectively affirm that this is a goal worthy of all our best efforts, we will continue to languish at the moment of death. At present this is too often a state of confusion, and sadness, and indeterminacy.

For me the issues presented by my 88-year-old patient are straightforward ones. But what if she had been severely ill when she stopped breathing? Or demented? Or depressed? Then the situation would have been much harder. Presently it is common for the judicial system to be invoked in order to resolve hard choices. Sanctity of life, sovereignty of individual choice, medical realities, and cost are all mixed. The bedside becomes a courtroom. To me this is a sadness, and an evidence of the lack of maturity of our culture. Still, we are working at it. For example, in March 1983, after a series of public hearings and numerous deliberations, the President's Commission for the Study of Ethical Problems in Medicine, led by Morris Abram, presented a report entitled "Deciding to Forgo Life Sustaining Treatment—Ethical, Medical, and Legal Issues in Treatment Decisions." It remains a basic reference even today. Furthermore, almost every hospital, every specialty medical society, and the AMA have deliberative bodies working on the dilemma. We all need to think on it. Death and dying need to be demystified. Death should once again become a natural act.

MAY WE FACILITATE A
"NATURAL DEATH"?

There is evidence that suicide is increasing among the old. Government records indicate a 25 percent rise in suicides of people aged 65 and older. This is counter to what is happening at all other ages and seems to contrast with the general view of increased health and prosperity of older persons. The rate is highest among white males—43.2 out of every 100,000 (four times the national average). The ratio of men to women is 4:1 in the 65 to 69 age group, and 12:1 for those over 85. Even these numbers are understated, as the exact cause of death in older people (who often have numerous medications in the medicine cabinet) is frequently obscure and casually attributed to heart failure or some kindred lethal event.

Further, I've had many older patients simply stop eating for no obvious medical reason. Life seems to have become too much of a burden, and the patients have given the signal that they have decided to die. Maybe this is like the leave-taking seen in primitive societies.

What of euthanasia? Can we condone the taking of another's life— under any circumstances whatsoever? Is this not murder? The accepted party line of the medical establishment is often expressed in Arthur Hugh Clough's simple couplet:

> Thou shalt not kill; but needst not strive
> Officiously to keep alive.

In March 1987, the Royal Dutch Medical Association formalized procedures for active euthanasia. These binding conditions include:

1. The patient must make repeated requests.
2. The patient must be fully informed and rational.
3. The patient must have a terminal illness.
4. The patient must be suffering.
5. Two doctors must agree on the action.

While the statistics are not accurate, it is assumed that between 6,000 and 20,000 persons are killed each year in the Netherlands in this fashion. This number represents 4 percent of the country's annual death rate.

At this time, euthanasia lacks formal legislative approval from the Dutch government, although it has strong support from both the people and the legal system. The usual technique involves the administration of a barbiturate and curare, a respiratory inhibitor.

A 1986 report of the experience of 25 family physicians in the Hague revealed that in the prior year the physicians, who care for about 500 patients who die each year, had received 17 requests for active euthanasia, and had carried it out in 9 of the 17—2% of total deaths.

Several refinements of the system were detailed in an article in the December 15th, 1989 JAMA by Dr. M.A.M. de Wachter of the Institute of Bioethics, Maastricht, the Netherlands, "It is not sufficient that the patient wishes to die or that the patient agrees with the termination of life. Instead, the patient must take the initiative. Nor should the physician solicit the patient to make the request. . . . There must be no family pressure on the patient to request euthanasia. . . . The patient's request must be persistent and consistent."

In our own country there are many indications of support for both "active euthanasia," such as the Dutch system, and "passive euthanasia," the withholding of so-called heroic efforts to keep the patient's body functioning long after "brain death" has occurred. A recent Roper public opinion poll affirmed general support for all euthanasia; while 80 percent of those polled by the AMA favored "passive euthanasia." A 1988 survey conducted among 2,218 Colorado physicians revealed that 60 percent felt they had had personal, professional experience with patients in whom they felt euthanasia would have been appropriate. Sixty percent of this group said that they would be willing to participate in euthanasia if it were legal; but little more than 4 percent actually admitted having done so regardless of present laws.

In 1989, a distinguished physician panel wrote in the *New England Journal of Medicine*, "It is not immoral for a physician to assist in the rational suicide of a terminally ill patient."

On the morning of the day I write this I removed the feeding tube of an 81-year-old man who six weeks ago suffered a massive stroke, and who has remained ever since in what is known as the "persistent vegetative state." Early on I had told his loving wife that I felt we should provide support for a reasonable period of time to see if he would improve, and then we should consider removing "life supports." She and I have conferred frequently; and last Friday, I suggested that she and other family members think it through one last time. If they concurred, I felt that today (Monday), the tube should be removed. We have now done so. My patient will die in a few days; his wife is very grateful.

It is not always so straightforward. I care still for another patient, age 45, who has been in the persistent vegetative state since a severe auto collision five years ago. I visit her monthly in the nursing home where she is sustained by a feeding tube. Her eyes are open but she shows no response or communicative capacity. She can't move. Her caring husband wants me to remove the tube, but her mother and brother do not. So the impasse is held up in the court. I am advised that were the husband sturdy enough to carry on the legal fight the court would probably rule in his favor—but who is to be sure, and at what financial and personal cost?

William Reichel, distinguished geriatrician and ethicist, tells me of a patient of his who was a terrible burden to his wife. He had had multiple strokes and was bedfast, incontinent, and miserable. For months she had begged Bill and others to let her husband die; when abruptly she died, he got better.

So the issues are complex; the answers hard. They should be hard. Beware of anyone with a slick scheme. Philosophically, I favor euthanasia. As I removed the tube from my patient this morning, I now await his death in a few days. Why wait? you may ask. If what the family, and I, and others all want is for him to have a dignified death, why not just give him a barbiturate and curare and hasten the event? The answer is that the medical system is not ready for that; and I'm not certain that we can ever develop procedures which will be "airtight" enough. We cannot, for example, involve health personnel who have sincere objections to such an active approach. What of the pharmacist asked to prepare the fatal mixture? What of the nurse who brings it at my call? And while I am certainly not a cynic, I have great reserve about the ability of our society to create adequate safeguards regarding euthanasia. Despite a seemingly failsafe set of guidelines, I fear that our capacity for misadventure when personal gain may be accomplished outweighs our moral and legal capacities.

The bottom line is that the issue of euthanasia should be largely hypothetical. The reasons people commit suicide or request euthanasia is the fear of the indignities of dying, dependency, pain and tubes. Physicians should bolster their stewardship by giving absolutely firm confidences that these three burdens will not be borne. The patient must be made to know that he or she will be fully franchised, fully empowered, fully in charge, until the last breath. Most important, pain must not be allowed to become an issue. There is no excuse for unrelieved suffering when we clearly have the technologic know-how to avoid the pierce of pain. Who cares if the terminal patient becomes "addicted"! Finally, tubes should be avoided strenuously except for temporary support systems. Currently, I believe I have only two or three patients on feeding tubes. I feel such devices are an indignity, and that the only excuse for their use is the temporary provision of calories. Anyone who ever approaches me or my family member with one is going to have one hell of a fight on his hands.

LEARNING TO LIVE
WITH DEATH AND DYING

Many of the living cannot face death and dying, and a major element of this incapacity evolves out of superstition and fear. The new knowledge of the Age Age will assist. We will mature. As we learn more, develop surer senses of what life is, how human life began, how it ends, and how we can shape such an end—then a major enlightenment will be upon us. Death and dying are integral to our aging. As we rationalize our ending, then its prelude will become easier and more opportunistic. In *Living To Be 100,* Osborne Segerberg reports the relationship to death which these centenarians exhibited. For most, death had lost its sting. It was noted further that for those who exhibited airs of resignation, "I have seen and done it all," death was close at hand. For those who had extended agenda, life went on further. We know that death is less common before birthdays or important ceremonies. Rene Dubos planted a tree on each birthday—as an investment in his own future. Psychologists feel that they can predict imminent death by psychologic inventories which reflect a loss of self-efficacy. A loss of control precedes death, "the terminal drop." Freud's most influential colleague, Carl Jung, based much of his own theory upon the precept that elements in our own life experience are shaped by how we manage the thoughts of our own mortality. He remarked, "Profoundly unprepared, we enter upon the evening of life. Worse still, we do so under the false assumption of the truth and ideals in which we have hither to believed. We cannot live through the evening in accordance with the morning's program."

Alan Leveton of the University of California, San Francisco, described the "ego chill" as "a shudder which comes from the sudden awareness that our nonexistence is entirely possible." This was expressed with humor in the last words of William Saroyan, "I know everybody has to die sooner or later, but I thought an exception would be made in my case." And by Woody Allen, "I do not wish to obtain immortality through my work. I wish to obtain it through not dying."

The tragedy and grief which surround death have their origins in three domains, two of which are preventable, and the third of which is "treatable." The first sadness about death is that it is nearly always inappropriate. Cecil Rhodes on his death bed at age 49 said, "So little done, so much to do." A child's death is most excruciating, for it cannot be rationalized. It hurts so much because it is so obviously an affront to any sense of order or right. But if this is the ultimate hurt, then any premature death bears with it too the element of "life unlived." A foreshortened design, an incomplete act, an abortion. As we extend life to its natural boundary, this source of grief and sadness will disperse.

A second contributor to the despair about death is the set of circumstances which surround death. Clearly pain is the most unacceptable companion to the last moments of life, and I solemnly promise any patient in whom death is soon likely that pain will not be theirs to bear. But pain is only one indignity. There are hosts of others, some bodily, many others psychologic—tubes and loneliness among them. The act of dying needs to be shortened. We die too long. As reflected in the King James version of *The Book of Job*, 5:26, we wish to ". . . come to the grave at a full age, as a sheaf of grain ripens in its season."

If independence until our heart stops is desired, then effort needs to be directed to sustaining that primal freedom. More of us are learning that it is both bold and correct to provide some clear statement of our wishes concerning our own individual deaths. Death should come as no surprise, and the style of exit is largely ours to make if we will only have the prudence to advise our loved ones and physicians of what we want. A living will or a durable power of attorney for health matters is readily available, and should be universally employed. It has been estimated that nearly 10 percent of Americans currently have such a document. Death can lose much of its sting when we and our families have the confidence that not only did death occur at the appropriate time, but also in the ideal manner. The fear of death has been subordinated to the fear of living too long.

We must learn to be mortal, but we should sustain mastery until our last breath. Only then will death become the final helplessness.

As this book neared completion, my mother died. She had had her hair done in the morning, had gone to a luncheon, and played bridge in the afternoon. I picked her up in my convertible at five o'clock to take her to the Palo Alto Senior Center, where I was to give a celebratory talk on their twentieth anniversary. The title of my speech was, "Redefining Human Aging." Ma was in her pretty, bright, orange-and-white flowered dress. We sat in the front row and hobnobbed with the local celebrants.

I started my speech by asserting that I had accepted the invitation to speak only on the proviso that I be allowed to sing—and then enjoined the crowd of 250 to sing "Happy Birthday" to Mother for her 95th birthday on the following Monday. Ma beamed; and afterward she had a glass of champagne, had her picture taken, and was generally honored.

I took her back to her apartment at seven o'clock, kissed her good-night, and suggested that she might like to ride around with me as I made several house calls the next day. She went in for supper; and just after saying to a friend that she didn't want any salad, she dropped to the floor dead. Resuscitation efforts failed, and I was called with this new reality.

She died like an Indianapolis race car driver hitting the wall at 200 miles per hour. Like a burst bubble. She never knew what happened. Her morbidity was compressed to a minisecond. She died healthy.

Mother's death exposed my own mortality. While she lived I never really pondered the possibility of my own death. She was the omega generation. Now, suddenly, I am. It is a major life passage, but of the three sources of grief mentioned above, I felt only one. Certainly she had lived a long and disease-free life. She had squeezed out most all of her good. Her mode of death was as ideal as one could design. Only the animal sense of energy loss accompanies me now.

Mother never expected to live this long. She was the last survivor of twelve children. Oftentimes she was bewildered by being as old as she was. She hadn't been primed or rehearsed for it. Oftentimes she was selfish in her demands for the time of others. She wanted company. I feel I did a good job as her parent toward the end. I miss her, a lot. But, as I said, she died healthy; that may be all a son should ask.

Dad, on the other hand, did much worse. Twenty years ago at the age of 74, he died in the hospital after a six-week illness and multiple organ system failures—heart, liver, and cancer of the prostate. One evening, I had temporarily resuscitated him when his heart arrested. His death is the only really bad thing that ever happened to me in my whole life. He died too soon. I didn't manage this at all well, while Mother did better. Dad was my champion, my design. I grieved miserably for six months. I still feel cheated for not having had him alive for more of my life. The only good thing Dad's death did for me was that my grief led me to adopt jogging as part of my life strategy.

IDEAL DEATH

The concept may seem alien at first, but there is such a thing as ideal death. Oliver Wendell Holmes defined it thus:

> All of a sudden and nothing first,
> Just as bubbles do when they burst.

The life which like the sun grows larger at its setting is the ideal.

Yet, for those who are left behind after the death—even the ideal death—emptiness remains. The sense of loss is evident even in animals which lack, probably, our capacity to sense the inappropriateness of most deaths. The loss of life is disordering and diminishing because an energy source is lost to us. This pang, this grief, is innate and inevitable if connectedness is to be part of our essence. Not to feel loss at the death of a loved one, even in the idealized fashion hinted above, is unnatural. During life we build our approach to immortality into which death provides access. This immortality is claimed in the lives of the survivors and in the life of our earth. The grief which arises from our sense of loss is "treatable," by ritual, by celebration, by humor, and finally by action. This too is part of the ideal.

Death is the ultimate expression of entropic decay—a rush to oblivion and disorder. The bodily elements are lost to the universe, but the energetic components of that life remain in all of us. Each life affects all. Each death affects all. As John Donne wrote, "Any man's death diminishes me because I am involved in Mankinde and therefore never seek to know for whom the bell tolls; it tolls for thee." The Second Law is immutable. We can't cure it, no matter how much money we spend. But the powerful truth appears as we study and understand it. The order, effectiveness, utility, value, importance, and meaning of all our lives is generated and maintained by an active energy flow. When the energy flow is interrupted, death follows surely. It is therefore clear that our lives *and* our deaths are made optimal by the same device—the ordering effect of energy. It is no accident that nature has conformed our beginning, middle, and end to the same design.

We live full length; we die at a moment when we are active in the fullest sense of being active. If we limit our energies, we will not only live as long as we are intended to live; but our decay process will be slow and miserable. Disuse invites decay and slow dissolution. Activity generates life and a sudden ending. Who can ask for anything more?

In 1956, Bertrand Russell wrote, "An individual's human existence should be like a river—small at first, narrowly contained within its bounds, and rushing passionately past boulders and even waterfalls. Gradually the river grows wide, the banks recede, the waters flow more quietly, and in the end, without any visible break they become merged in the sea, and painlessly lose their individual being."

Death becomes integrating.

It is therefore the ideal pattern and supreme irony that it is the same design, a life actively lived, that enables not only the idealized life but the idealized death.

TWELVE

THE GREENING OF GRAYING

Had we been born fifty years earlier, we would
have wondered, pondered, speculated about
these issues, but we could have done nothing about
them. Had we been born fifty years later, the
answers would, I think, already have been in. Our
children will have been taught the answers
before most of them will have had an opportunity
even to formulate the questions. By far the
most exciting, satisfying and exhilarating time
to be alive is the time in which we pass from
ignorance to knowledge on these fundamental
issues; the age where we begin in wonder and end
in understanding. In all of the four-billion-
year history of life on our planet, in all of the
four-million-year history of the human family,
there is only one generation privileged to
live through that unique transitional moment:
that generation is ours.

Carl Sagan, *Broca's Brain*

I t may be the vanity of each generation down through the ages that it
uniquely has inherited the fulcrum point of history—that all prior time
has been consecrated to its special time—from which all future events will
derive as a residue of the judgments and actions of its particular moment. I
contend, however, like Carl Sagan, that we now can with legitimacy claim

this credential as our special own. For the first time in history we know from where we have come and how we have come. We have our genetic code. We know our universe near to its farthest reaches—we know our beyonds and our innards and our time dimension. But we know too for the first time, as part of this knowledge implosion, what our own personal limits are—our dimensions—and the events and forces which decree how we reach them. We have our map and our calendar.

This is precious knowledge, a basic treasure that until now has been hidden in ignorance and superstition. Yesterday we fantasized about our lifetimes. We implored the spirits, we inveigled the astrologers, we spurred on the alchemists. Yesterday life was an uncertain affair, unable to be bought or conjured or understood. Its uncertainties bred fatalism and passivity. Death didn't make any sense, nor did life. It wasn't rational. It was a crap shoot. Today these shadows are illumined. We know our limits. We know our requirements and our potentials. We see our whole blueprint.

The characterization of our epoch as the Age Age stems naturally from this achievement of self-knowledge. Not only in our generation are there millions more of our older selves, but concomitant with this is our understanding of the dynamics which have shaped this immense demographic event. We are fortunate that new insight accompanies the number. Were we in the position of growth without reason or understanding, our millions of gray persons could constitute a potential cancer on our society, consuming and pressuring. As it is, there is enlarging debate on the issue of "intergenerational equity"—which in effect represents a social search into the nature and the definition of our burgeoning aging selves.

Several slogans have appeared in the attempt to put a label on the strategy of how the new system can work. For me the term *useful aging* works best. "Useful aging" connotes not only the notion that our biology works and that our health is made optimal by use; it also connotes the idea that our gift of found lifetime makes sense if the added years have an identified purpose.

Lewis Thomas wrote, "We have genes for usefulness, and usefulness is about as close to a common goal for all of nature as I can guess at."

In an earlier time Tennyson wrote in "Ulysses,"

> I am a part of all that I have met;
> Yet all experience is an arch wherethro'
> Gleams that untravell'd world, whose margin fades
> For ever and for ever when I move.

How dull it is to pause, to make an end,
To rust unburnish'd, not to shine in use!

On his 90th birthday, Oliver Wendell Holmes said, "For to live is to function. That's all there is to living."

The term *useful aging* also captures the thermodynamic implications inherent in human aging. It connotes a directed energy flow, ordered and ordering. Useful at the cellular level, useful at the organism level, useful at the societal level.

My good friend and geropsychologist Martin Connelly favors the term *responsible aging* to reflect the issue of accountability of our emerging aging society. It implies responsibility not only of the aging individual for his or her part of the general domain, but of the aging society itself as an ecosystem of its own. If our older selves adopt a posture of dependency then the equation can't balance, and enlarging discord will be ours. *Responsible aging* has an exhortative ring to it—which I like.

Rollo May wrote, "A new ethic is needed for our age, an ethic of interaction based on the assumption that each man is responsible for the effects of his own actions."

The Gray Panthers buy into this notion.

Robert Butler, M.D., first director of the National Institute on Aging, proposes the term *productive aging* as the signpost to identify the road to travel. This phrase was first elaborated at a Salzburg International Seminar in 1983, and has since been institutionalized at the Center for Productive Aging within the Department of Geriatrics at Mt. Sinai in New York, where Butler now works. The Salzburg Seminar concluded, "Productive participation in society is essential to health."

Alan Pifer wrote in *The Aging Society,* "The most essential ingredient for implementing the proposed changes in policies and practices for the aging is the societal expectation that people will remain productive in the broad sense, throughout the third quarter of life, and will thus be accepted as full contributing members of the community."

Productive aging has a compelling financial urgency to it which is inevitable and welcome in our time of competing interests.

Successful aging is the theme developed by John Rowe in his important 1987 article in *Science,* co-authored by Robert Kahn. In this work Rowe and Kahn propose *successful aging* as a term to differentiate the full potentials of the aging person from "usual aging"—the standard norm. To me, "successful aging" subsumes "useful," "responsible," and "productive." All

are strategies for achieving successful aging, connoting an active involvement in and full role playing of life's design.

These various tags for the steps necessary to drive our planning apply
to the individual and to the society. Micro- and macrostrategies are necessary. Norman Cousins writes perceptively of the central role that options
play in the fulfillment of the human condition. Indeed, our species is virtually identified by the supreme degree that we, uniquely in all of nature,
have explored and exploited the myriad niches of opportunity which our
universe provides. Our freedom is defined by our ability to pursue our
options.

As the full exercise of options is a marker for the successful life,
constriction of options represents a diminishment of that success. The aging
process bears within it the risk of narrowed options. But it holds too the
prospect of enlarged options through accumulated experience and wisdom.
Age has its advantages as well as its disadvantages. It can be either gain or
loss, disabling or enabling. Both successful aging and successful living inherently mean vigorous efforts to maintain options. Maintaining such effort is a
job for all of us—young and old alike. We are designing ourselves. There is
no more sacred task.

Anne Somers remarked, "I must emphasize that this positive approach remains a *policy option, not a prediction.* Inadequate conviction,
inadequate resources, inadequate courage, above all, inadequate vision, or
just plain selfishness—on the part of the elderly as well as the young—could
result in failure by default and lead to the type of self-defeating intergenerational conflict and stalemate already predicted by some pessimists."

The bumper sticker AVENGE YOURSELF—LIVE LONG ENOUGH TO
BECOME A BURDEN TO YOUR CHILDREN strikes too close to home. For many,
the older years provide an excuse for antisocial reactions. I have dozens of
ornery old patients. They were probably ornery when they were young,
too, but being old gives their orneriness extra leverage. "I've worked, and
sweated, and sacrificed all these years, and now look what it's gotten me!" I
hear it often.

Leo Stavskis, 80, a widower, was angry with his son every time I saw
him. By every evidence I could muster, his son was loving and supportive,
responding to the stream of unreasonable demands which Leo made of
him. Leo was deaf and had bad arthritis; when he lost control of his urine,
his son took the option of putting Leo in a nursing home. Leo was livid. He
cursed his son and refused to talk with him. No reasoning was possible.
"After all I've done for him!" was the constant refrain. Leo became so

enraged about this that he stopped eating and died shortly thereafter. This served only to heighten the son's anguish and sadness.

I struggled against my own angry reactions to Leo when I saw him; his innate bitterness toward the world in general gave few ports of entry into his good side—if he had one.

Where along the way could Leo have steered a different course? One which would have allowed him to end his life in a way that would have been more positive to all involved. Sometimes the intergenerational system just doesn't work out; but more frequently, conflicts like the one between Leo and his son are rare. Primarily I see relationships which are far more productive. Generally the omega generation and the ones beneath share common goals. Indignity and discomfort for one is indignity and discomfort for all.

A STRATEGY FOR AGING

A total age strategy has multiple parts, some small, some large. These parts are independent, yet interdependent. If we as a congruent society are to make our older years worthy, we must live all of our time. How much is a year of life worth? Ask a very sick young person or his family. We are the ultimate resource, and time is one of our basic definitions.

Based on multiple evidences from multiple sources, I presume to offer the following protocol to fulfill our design. The architect has given us the blueprint—now we have both the intellect to understand and the tools with which to build. We have finished the whereases—the resolves follow.

Be it now resolved that a set of national policy initiatives be instituted that hold the promise of removing adverse incentives that presently inhibit and penalize us for growing old.

I propose that we should have an Age Constitution that addresses particularly the rights and responsibilities of our older selves—especially the responsibilities. As a new grandparent, I feel a heightened sense of obligation to the children. They are my window to helping the world to be a better place. This new Constitution should emphasize the opportunities that added years avail, and how our society should guarantee and extend these extra chances. The Constitution should extend the utility of our older years.

All of us, the meek and the mighty, perceive daily how our world could be better. Between bitching about poor service at the post office, to the aggravation of computerized telephone service, to the inefficiency of the doctor's office, we all see how things are—and wish they were different. I often ponder how we could aggregate, bundle, and exploit this immense collective yearning to improve our world. Which is the mechanism that could effect this?

Old people have seen more, known more, felt more, smelt more, spent more, lived more. How can we harness their collective judgments as to how our world can be improved? When I was a young doctor, my uncle Walter, in his mid-nineties, was still practicing general medicine in western Pennsylvania. At that time I wanted desperately to rub off onto myself some of the patina of his immense experience in caring for people. I didn't know how. Instead, he died, and all of that was lost. How can we bank the treasures that older people have garnered incrementally? They are—and we will be—a huge resource that must be tapped. Perhaps everyone 90 or so should be drafted into an Age Corps that has a decade of public service inherent in it. The Age Corps should constitute a faculty for the rest of society, enriching it, providing it with the template for continued growth. Who better to teach government than our elder statesmen? Who better to teach music than our elder maestros and retired orchestra members? Who better to teach anything than someone who has spent ninety years study-ing, testing, failing, and succeeding? But that is not our societal design. Our oldest decades are cast into the dependent mode, receiving rather than generating energies and enthusiasm. Old age should be earned, not given. It should be a privilege, not a right.

It is easier to model up a new life/living design within our own family units—the rewards seem so much closer at hand. In midlife I feel a real consecration to being fit, so that I may act as a vital resource for my grand-children and beyond. Try a centripetal, rather than a centrifugal, strategy. A family building and bonding—moving toward the center, rather than away from it. In such a centripetal scheme, the family unit is stronger with much more energy; entropy is offset; chaos and disruption are avoided; order prevails. All of the sadness of aging would evaporate if we could create a vision of our tomorrows that has such a vibrant good as its soul.

WHAT OF GOVERNMENTAL IMPACT?

In the fall 1984 issue of the *Millbank Memorial Fund Quarterly,* Lynn Etheredge wrote an essay entitled "An Aging Society and the Federal Deficit." Among other things, he observed that aging and its governmental programs affect every dynamic of our federal government. Social Security, Medicare, and other age-related entitlements are central to our lives. In 1989, the estimated federal budget was $1.34 trillion: $419 billion for defense, $297 billion for Social Security and retirement plans, $152 billion for health, $219 billion for interest on the national debt, and $255 billion for everything else. Thirty-three percent of all federal dollars go for aging-directed programs, while 31 percent goes for defense. If we presume that the rest of the budget is untouchable, it is evident that programs for the elderly are competing actively with the military in the budgetary process. A bomber or home-health benefits—the conflict is real. Economist Barbara Torrey calls it the confrontation of guns and canes. Medicare benefits versus Star Wars. Alzheimer's disease research projects versus the stealth bomber. The American Association of Retired Persons (AARP) versus the military-industrial complex.

But this competition is not new—it goes back millions of years, and reflects the debate within the aboriginal family when an elder became disabled. Does the family commit its marginal resources to protect the elder, with his attendant risk-taking? Or does it act aggressively to protect itself with lessened regard for succor of the disabled? Tough, long-standing questions.

Further, Malcolm Morrison points out that if present levels of expenditures for programs for the elderly persist, we, in 100 years, will be spending 60 percent of our federal moneys on elder-based programs. Other predictions, such as that of ex-Health and Human Services chief Dr. Otis Bowen, are even worse: 67 percent of the entire federal budget to the elderly by 2010.

Such projections do not go unnoticed. The Washington lobby for elder programs is under much pressure. Education and health programs for our older selves are thought to be consumption. The cries of intergenerational equity are being heard louder and louder. Dying seems like it costs a lot of money, and it does—1 percent of our gross national product. We can and should do a better job here, but I don't think the government is the place to start addressing this issue.

Daniel Callahan asked in *Setting Limits,* "Are the aged a biologically surplus and financially burdensome group?" Clearly the answer lies in the definition of "the aged." If they are functionally inert and energetically draining, then massive allocations of the resources to their welfare is debilitating. But if the aged can be embraced into a new and vital participatory role, then investment becomes the guide—not consumption.

The Eriksons wrote:

> By relegating this growing segment of the population to the onlooker bleachers of our society, we have classified them as unproductive, inadequate, and inferior—offering them, on occasions, status honors and honorary memberships shows respect and may be gratifying to them. Taking care of them in innumerable organized ways is being responsible. Entertaining them with bingo games and concerts is, however, patronizing. Surely the search for some way of including what they can still contribute to the social order in a way befitting their capacities is appropriate and in order. . . . What steps can be taken now to insure that the elderly in the future will remain an integral part of the social fabric? . . . Society owes its citizens encouragement and opportunity to develop their well-being and should provide as many avenues as possible for the maintenance of stamina in old age.

Many others have made similar observations. Alan Pifer commented on the striking lack of governmental perception that the old may constitute a resource rather than a burden. In the introduction to the important book *Other Ways of Growing Old,* Carl Eisdorfer noted that in other primitive cultures:

> . . . most successful elders are all contributing valuable services and thus earning their respected social place. In our society maximizing the social utility and value of the old might include involving them in a program of retraining and education to avoid obsolescence; developing alternative social roles to play through a range of voluntary efforts and part-time employment, and identifying alternate ways to finance retirement, for example economic alternatives and supplements to Social Security that would provide for proportional 'investment' in the economy as opposed to an eventual publicized depletion of general fund revenues." Eisdorfer went on to say, "The social rank of the old is determined by the balance be-

tween the cost of maintaining them and the contribution they are perceived as making.

Anne Somers writes, "In our large, complex, heterogeneous, and highly organized democracy the relationship between rights and responsibilities often becomes attenuated and at times almost disappears from view. In the last analysis, however, we ignore the relationship at our own peril. U.S. aging policy, as in other ones, must reflect the balance of rights and responsibilities on the part of both the individual and society."

A 1987 survey conducted by Arthur Andersen found that a wide diversity of concerned groups, from executives to consumers to governmental agencies, agreed that the number-one health care issue coming in 1995 is the growth of the elderly population—bigger than the concern about AIDS, or the size of the federal deficit, or anything else.

Thomas Jefferson wrote, "If we can prevent the government from wasting the labor of the people under the pretense of caring for them they will be happy."

Our Social Security system is severely faulted. For far too many of us it serves as a premature signal for disengagement. It may have been okay fifty years ago, but today the age 65 has no functional significance at all. Social Security penalizes meaningful involvement. It is a dropout signal. For far too many of us it means the main exercise is going to be to the mailbox to await the monthly check. Continued gainful employment is legislated against. In my view we should rapidly increase the eligibility age to 70 and above; and it should include a means test. Sending monthly checks to the 200,000 millionaires over 65 years of age makes no sense. Sociologists Matilda and John Riley said it best: "Capable people and empty role structures cannot exist for long." As economist Michael Boskin calculated in his 1986 book, *Too Many Promises: The Uncertain Future of Social Security*, each one-year increase in the "average length of retirement" statistic boosts payments from the Social Security trust fund by half a trillion dollars.

In a similar way I feel that our government needs to reshape Medicare *totally*. Presently its deficiencies are periodically tinkered with to ease, supposedly, our social conscience about its flaws. But nothing less than a complete overhaul can work. Medicare is both fiscally and philosophically bankrupt. It is a system based on the traditional illness model, an acute-phase model, grafted onto a time of life when chronic problems predominate. Aging is incurable as are most of the common medical problems of older people. Most medical problems in old people aren't—*can't* be—

cured. They can be treated and moderated, but not cured. But Medicare does not address chronic problems. The archives overflow with major failures of the system when Medicare stops paying. Denials of coverage are usually arbitrary and capricious. Fighting with the system is a regular and debilitating part of each of my working days. We need a new system.

My recommendation is that the highly respected Institute of Medicine of the National Academy of Sciences convene a widely representational blue-ribbon group of elders, scholars, administrators, insurance people, physicians, and others to look at the wide body of experimental programs and proposals which exist, and from such study submit to Congress a totally restructured health insurance program for older Americans. One of the principal rules of therapeutics is that if the present therapy isn't working, change to another therapy. Certainly the present remedy doesn't match the ills. With diligence and prudence, such a proposal should be a win-win situation. While it will require major reallocations of priorities, such a system can cost less than we are currently spending by emphasizing prevention and home health services.

Rationing of increasingly expensive medical technology is inevitable; and so my plan would mandate careful scrutiny of expensive, highly technologic maneuvers. Technologic immortality is an unworthy goal. In all of this I agree with Dan Callahan, *but* age should not be the discriminator for allocation. That role goes to "function." And better efforts at functional assessment and outcomes measurement should be mandated.

Individual responsibility and family responsibility must be rewarded. Antisocial, self-destructive behavior should be discouraged in every way possible. I advocate "sin taxes." Lower insurance rates for good health practices makes every sense to me. Earlier I spoke of my 63-year-old box-manufacturer patient. This man should have originally been tagged with a very high insurance bill (like a male teenage driver); when he restructured his life, his rates should have been cut.

Kenneth Manton recently calculated that there are two hundred federal programs which affect the elderly. These programs are under the jurisdiction of forty-nine congressional committees and subcommittees, and are administered by seven departments within the Executive branch and five independent agencies. This is a madness that can only confound our present inadequacies at creating social policies for our older selves. Maybe we need a cabinet-level Secretary of Aging—period.

Further, we need to arm our governmental leaders with good information. I confess to a general naïveté and trust in the way the world works. As I mentioned in an earlier chapter, my presidency of the American

Geriatrics Society allowed me the opportunity to meet with a number of elected governmental officials and their staffs. I liked them all and respected their good intentions, but I found out what a shallow knowledge base underlies many of these momentous decisions that are reached in Washington. Beyond government, I found even some of the lobbyists for the elderly to be woefully short on wisdom. Political expedience rules. This cynical verdict, however, is tempered by my genuine belief that all of these people need and deserve our help. They want to do right if they can only get the right information. Not to work at such a process invites helplessness and hopelessness, and our political process certainly cannot stand this.

Occasionally at the end of a speech I urge the audience to write a few letters to our leaders to give counsel and offer assistance. We all make a difference.

For our leaders themselves I would wish a heightened awareness of their own aging processes. For decades Congressman Claude Pepper (Democrat; Florida) was a tower of zeal and energy in the battle to increase sensitivities to aging issues. Pepper (like other older legislators) had the advantage, because he knew what it was like to be old. Celebration of effective elders is a master strategy for sustaining self-efficacy as we age.

AGING AND THE COMMUNITY

At the community level, a number of resolves are appropriate. Most of them concern role definition. What place are we to take in our community—in our family—as we age?

For most of us work defines our existence, and we clearly need a major rethinking of our employment practices with regard to aging. Now we have an average of nineteen years of retirement; by the year 2000 we will have twenty-five years of retirement. What about this?

Norman Cousins wrote:

A whole new world of potential leisure has sprung up for which people are unprepared. The shorter work week may produce premature retirement symptoms rather than a condition of creative liberation. That is, available new hours are more likely to lead to helplessness and floundering than to active discovery of exciting new options.

Retirement, supposed to be a chance to join the winner's circle, has turned out to be more dangerous than automobiles or LSD. Retirement for many people is literal consignment to no man's land, it is the chance to do everything that leads to nothing. It is the gleaming brass ring that unhorses the rider.

In 1947, 48 percent of those over the age of 65 worked. In 1979, 20 percent did. In 1930, our population consisted of ten producers for every dependent. By 2030, there will be only three producers per dependent. Fewer and fewer old people are working. Instead of retirement being delayed, it seems to come earlier and earlier. Victor Fuchs, noted Stanford University economist, observed that this earlier withdrawal from work is not so much the result of mandatory retirement from work or of mandatory retirement policies, but rather the result of generous pension plans and Social Security payments, which have risen faster than the cost of living. This shift, Fuchs points out, leads directly to millions of Americans living on sources over which they have no control.

I count myself very fortunate to be a physician, not only because it allows the work of each day to be dedicated to doing good things for other persons, but because the career can be extended indefinitely. I hope to be able to practice medicine, like Uncle Walter, into my nineties and beyond, in Palo Alto, or Ethiopia, or Borneo, or wherever. The corollary benefits of controlling my own financial destiny, and of not becoming a burden of any sort to our children, grandchildren and beyond, only confirm the appropriateness of this decision.

Most occupations do not provide such an open-ended continued productivity, but our system needs to think hard about this—to redefine retirement—and to ask ourselves, "retire to what?"

INEVITABLE CHANGES
REGARDING THE OLDER WORKER

Loss of the opportunity to work is constricting and debilitating. One of the really hopeful conversations I have had lately was with a national manpower specialist next to whom I sat on a flight home from Los Angeles. She told me that in a decade or two the nation's older people are going to have to work merely to keep our country running. The demographic shifts are operating in such a way that the projected labor pool will be insufficient to run our nation. Now that's exciting! Old workers have been shown to be cost effective with their lower rates of absenteeism and medical costs for company insurance plans. While modernization has tended to lower the social rank of older workers, there is much to be retained and nurtured.

The Eriksons have written, "it is an across-the-board simplification of attitude and practice to devalue wit, creativity, and experience by equating these qualities and weighing them against mere speed and the more up-to-date information of the young."

When we retire from life, life retires from us. Presently a few plans, such as phased retirement, retraining, altered pay schedules, and consultancy, are emerging. However, we still need major incentives which will keep older persons active. Disuse is debilitating for all of us. When you stop being energetic, you take my energy. I resent that, and I don't want to have to pay for it.

We should resolve to augment the sense of control of our older persons; solicitousness and gratuitous gestures are ultimately weakening. Useful roles need to be found and cultivated. The old need to be thought of as a vital national resource. The cost effectiveness of this awareness would be enormous.

In this regard the entire notion of education needs to be opened up for a fresh look. What has been the effect on our nature of confining educational efforts to our first two decades of life? Who thought that up? Certainly in medicine we practitioners are forced to maintain continuing education efforts; because if we don't, our competence deteriorates. I am certain that the same holds for all of us. Use it or lose it is heard over and over again. The brain cell knows when it isn't being stimulated; and it, like my leg in the cast, shrivels up. When society emphasizes the potential for self-development throughout the life span rather than the stereotypical decline of age, the older person is most likely to lead a productive and fulfilling life. A sense of mastery is gained by lifelong learning. The Elderhostels have become a huge success. This nonprofit organization continues to provide study programs and vacation packages for anyone over the age of 60. They have enrolled hundreds of thousands of elderly. It should be millions. Our great academic centers need to broaden their horizons so that they may serve each individual's growth needs for his or her lifetime—not merely for adolescence.

The community should encourage volunteerism for older persons. James House, of the University of Michigan Survey Research Center, looked at 2,700 people in Tecumseh, New York, and concluded that "regular volunteer work, more than any other activity, dramatically increased life expectancy." House reaffirmed that social contacts are essential to longevity. One hopeful development is the creation of cross-generational projects that put elders to work with young children in day-care centers and nursery schools. It's a toss-up who benefits more. Thousands of seniors have served in the Peace Corps. I look forward to this personally as I have consigned my tenth decade to working with the Peace Corps in East Africa.

Eileen Rockefeller Growald, founder and president of the Institute for the Advancement of Health, has reported on the manyfold benefits which accrue from such "altruistic egotism"—among them, that doing good helps the immune system.

"Exercise regularly, eat a balanced diet, and do something nice for someone." This platitude sounds too bland. Exercise and diet are boilerplate; but now we have increasing medical evidence that volunteering has major health benefits, for both those who give and those who receive. People who need people are healthier. Richard Leakey preaches that rather than aggression being our dominant primal habit, cooperativeness is. Being nice to someone has major effects on the neurotransmitters and on the immune system as well. Good Samaritanism may be the new prescription, as the life benefits are tallied.

Conversely, several studies, including those from Tecumseh and one by Lisa Berkman, of Yale, and H. Leonard Symes, of the University of California at Berkeley, showed that persons who retire from active personal involvement into "relaxing" and watching TV have double the chance of dying than do those who are still involved. Absence of friends and family is not conducive to healthy aging. Our communities should identify and react to this. Here in Palo Alto, I suspect that our seniors' center has done more good for the well-being of our older citizens than the corps of physicians which linger nearby.

Environmental cleanup and protection, city council activities, library research work, genealogy, the arts—on and on go the exciting opportunities which our communities should encourage our older persons to explore.

I am a physician, and one who loves my profession, yet I see within it mountains of opportunity to do things better with regard to our older patients. In 1982, the National Institutes of Health published a document called "A National Plan for Research in Aging." The four identified priorities were: (1) better understanding of the basic processes of aging, (2) better understanding, preventing, and control of the clinical manifestations of aging and aging-related disorders, (3) better understanding of the interactions between older people and a dynamic society, and (4) increased opportunity, motivation, and support for older people to contribute productively to society. I feel it was farsighted that these planners recognize that the health of older people is inextricably linked to the society in which they are aging. Medicine is a social science as well as a biologic one. The two interact intimately.

THE ROLE OF MEDICINE

I feel medicine should emphasize function and de-emphasize disease, as discussed extensively in chapter 4. We should emphasize health and not illness. As I emphatically stated earlier, age cannot be viewed as something to be cured. Instead, we should insist upon prevention. We need a new awareness of the time dimension of health problems in older people. Many favor the creation of a specialty of geriatric medicine such as in Great Britain. I have argued against this as I feel the medical care of older people should be the job of *all* physicians—not merely consigned to an elite few superspecialists. Continuity of care is a precious component of the medical care of older persons, and I fear for a circumstance in which a person is transferred from the usual care mode to another based merely on age. The principles of geriatric medicine should be thoroughly ingrained in all medical school curricula. After all, the medicine of tomorrow, as is clearly evidenced from the gray heads in today's hospitals, will be almost exclusively geriatrics. For example, the medical profession, with its research allies, *must* get rid of Alzheimer's disease. As noted earlier, if this giant step is not guaranteed, then the remainder of the logistics to improve the quantity and quality of our lives will all become irrelevant. We need an intense societal campaign, such as those mounted recently against AIDS and heart disease, if we are to stop AD from killing and maiming millions.

THE ROLE OF THE FAMILY

The family unit needs to be reworked to accommodate the gift of added years. My mother certainly did not plan on living 94 years, and in some ways she was bewildered by it. She didn't plan on being a great-grandmother; in fact, I don't think she even planned to be a grandmother. But from our generation onward we have no such excuse. The four-generation family is becoming commonplace, and each generation from alpha to omega needs roles to play. My wife and I, now enjoying the bliss of grandparenting, have all sorts of plans for their generation—and the next. We need to build our vigor, experience, and understanding to play these intergenerational roles in the best fashion we can. To be an effective parent is no longer enough. Each person should be a resource for the entire family over his or her entire life span.

Living long enough to become a burden to our kids is not for my wife and me. The atomic family of one or two isolated members is not a healthy ingredient for a society. A rich network of family ties, mutually supporting and extending, if nurtured and identified as a basic good, could go a long way toward rendering moot many of the support devices we have created for our older selves.

In *The Greening of America,* Charles A. Reich exhorted, "Stay together." This is a strong message.

YOU STILL HAVE THE
ULTIMATE RESPONSIBILITY

We need a new oath.

"I pledge allegiance to the last third of my life, and to the whole in which it stands, one life, indivisible, with opportunity and responsibility throughout all."

My Granddaddy Bortz, butcher in Greensburg, Pennsylvania, is at the edge of my memory. I recall he used to reward my chore performance in his store with a glazed doughnut. He died when I was only 8 years old; but I remember his counsel, "Make yourself necessary." No matter how enlightened our national or community aging policies become, the sum is only as good as its parts—and we, the people, are the ones who must inevitably bear the responsibility for our own aging.

Granddaddy's advice was right on. As we traverse Erikson's life phases, being necessary is a fundamental strategy. If we aren't necessary to someone, to something, why live? This is why this study of aging yields so much about the nature of living. We need to plan for our vital involvement in our own aging. An important corollary to this is that it is never too late to start. Our renewal capacities are immense.

As we must plan individually for our lives we must plan for our own deaths. Our new knowledge base helps immensely. Until the present we had the idea that each of us was the ultimate incarnation, the distillation of some almighty handiwork which occurred a few years ago and was likely to end sometime soon. We were divine creatures whose eternity was to be spent in golden fields and eternal springtime, or alternatively in some fiery pit brimming with every conceivable cackling demon. Death was a significant branch point. We trembled and repressed. Our vanities soared. Knowledge has destroyed this conception. The egotism of our earlier self-portrait has given way to the understanding that the human being is a part of a universal continuum that began inanimately billions of years ago and has billions of years to go until it ends. Mankind has come only recently on the scene, and is but one of a host of living, breathing creatures in our world. We are not alone. This cumulative assault on our vanity does not limit us—far from it. It gives us a view of who we are which is far more grand, comprehensible, and whole.

In *The Cloud*, Percy Bysshe Shelley wrote,

> I am the daughter of earth and water,
>   And the nursling of the sky;
> I pass through the pores of the ocean and shores,
>   I change, but I cannot die.

Confucius said, "As you learn about life, you will learn about death."

As we learn of our place in the universe, spatial and temporal, it gives our planned existence truth and relevance. We do not retain for ourselves the unnecessary vanities of ignorance. Our coming and going is seen not as a start and an end, but rather as a continuum of energy—becoming, not being. Process, not product. Insofar as we, through our life energy, can bring life to someone else, then we have approached immortality. As we become better able to measure our own deaths in terms of the greater whole, we change; but in a cosmic sense, we—like the cloud—do not die.

As we confront the inevitably difficult decisions which swirl around the end of life, we are newly able to address them rationally and with a sense of compassion born out of understanding rather than out of ignorance. Ideally death should not be a time of despair and misery—it should be an acknowledgment that life has been lived to its outer limits, and that much of the energy lives on, dispersed, but still an extension of our lifetimes.

William James, the great philosopher and psychologist from Harvard wrote, "We live lives inferior to ourselves." To me, these words are powerful and exhorting.

WHAT CAN YOU DO *TODAY* TO AGE SUCCESSFULLY?

1. Do at least 30 minutes of sustained, rhythmic, vigorous exercise four times a week. Seek out patterns, times, places and contacts that make exercise as much a part of your day as eating and sleeping.
2. Eat like a bushman. Return to the habit of eating what nature first laid on our tables: fruits, whole grains, vegetables and *lean* meat.
3. Get as much sleep and rest as you need. Make quiet time a major priority. Exercisers, in particular, must acknowledge that their bodies require respite from workouts and the general clamor of the day.
4. Maintain your sense of humor and deflect anger. Make each day an opportunity for optimism for yourself and others. A positive mind-set creates the expectation that something good is about to happen and opens the door to new options for success.
5. Set goals and accept challenges that force you to be as alive and creative as possible. Nature operates in such a way that growth and living are nearly synonymous. When one stops, so does the other. Creativity is not confined to the first part of your life. In fact, accumulated knowledge and experience should make the later decades even more congenial to new accomplishment.
6. Don't depend on anyone else for your well-being. A well-developed sense of self-efficacy is the crucial link to a long and meaningful existence. We all need to maintain mastery, autonomy and independence in our daily lives.

7. Be necessary and responsible. Live outside yourself. Beyond independence, we also need to see each day as a chance to help someone or something. Associate with other active, involved individuals. Sharpen your sense of duty to the Earth, which nurses us all.

8. Don't slow down. Stick with the mainstream. Avoid the shadows. Stay together. Universal law dictates that natural order is ordained by only one mechanism—a well-directed, purposeful flow of energy. Aging need not be characterized by loss. Maintaining your energy flow is the antidote.

Some physicist/philosopher might logically propose that the world and all that it contains is in a zero-sum equilibrium. Positrons equal the electrons. Day and night. Yin and yang. Good and evil. Beauty and ugliness. Truth and falsehood. Inhaling and exhaling. Wisdom and ignorance. Optimism and pessimism. Independence and dependence. Up and down. In and out. It all seems so balanced—so symmetric, so sensible, so immutable, and so inhuman.

When I was a little boy I was enchanted by the story "The Little Engine That Could." My folks must have read it to me a thousand times. "I think I can. I think I can. I think I can," echoes loudly in a chamber of my boyhood memories.

I wonder over and over whether this little moral lesson was essentially life-shaping for me. Its affirmative message creates expectancy; it distorts the zero-sum equilibrium. Physicist Robert B. Lindsay proposes that an ethical code can be derived from thermodynamics. He calls this rule the "thermodynamic imperative." It implies that each of us has the responsibility to work against the exit flow of energy as entropy. The inanimate world has no such imperative. It lacks the structure. The animal world, except for us, lacks the insight and organized skills to alter destiny. Only we, in our recognized universe, have the capacity—the responsibility—to see things as they might be, and ask, "Why not?" We need to create order out of the chaos of our environment—to bundle, tend, and exert our energies toward making the world not just as good as it was and is but better. As far as I can determine, the human spirit is the only force in the universe that has within itself the chance to create a nobler life.

Dylan Thomas declared:

> Old age should burn and rave at close of day;
> Rage, rage against the dying of the light.

This is a heraldic cry to conform our life plan to the cosmic forces which gave it birth, and will ultimately consume it. In the interim we have the chance—for the first time—to live long and die short.

It is our finest option.

REFERENCES

Preface

Bortz, Edward L., and Walter M. Bortz. "Major Issues of Aging." *General Practice* 20:84–93, 1959.

Bortz, Edward. *Creative Aging.* New York: Macmillan, 1963.

Chapter 1

Leakey, Richard, and Roger Lewin: *Origins.* New York: Dutton, 1977.

Manton, Kenneth. "Changing Concepts of Morbidity and Mortality in the Elderly Population." *Millbank Memorial Fund Quarterly, Health & Society* 60:183–244, 1982.

Guinness Book of World Records. New York: Bantam, 1989.

Leaf, Alexander: "Search for the Oldest People." *National Geographic* 143:93–119, 1973.

Siegel, Paul, and Cynthia Taeuber. "Demographic Perspectives on the Long Lived Society." *Daedalus* 77:117, winter 1986.

Fries, James, and Lawrence Crapo. *Vitality and Aging.* San Francisco: Freeman, 1981.

Mazess, Richard, and Sylvia Forman. "Longevity and Age Exaggeration in Vilcabamba, Ecuador." *Journal of Gerontology* 34:94–98, 1979.

Thomas, Lewis. *The Medusa and the Snail: More Notes of a Biology Watcher.* New York: Viking, 1977.

Cutler, Richard. "Evolution of Longevity in Primates." *Journal of Human Evolution* 5:169–202, 1976.

Shock, Nathan. "Mortality and Measurement of Aging." In *Biology of Aging*, B. Strehler (ed.). Washington, D.C.: Avis, 1960.

Hayflick, Leonard. "Aging Under Glass." In *Advances in Cell Culture*, K. Maramorosch (ed.). Orlando: Academic Press, 1988.

McGrady, Patrick. *The Youth Doctors.* New York: Coward-McCann, 1968.

Pifer, Alan, and Lydia Bronte. *The Aging Society.* New York: Norton, 1987.

Chapter 2

Helton, Roy. "Why Things Grow Old." *Harper's* 174:1–12, 1936.

Hawking, Stephen. *A Brief History of Time: From the Big Bang to Black Holes.* New York: Bantam Books, 1988.

Prigogine, Ilya, and Isabelle Stengers. *Order Out of Chaos.* New York: Bantam Books, 1984.

Atkins, Peter. *The Second Law.* Scientific American Books. New York: Freeman, 1984.

Schrodinger, Edwin. *What Is Life: The Physical Aspects of Living Cells.* New York: Cambridge University Press, 1967.

Duffy, Peter, et al. "Effect of Chronic Caloric Restriction on Physiological Variables Related to Energy Metabolism in the Male Fischer 344 Rat." *Mechanisms of Aging and Development* 44:117–33, 1989.

Mayr, Ernst. *The Growth of Biological Thought.* Cambridge: Harvard University Press, 1982.

Barrow, John, and Frank Tipler. *The Anthropic Cosmological Principle.* Oxford: Clarendon Press, 1986.

Gleick, James. *Chaos: Making a New Science.* New York: Penguin Books, 1987.

Comfort, Alex. "The Biological Basis for Increasing Longevity." *Medical Opinion and Review,* April 1970, pp. 18–25.

Morowitz, Harold. *Entropy for Biologists: An Introduction to Hemodynamics.* New York: Academic Press, 1970.

McKay, Clive. "The Effect of Retarded Growth upon the Length of Lifespan and upon the Ultimate Body Size." *Journal of Nutrition* 10:63–73, 1935.

Masoro, Edward. "Food Restriction in the Aging Process." *Journal of the American Geriatric Society* 32:296–330, 1989.

Wolford, Roy. *Maximum Lifespan.* New York: Norton, 1983.

Rubner, Max. *Das Problem des Lebensdauer.* Munich/Berlin: Oldenbourg, 1908.

Pearl, Raymond. *The Rate of Living: Being an Account of Some Experimental Studies in the Biology of Life Duration.* New York: Knopf, 1928.

Dyson, Freeman. "Time Without End: Physics and Biology in an Open Universe." *Review of Modern Physics* 51:447–60, 1979.

Selye, Hans. *The Story of the Adaptation Syndrome.* Montreal: Acta, 1952.

Cousins, Norman. *The Celebration of Life.* New York: Harper & Row, 1974.

Gould, Stephen. "Our Allotted Lifetimes." *Natural History* 34–41, Aug.–Sept. 1977.

Bortz, Walter. "Aging as Entropy." *Experimental Gerontology* 21:321–28, 1986.

Chapter 3

Aaron, Henry, and William Schwartz. *The Painful Prescription.* Washington, D.C.: Brookings Institute, 1989.

Sagan, Leonard. *The Health of Nations.* New York: Basic Books, 1987.

Fuchs, Victor. *Who Shall Live?* New York: Basic Books, 1974.

Knowles, John. "The Medical Center and the Community Health Center." In *Social Policy for Health Care.* New York Academy of Medicine, 1969.

Elwood, Paul. "Shattuck Lecture: Outcomes Management, a Technology of Patient Experience." *New England Journal of Medicine* 318:1549–56, 1988.

Lukagiewicz, Julius. "The Knowledge Explosion." *Transactions, New York Academy of Science* 34:373–90, 1972.

Stewart, Anita, et al. "Functional State and Well-Being of Patients with Chronic Conditions." *Journal of the American Medical Association* 262:907–13, 1989.

Gailar, John, and Edward Smith. "Progress Against Cancer." *New England Journal of Medicine* 314:1226–1323, 1986.

Health Policy Agenda for the American People. American Medical Association, 1987.

Chapter 4

Breslow, Lester, and Anne Somers. "The Lifetime Health Monitoring Program: Practical Approach to Preventive Medicine." *New England Journal of Medicine* 296:601–09, 1977.

Pearson, Durk, and Sandy Shaw. *Life Extension.* New York: Warner Books, 1983.

Steel, Knight, and K. Franklin Williams. "Geriatrics: The Fruition of the Clinician." *Archives of Internal Medicine* 134:1125–26, 1974.

Somers, Anne, et al. *Preventive Health Services for the Elderly: Rutgers Medical School Project Inquiry,* fall 1982, pp. 190–98.

Belloc, Nedra, and Lester Breslow. "Relationship of Physical Health Status and Health Practices." *Preventive Medicine* 1:409–21, 1972.

Chapter 5

Cousins, Norman. *Head First: The Biology of Hope.* New York: Norton, 1989.

Seligman, Martin. *Helplessness: On Depression, Development and Death.* San Francisco: Freeman, 1975.

Engle, George. "Sudden Death of the 'Medical Model' in Psychiatry." *Canadian Psychiatric Association Journal* 15:527–38, 1970.

Brohn, John G., Betty Chandler, Thomas Lynn, and Stewart Wolf. "Social Characteristics of Patients with Coronary Heart Disease." *American Journal of Medical Science* 251:629–37, 1966.

Mace, Nancy, and Peter Rabins. *The Thirty-Six-Hour Day.* Baltimore: Johns Hopkins University Press, 1981.

Gardner, John. *Self Renewal.* New York: Norton, 1981.

Cannon, Walter. "Voodoo Death." *American Anthropologist* 44:169–81, 1942.

Richter, Curt. "On the Phenomenon of Sudden Death in Animals and Man." *Psychosomatic Medicine* 19:191–98, 1957.

Frank, Jerome. *Persuasion and Healing.* New York: Schocken Books, 1974.

Pruyser, Paul. "Aging: Downward, Upward, or Forward?" *Postgraduate Psychology* 24:102–117, 1975.

Chapter 6

Harding, Robert, and Geza Teleki (eds). *Omnivorous Primates.* New York: Columbia University Press, 1987.

Lee, Richard, and Irven DeVore. *Man the Hunter.* Chicago: Aldine, 1986.

Currens, James H., and Paul White. "Half a Century of Running: Clinical, Physiological and Autopsy Findings in the Case of Clarence DeMar ('Mr. Marathon')." *New England Journal of Medicine* 265:988–93, 1961.

Mayer, Jean. "Decreased Activity and Energy Balance in Hereditary Obesity-Diabetic Syndrome of Mice." *Science* 11:504–05, 1953.

Bortz, Walter. "Physical Exercise as an Evolutionary Force." *Journal of Human Evolution* 14:145–56, 1985.

      "Disuse and Aging." *Journal of the American Medical Association* 248:1203–09, 1982.

      "The Effect of Exercise on Age: The Effect of Age on Exercise." *Journal of the American Geriatric Society* 28:49–55, 1980.

DeVries, Harold. "Physiologic Effects of an Exercise Training Program on Men Age 52–88." *Journal of Gerontology* 25:325–35, 1970.

Morowitz, Harold. *Cosmic Joy and Local Pain.* New York: Scribner's, 1987.

Bortz, Walter. "Redefining Human Aging." *Journal of the American Geriatric Society* 37:1092–96, 1987.

      "The Disuse Syndrome." *Western Journal of Medicine* 141:69–98, 1984.

Kraus, Hans, and Wilhelm Raab. *Hypokinetic Disease: Diseases Produced by the Lack of Exercise.* Springfield, IL: Thomas, 1961.

Fries, James. "Aging, Natural Death, and the Compression of Morbidity." *New England Journal of Medicine* 303:130–36, 1980.

Bortz, Walter. "Disuse and Extended Morbidity." *Gerontologic Perspectives* 1:52–55, 1987.

Rifkin, Jeremy. *Entropy: A New World View.* New York: Bantam Books, 1980.

Chapter 7

Masters, William, and Virginia Johnson. *Human Sexual Response.* New York: Bantam Books, 1966.

Davidson, Julian. *Gonadal Hormones and Human Behavior.* New York: Academic Press, pp. 123–30, 1978.

Kinsey, Albert. *Sexual Behavior in the Human Male.* New York: Saunders, 1948.

Brecher, Edward. *Love, Sex and Aging.* New York: Consumers Union, 1984.

Bretschneider, Judy, and Norma McCoy. "Sexual Interest and Behavior in Healthy 80- to 102-Year-Olds." *Archives of Sexual Behavior* 17:109–29, 1988.

Morley, John, et al. "UCLA Geriatric Ground Rounds: Sexual Dysfunction in the Elderly Male." *Journal of the American Geriatric Society* 35:1014–22, 1987.

Morrell, Martha, et al. "The Influence of Age and Cycling Status on Sexual Arousability in Women." *American Journal of Obstetrics and Gynecology* 148:66–71, 1984.

Crenshaw, Theresa. *Beside Manners: Your Guide to Better Sex.* New York: McGraw-Hill, 1983.

Starr, Bernard, and Marcella Weiner. *The Starr-Weiner Report on Sex and Sexuality in the Mature Years.* New York: Stein & Day, 1981.

Chapter 8

Gould, Stephen. *Ever Since Darwin.* New York: Norton, 1977.

Jerison, Harry. *Evolution of the Brain and Intelligence.* New York: Academic Press, 1977.

Lenard, Lane. "The Dynamic Brain." *Science Digest*, December 1983.

Gould, Stephen. *The Mismeasure of Man.* New York: Norton, 1981.

Diamond, Marian. "Extensive Cortical Depth Measurements and Neurone Size Increases in the Cortex of Environmentally Enriched Rats." *Journal of Comparative Neurology* 131:357–64, 1967.

Treffert, David. "The Idiot-Savant: A Review of the Syndrome." *American Journal of Psychiatry*, May 1988.

Singh, J., and Robert Zingg. *Wolf Children and Feral Man.* Denver: Archon Books, 1966.

Schaie, K. Warner, and Sherry Willis. *Developmental Psychology* 22:223–30, 1986.

Dustman, Robert, et al. "Aerobic Exercise Training and Improved Neuropsychologic Function of Older Individuals." *Neurobiology of Aging* 5:35–42, 1984.

Bashore, Theodore. "Age, Physical Fitness and Mental Processing Speed." In *Annual Review of Gerontology and Geriatrics*, MP Lawton (ed.), vol. IX, *Clinical and Applied Gerontology*, New York: Spring, 1989.

Gose, Kathleen, and Gloria Levi. *Dealing with Memory Changes as You Grow Older.* New York: Bantam Books, 1988.

Lapp, Danielle. *Don't Forget: Easy Exercises for a Better Memory at Any Age.* New York: McGraw-Hill, 1987.

Baltes, Paul, and K. Warner Schaie. *Psychology Today*, March 1974.

Chapter 9

Dubos, Rene. *The Dreams of Reason: Science and Utopias.* New York: Columbia University Press, 1961.

Thompson, Paul, et al. "Death During Jogging or Running." *Journal of the American Medical Association* 242:1265–67, 1979.

Paffenbarger, Ralph, et al. "A Natural History of Athleticism and Cardiovascular Health." *Journal of the American Medical Association* 252:491–95, 1984.

Pauling, Linus. *How to Live Longer and Feel Better.* New York: Avon, 1986.

Vaillant, George. "Natural History of Male Psychologic Health: Effects of Mental Health on Physical Health." *New England Journal of Medicine* 301:1249–54, 1979.

Astrand, Per Olaf. *Experimental Studies of Physiologic Working Capacity in Relation to Sex and Age.* Copenhagen: Munksgaard, 1952.

Bortz, Walter. "Metabolic Consequences of Obesity." *Annals of Internal Medicine* 71:833–43, 1969.

Schneider, Edward, and John Reed. "Life Extension." *New England Journal of Medicine* 312:1159–68, 1985.

Horne, James. *Why We Sleep.* New York: Oxford University Press, 1988.

Blair, Steven, et al. "Physical Fitness and All Cause Mortality." *Journal of the American Medical Association* 262:2395–2401, 1989.

Chapter 10

Bandura, Albert. *The Social Foundations of Thought and Action: A Social Cognitive Theory.* Englewood Cliffs, NJ: Prentice Hall, 1986.

Erikson, Erik, Joan Erikson, and Helen Kivnick. *Vital Involvement in Old Age.* New York: Norton, 1986.

Cousins, Norman. *Anatomy of an Illness.* New York: Bantam Books, 1981.

Abler, Rose, and Bruce Fretz. "Self-Efficacy and Competence in Independent Living Among Oldest Old Persons." *Journal of Gerontology* 43:S138–43, 1988.

Langer, Ellen, and Judith Rodin. "The Effects of Enhanced Personal Responsibility for the Aged." *Journal of Personality and Social Psychology* 34:191–98, 1976.

Langer, Ellen. *Mindfulness.* Reading, MA: Addison-Wesley, 1989.

Segerberg, Osborn. *Living to Be One-Hundred.* New York: Scribner's, 1982.

Clark, Etta. *Growing Old Is Not for Sissies.* Corte Madera, CA: Pomegranate Calendar and Books, 1986.

Beard, Beth. "Some Characteristics of Recent Memory of Centenarians." *Journal of Gerontology* 23:23–30, 1968.

Chapter 11

President's Commission for the Study of Ethical Problems in Medicine and Biomedical and Behavioral Research, Deciding to Forego Life Sustaining Treatment. Washington, D.C., U.S. Government Printing Office, 1983.

Guidelines on the Termination of Life Sustaining Treatment and the Care of the Dying. A Report of the Hastings Institute, Hastings Center, New York, 1987.

The Physician and the Hopelessly Ill Patient. New York: Society for the Right to Die, 1985.

Wanzer, Sidney, Daniel Federman, et al. "The Physician's Responsibility Toward Hopelessly Ill Patients." *New England Journal of Medicine* 320:844–49, 1989.

Law Reform Commission of Canada. "Euthanasia: Aiding Suicide and Cessation of Treatment." Minister of Supply and Services, Canada, 1982.

Callahan, Daniel. *Setting Limits: Medical Goals in an Aging Society.* New York: Simon & Schuster, 1987.

Holmes, Oliver Wendell. "The Deacon's Masterpieces: Or the Wonderful One Hoss Shay." *From* The Autocrat of the Breakfast Table, 1857–58, *The Complete Poetical Works of O.W. Holmes.* Boston: Houghton-Mifflin, 1908.

Scitovsky, Ann. "Medical Care Expenditures in the Last Twelve Months of Life." APHA Meeting, New Orleans, 1987.

Bortz, Walter. "The Trajectory of Dying: Functional Status in the Last Year of Life." *Journal of the American Geriatric Society* 38:140–50, 1990.

Jonsen, Al, et al. *Clinical Ethics: A Practical Approach to Ethical Decisions in Clinical Medicine,* second edition. New York: Macmillan, 1986.

Chapter 12

Sagan, Carl. *Broca's Brain.* New York: Random House, 1974.

Tennyson, Alfred. *Ulysses.* The Harvard Classics, Charles E. Elliott (ed.), vol. 32. New York: Colon & Sons, 1910.

Rowe, John, and Robert Kahn. "Human Aging: Usual and Successful." *Science* 273:143–49, 1987.

Other Ways of Growing Old: Anthropologic Perspectives. Amoss, Pamela T., and Steve Harell (eds.) Stanford: Stanford University Press, 1981.

Cousins, Norman. *Human Options.* New York: Norton, 1981.

Gardner, John. *Excellence.* New York: Norton, 1978.

Etheredge, Lynn. "An Aging Society and the Federal Deficit." *Millbank Memorial Fund Quarterly Health and Society* 62:521–44, 1984.

Miller, G. Tyler. *Energetics, Kinetics and Life: An Ecologic Approach.* Belmont, CA: Wadsworth, 1971.

Somers, Anne. "Aging in the 21st Century: Projections, Personal Preferences and Public Policy, A Consumer's View." *Health Policy* 9:46–58, 1989.

Lindsey, Robert B. *The Role of Science in Civilization.* New York: Harper & Row, 1963.

De Chardin, Teilhard. *The Phenomenon of Man.* New York: Harper Brothers, 1959.

Piper, Watty. *The Little Engine That Could.* New York: Platt & Munk, 1930.

Lubitz, James, and Ronald Prihoda. "Use and Cost of Medicare Services in the Last Two Years of Life." *Health Care Financing Review* 5:117–31, spring 1984.

Schneider, Edward, and Jack Guralnick. "The Aging of America Impact on Health Care Cost." *Journal of the American Medical Association* 263:2335–40, 1990.

Manton, Kenneth. "A Dynamic Model of Population Aging and Health Status Change: Implications for the Development and Implementation of National Health Policy." Presentation to the National Health Policy Forum, April 1983, Washington, D.C.

America's Aging: Productive Roles in an Older Society. Committee on an Aging Society, Institute of Medicine and National Research Council, 1986.

Tavris, Carol. "Old Age Is Not What It Used to Be." *New York Times Good Health Magazine*, September 27, 1987.

INDEX

Massachusetts Medical Association, 66
Mastery experiences, creating of, 227–33
Matter, as component of aging, 27
May, Rollo, 261
Mayer, Jean, 131, 203
Mayr, Ernst, 28
Mazess, Richard, 9
Mean lifetime potential (MLP), 13
Medicaid, 248
Medical Aspects of Human Sexuality, 147
Medical Care. *See* Health care
Medical insurance, 81–84, 246–48, 265, 267–68
Medical Nemesis (Illich), 243
Medicare, 81, 83, 246–47, 265, 267–68
Medicine. *See* Health care
The Medusa and the Snail (Thomas), 12
Medvedev, Zhores, 9
Memory, and aging, 179–83
Menopause, sexuality and, 140, 142, 152
Menstrual periods, sexuality and, 140
Metabolism, 31–33, 37–42
Metschnikoff, Eli, 47
Middle age, parameters of, 23
Millbank Memorial Fund Quarterly, 265
Miller, Stanley, 31
Mindfulness (Langer), 228
The Mismeasure of Man (Gould), 158
MLP. *See* Mean lifetime potential
Mobility. *See* Physical mobility
Morley, John, 148
Mormons, mortality rates in, 65
Morowitz, Harold, 32–33, 113, 212
Morrell, Martha, 152
Morrison, Malcolm, 265
Mortality, rates in Mormons, 65
Mortality, *see also* Death and dying
Mother Teresa, 244–45
Motivation, and learning, 177
Mozart, Wolfgang Amadeus, 163
Multiple Risk Factor Intervention Trial (MRFIT), 191
Musculoskeletal system,
  age changes and, 130–31
  fragility due to inactivity, 135
  longevity and, 13
Myers, R.D., 35

NASA, 123–24
Nascher, D.G., 20
National Geographic, 8
National Health Interview Study, 187

National Institute on Aging, 10, 17, 20, 128, 174, 189, 261
National Institutes of Health (NIH), 13, 20, 38, 97, 108, 272
Natural selection, 114
Netherlands, euthanasia in, 251–52
Neurobiology, 158–60, *see also* The Brain
New England Journal of Medicine, 57, 66, 128, 132
New York Academy of Sciences, 51
Niehans Cellular Therapie Clinic, 18
Niehans, Paul, 18
NIH. *See* National Institutes of Health
Nocturnal penile tumescence (NPT), 150, *see also* Impotency
Non-smokers, and longevity, 219
Nonequilibrium thermodynamics, 27
Nonlinear thermodynamics, 32
Novak, Mark, 16
Nutrition, improvements in, 48
Nutrition, *see also* Diet

Obesity, 77
  disuse and, 131–32, 135–36
Ochsner, Alton, 64, 80
Okel, Ben, 73
Old age,
  death from, 47
  defining of, 8–9
  parameters of, 23
  representation in cultural expression, 17
Old age, *see also* Aging; Longevity
On the Origin of Species (Darwin), 114
Order Out of Chaos (Prigogine; Stengers), 29, 113
O'Rourke, Paul, 106
Osler, William, 100, 230
Osteoporosis, 130–31
Other Ways of Growing Old (Eisdorfer), 266
Oxygen transfer, 125–28

Paffenbarger, Ralph, 189–90, 192
Page, Henry, 219
Page, Irvine, 55
Paige, Satchel, 89
The Painful Prescription (Aaron; Schwartz), 49
Palliative health care, 64
Palmore, Erdman, 219
Parkinson's disease, 134, 178
Patterson, E. Mansell, 245
Pauling, Linus, 31–32